11-07

For George and Marguerite—
Thank you for all
your support and love over the
last few years while I was trying
to write this baby.

Jim

WRESTLERS AT THE TRIALS

Their stories of trying to make
the US Olympic Wrestling team
1960-1988

By James V. Moffatt

Wrestlers At The Trials
Their stories of trying to make the US Olympic Wrestling team 1960-1988

Published by Exit Zero Publishing, Inc.
www.exitzeropublishing.net

Book design by Jack Wright
Cover design by Victor Grasso

First edition: November 2007

ISBN 978-0-9799051-0-0

CONTENTS

This book is dedicated to the Board, the staff and all the generous supporters of the College Sports Council — the not-for-profit national coalition that is dedicated to saving Olympic sports such as amateur wrestling from the devastation caused by Title IX's ('a good law, poorly regulated') quota enforcement. For more information on how you can help with this worthy cause, go to www.savingsports.org.

INTRODUCTION

THIS isn't just a book about wrestling. You could say it's a book about *wrestlers*. But it's more than that. It's a book about passion. And dedication. It's a book about men who went above and beyond the normal boundaries of physical and mental exertion. All because they had a dream.

Their dream was to represent the United States of America on the Olympic wrestling team. And, boy, they traveled a long, hard road just trying to get there.

Before even being invited to the Trials, these men spent thousands of hours in training, perfecting their moves, strengthening their bodies, building their stamina and battling the toughest foes thrown their way.

These men were often subjected to a brutal regime — fighting fatigue, dehydration and pain. Intense pain.

And then there were the Trials, where their foe was not always just the man on the other side of the mat, the man who wanted to put them on their back. They also had to contend with injuries, bad calls, prejudices and politics.

This is what makes the men in this book so special. Yes, many of them were born with natural athleticism, speed and power. But all of them had to dig down for the focus, the discipline and the passion. Especially the passion.

McCann, Bettucci, Blubaugh, Lahr, Douglas, Sanders, Behm, Baughman, Camilleri, Wells, Gable, Farrell, Peterson, Schalles, Dziedzic, Kemp, Banach, Fraser, Mills, Weaver, Lewis, Dellagatta, Smith, Carr, Schultz, Houck, and Monday. These guys were warriors. These guys were my heroes. Matter of fact, they still are.

They inspired me to write this book. I wanted to hear their stories... and share their stories.

Read a few of them and you will see what I mean. Passion permeates just about every page in this book. That's not my doing. It comes from these men. The passion doesn't go away in men like these. Their stories come forth with such a resonance that it is impossible not to share their emotions.

You will also notice a camaraderie and respect among these men that I am proud to associate with wrestling.

That's usually the way with warriors.

Let the stories begin...

1960
OKLAHOMA
RULES

> " That Oklahoma Trials Camp was a real shock to me... training that hard. I was only 20 at the time and never saw anything like it. One day after practice I was exhausted and whispered to the guy sitting next to me in the locker room: 'Hey, Blubaugh, are they trying to kill us?' To which the veteran Blubaugh calmly replied: 'Simons, they can't make it tough enough for me.'
>
> — Gray Simons, winner of the 114.5-pound 1960 Olympic Freestyle Trials

IN 1960, more than one thousand wrestlers tried to make the United States Olympic team. From April to August, the grapplers battled their way through the Trials process. Most of them dropped by the wayside — first at the Regional Qualifiers, then at the 'Final Trials' in Iowa. Finally, during a sultry mid-summer fortnight in Oklahoma, 16 men emerged from a series of wrestle-offs to earn the right to represent their country on the 1960 US Freestyle and Greco-Roman Olympic team.

Old-timers recall the '60 Trials primarily for the intensity of the survivor-like training regime designed by famed University of Oklahoma wrestling coach Port Robertson. Adding to the mix were charges of favoritism and territorial disputes involving Oklahoma's wrestling insiders and some hard-scrabble guys from New York. And there were some classic individual rivalries on the line, none more so than the long-standing one between two of Oklahoma's greatest middle-weights — Doug Blubaugh and Phil Kinyon.

Based on international results of US wrestlers in the late '50s, expectations for Olympic medals in Rome, Italy were not high. The US had not competed in the FILA World Championships since 1954, when we finished 7th. The US wrestled the Russian team on several occasions in 1958 and 1959, but only

Previous spread: Shelby Wilson throwing Ben Northrup during the 1960 Trials *Photograph courtesy of* They Call It Wrestling, *by Wade Schalles*

one American won a match — the unstoppable Terry McCann. Few others were given much of a chance to bring home a medal.

Looking back, 1960 was a far different, gentler time to be living in the United States. Dwight David (Ike) Eisenhower was our president — closing in on the end of his eight-year term of office. In the upcoming Presidential election, Ike's Republican Party was looking to Vice-President Richard Nixon as the heir apparent. The Democrats tabbed a young charismatic senator from New England, Jack Kennedy, as their nominee. Like the aspiring Olympic wrestlers at the Trials, these two would spar in an intense rivalry over the summer, with the victor taking his place in history with a dramatic win in the final minutes.

Most Americans in 1960 were not aware of it, but our society was about to say goodbye to the days of the *Ozzie & Harriett* and 'I Like Ike' mentality. After all, Vietnam, Lee Harvey Oswald, the Watts riots and the New York Mets were still to come — as were computers and a whole new way of doing business.

On the foreign front, Americans mostly feared the Russians and their head man, Nikita Khrushchev, and were wondering which nation would emerge victorious in the race for the title of the 'World's #1 Superpower'. Domestically, an eloquent, energetic Baptist preacher from Georgia, Dr. Martin Luther King, Jr., was emerging as the spokesman for equal-rights for all people. Both the Republican and Democratic parties offered an equal-rights election platform - but their tone and substance varied.

For those fortunate enough to have a few dollars to invest in the stock market, the Dow Jones Industrials average hovered around the 600 mark during the summer of 1960. The companies whose stocks had the highest trading volumes were: Universal Match, American Motors, Standard Oil of New Jersey, Sperry-Rand Corporation and Bethlehem Steel.

The Trials Process

THE National AAU organized three levels of Trials that constituted the elimination process for selecting the eight Freestyle and eight Greco-Roman wrestlers who would represent the US in the Olympics in August. First, in the spring, wrestlers competed in one of eight Regional Qualifiers. You had to place 1st or 2nd to be invited to the 'Final Olympic Team Trials' tournament held in Ames, Iowa. However, these weren't really the final 'Final Trials'.

The Olympic Wrestling Committee declared that a two-week-long Final Olympic Training Camp (the 'Camp') would take place starting July 22 on Olympic-team Coach Port Robertson's hallowed ground — the University of Oklahoma campus in Norman. This Camp would provide intensive training for the competitors, plus the ultimate and deciding round of wrestle-offs. To qualify for the Camp, wrestlers had to place in the top three in their Freestyle weight class at Ames or win the Greco competition.

The Committee voted to give the winner at Ames an advantage. The top man coming out of Ames would have to be defeated twice in a row by a challenger — determined by a wrestle-off between #2 and #3. In the wrestle-offs, draws were considered 'no match'. Freestyle wrestlers at the Camp who also finished in the top three at Ames in Greco could challenge for the Olympic berth in both styles.

The Final Olympic Team Trials — Ames, Iowa, April, 1960

COMING out of the Regional Qualifiers were approximately 150 wrestlers who entered the Freestyle competition. Another 80 tried out for the Greco-Roman team. A handful entered the competition in both styles, hoping to maximize their chances of earning a trip to Rome.

The majority of the Ames contestants were dedicated wrestlers who had competed in college during the decade of the '50s and then honed their skills to learn the international Freestyle and Greco-Roman styles (then referred to as AAU-style). Many wrestled after college in the Armed Services. Amongst the competitors were a sprinkling of grizzled veterans such as Newt Copple, Bill Kerslake, San Francisco veterinarian 'Doc' Northrup, and the 36-year-old Navy cook Hallow Wilson (weighing in at 334 pounds); they were still hungry for competition after decades of wrestling. There were some impressive high-school grapplers in the mix as well.

The teenagers included Chuck Bush of Windsor, New York at 114.5; Wayne Simons — who just won his fourth Virginia high school state title - from Norfolk at 125.5; Frank Lucas from Tucson, Arizona at 136.5; and Roger Olesen, only a sophomore at Washington, New Jersey high school, competing at 160.5 pounds. Young Simons was the most impressive, pinning his first three opponents before getting bounced out of the tournament by Dave Auble. Bush, Lucas and Olesen didn't fare as well, losing opening-round matches to veterans Gil Sanchez, Dick Santoro and Doug Blubaugh, respectively.

There were several close, memorable matches. Dick Wilson and Andy Fitch drew and ended up tied for 1st in the 114.5 Freestyle class, with Wilson declared the winner on a weigh-in tie-breaker. At 147.5, Frank Bettucci and Shelby Wilson drew 0-0 in the final round-robin, giving Bettucci 1st place since Wilson had one more black mark. And at 160.5 Doug Blubaugh and Phil Kinyon also wrestled to a scoreless draw (this was not unusual for these two Oklahoma standouts; they had met five times previously – all draws, the last four scoreless) with Kinyon earning the coveted 1st place due to one-half fewer black marks. At 191 pounds, in an extremely tight match, Dan Brand emerged the winner, as he drew in the finals with Frank Rosenmeyer, who earlier in the day narrowly defeated Bill Farrell by a split-decision. Likewise at heavyweight, Bill Kerslake won the Freestyle title with a split-decision victory over Walt Goltl.

Among those Freestyle wrestlers who tried their hand at Greco-Roman, Toledo, Ohio native Dick Wilson at 114.5 was the only wrestler to win in both Freestyle and Greco, though half-a-dozen others qualified in both styles. This brings us to an interesting story from Oklahoma State graduate Shelby Wilson:

I remember well one of my first Freestyle matches of the Trials at 147.5 pounds. It was with a huge, tough guy in the Marines (Fred Parker). I'm weighing around 153 pounds naturally, and these guys are coming down from 160-170 or so. This was my first hard competition all year and it just about killed me. I thought I would die after the first six minutes, but luckily I was ahead by three points at the break, so I didn't have to go and wrestle down on the mat. I countered his takedown attempt with a whizzer, stuck my head in his chest and threw him right on his back for a fall. My God, I was so tired I was ready to go home.

Luckily, an hour later I recovered and was refreshed for my next bouts. From then on I never felt so tired again. I beat the next couple of guys and then met Greg Ruth. He was huge and very tough but I tied him, which eliminated him and assured me a spot in the top three. Finally, I met up with the favorite, Frank Bettucci, in the finals. He was a 1956 Olympian, a lot older and a more experienced Freestyle wrestler. We wrestled to a draw; he would never open up and really wrestle since he knew a tie would give him 1st place. I ended up 2nd, just ahead of Veryl Long.

At this point, I made a smart, calculated

move to enhance my chances to make the Olympic team. I decided to compete in the Greco-Roman Trials which immediately followed the Freestyle Trials. I was pretty scratched up from the Freestyle tournament, but hoped to finish in the top three in Greco. That would make me eligible to challenge for a Greco spot on the team in Norman if I didn't win in Freestyle.

Going into the Greco Trials, the top two guns at 147.5 were Ben Northrup, 'Doc's' son, and Mike Rodriguez, a big stud and twice a NCAA runner-up from Michigan. Now Rodriguez, in my opinion, was the superior wrestler but he had one problem. He would get angry easily and lose his cool. Northrup knew this and when he went to wrestle Rodriguez, he started baiting him and rubbing his headgear against Rodriguez' – who wasn't wearing a headgear, nor was hardly anyone else in those days – ear. Rodriguez got mad, stormed towards Northrup and threw him off the mat into the chairs. Back in the middle Rodriguez charged again, but this time Northrup used his favorite side-headlock, caught Rodriguez off-guard and pinned him.

Now, an interesting situation came about. I had clinched 3rd place - which I needed to do to be eligible for a Greco wrestle-off spot at the Camp - but still was due to wrestle Northrup. Greco coach Briggs Hunt and the Olympic Committee wanted Rodriguez on the Greco team rather than Northrup. Only the winner of the Greco competition was eligible for the wrestle-offs in Norman, plus the top three in freestyle. If I beat Northrup, Rodriguez would finish 1st. Coach Hunt came to me before my match with Northrup and told me to make sure that I beat him ('put him out of this thing,' said Hunt), because that would ensure that Rodriguez, not Northrup, would advance to the final wrestle-offs in Norman.

Well, I was no dummy. I knew I could beat Northrup any day of the week, but was not at all sure I could beat the tough Rodriguez. Why should I put myself in the position of having to beat Rodriguez at Norman? I would much rather have to compete against Northrup for a berth on the Greco Olympic team. So, I purposely wrestled Northrup to a draw, and then went home. I had guaranteed Northrup a trip to the Final Olympic Training Camp.

Olympic Trial winners in Freestyle at Ames, Iowa. From left: Bill Kerslake, Dan Brand, Ed DeWitt, Phil Kinyon, Frank Bettucci, Linn Long, Dave Auble and Dick Wilson *Courtesy of* Amateur Wrestling News

The 136.5 Freestyle weight class was shaping up as a dog-fight between Lou Giani and Linn Long. Giani, a native of Huntington, New York, was an alternate on the '56 Olympic team and won the 1959 Pan-American championship. Giani recalls his most memorable Ames experience:

I remember hurting both my knees as the tournament progressed. I had wrestled four or five matches, defeating Norm Young in the next to last round, so it was just me and Linn Long left. Long had beaten me at the AAUs earlier that year on weigh-in criteria. When the time came for the Trials finals I could hardly walk. I should have forfeited the last bout to Long, but I wrestled anyway and lost. I really didn't want to wrestle, but my NYAC team members coaxed me into it.

In hindsight that loss gave me the motivation to come back and win at the Camp. What motivated me the most happened at the conclusion of my match with Long. An older man — I believe it was Long's father — comes running out on the mat and acts as the referee, grabbing our hands and raising Long's. That bothered me and stayed with me. Long was a fierce competitor, yet I was determined that I'd be ready for him in Oklahoma.

Linn Long was the wrestling coach at the University of Colorado in 1960 and won the National AAUs that year at 136.5. He tells this story about his rival, Giani:

About 45 minutes before I was to meet Giani in the finals, Lou came up to me and said, 'I'm not wrestling. I'm hurt.' I didn't believe him and sure enough he came out on the mats when it was time to wrestle. The rumor was that the good 190 pound

guy from the NYAC, Henry Wittenberg, told Giani he wasn't going to forfeit. I pinned him.

At the conclusion of the Freestyle competition, the eight winners in these Trials were asked to come together on the center mat to have their picture taken. They didn't know it then, but only three of the eight would end up representing the US in Freestyle at the Rome Olympics. Dick Wilson, Dave Auble, Linn Long, Frank Bettucci, and Phil Kinyon all won the Ames Trials but did not make the eventual Olympic Freestyle team.

As the wrestlers were about to depart Ames, Freestyle coach Robertson and Greco-Roman coach Briggs Hunt called together the 32 men who had qualified for the Camp. They told the wrestlers about travel arrangements and how the ladder system would work. The wrestlers were warned to train well at home over the next three months and to make sure that they came to Norman in excellent condition. Very few knew what they were in for.

Intermezzo

ACTUALLY 35, not 32, wrestlers were invited to the Camp to tryout for the team. For the first time in history, several US wrestlers received an invitation to wrestle-off for an Olympic team berth even though they did not participate in the preceding Trials. The 14 person Olympic Wrestling Committee voted (11 'yes' votes were needed for approval) to extend invitations to three hardship cases — accomplished wrestlers that were unable to compete at Ames due to injury or illness. The invitees were: Jim Burke of Boulder, Colorado, the 1959 Pan American champion at 147.5; Terry McCann of Tulsa, a two-time NCAA champion and a three-time National AAU champion at 125.5; and, Gray Simons, the current NCAA champion from Lock Haven, Pennsylvania.

Not everyone endorsed this move. *The Amateur Wrestling News* (AWN) editor, Jess Hoke of Oklahoma City, wrote in an editorial in the May 16, 1960 edition:

Faced with logic, and possibly a sampling of public opinion, the US Olympic Wrestling Committee reluctantly voted to extend Terry McCann an invitation to join the training squad from which the eventual US Olympic wrestling team will be chosen. Invitations were also extended to two others who were prevented by illness from qualifying, one with limited experience in international-style wrestling, the other with none. Since we advocated suspension of rules to give McCann a chance to make the Olympic team, we were pleased with the committee's action in extending him an invitation. Invitations to the other two are not readily understandable, however, and there is a suspicion that they may have been politically or emotionally inspired.

One might ask — What was *AWN*'s suspicion of politics and emotion when it came to adding Burke and Simons, but not McCann?

McCann and Simons both recall their invitation. Says McCann:

Two weeks before the Ames Trials, I was working out at the Tulsa Y and tore cartilage in my knee. 'That was it for me,' so I thought. However, Clay Roberts, who headed up the

Gray Simons – slick on his feet
Courtesy of Bobby Douglas from his book, The Takedown

Tulsa Y wrestling program, appealed my case to the Olympic Committee. A couple of weeks later I receive a call from Roberts saying, 'I got you an exemption. You will be able to try out for the Olympic team at the summer camp.' I immediately got myself a special knee operation that would fix the torn cartilage so that I could get back on the mats quickly. It was a great idea. Soon after the operation I was up walking, then jogging, and I slowly worked myself into condition over the summer.

Simons doesn't remember the particular problem (reported in the press as "having the mumps"), but he dropped out of the Regional Trials, thus was ineligible for the Ames tournament and everything else. Simons recalls:

My college coach, Hubert Jack, who along with my high school coach, Billy Martin, inspired me to try out for the Olympics in the first place, were well acquainted with one of the Olympic Wrestling Committee members, Rex Peery. Hubert went to Rex, who of course knew me from the NCAA wrestling scene, and pleaded my case. Rex's influence must have counted a lot. I was just a young college sophomore with no international experience. Still, I got a call right after the Ames tournament informing me that I was voted an exemption and should be ready to report to the Norman Camp for final training and wrestle-offs in late July.

That summer I got in my wrestling training back home in Virginia, plus I worked in a concrete plant. My workout partner was Mike Grandstaff, who was an ex-Granby and Norview High wrestler and had finished 3rd in the Ames Trials. I thought I was ready for the Camp.

The Training Camp, Norman, Oklahoma — July/August, 1960

IT WAS like a Penal Colony," recalls Andy Fitch, a competitor at 114.5.

"Toughest camp I've ever witnessed," says Wayne Baughman, who was a Camp observer, spending the summer between his college freshman and sophomore years in Norman.

The 35 Final qualifiers arrived in Norman on July 21. Two-a-day practices started on

Friday morning, July 22 and went through the following weekend when the preliminary wrestle-offs began. Everyone agrees that the conditions were brutal and the Oklahoma heat was miserable. The wrestlers were housed on-campus at the football team dormitory, Washington House. There was neither air conditioning nor fans to stave off the 100-degree-plus temperatures. The wrestlers were assigned two to a room, with 10-12 men cramped in each of the dorm sleeping quarters. Most everyone had trouble sleeping. Gray Simons remembers:

At first, I couldn't sleep at all, it was so darn hot in the dorm. I called my college coach, Hubert Jack, and he gave me some good advice — 'just before climbing into bed at night, get a bottle of water, throw it on the bed and wet the whole sheet down.' I slept a little better after that.

Simons recalls the rugged workout schedule:

It went something like this: get up at 6am, run two miles out and two miles back with weights on your arms and ankles. I was hoping maybe a car would hit me. Then we'd immediately go into the gym and do a half-hour of calisthenics; then wrestle two 12 minute simulated matches against two different opponents. In the afternoon session from 3:30 to 6pm, we would have another half-hour of calisthenics which included running around the room with another guy on your back, an hour of technique training and drills, followed by a half-hour of running up and down the football stadium steps with those weights on once again, followed by some 100-yard wind sprints.

Opinion is divided as to the effectiveness of the rigor. McCann thought:

We were in the best shape come time for the Olympic Games. Our wrestling in the Oklahoma heat gave us an advantage in the Rome heat.

Simons declares:

Just being able to survive was an accomplishment. I remember in my final wrestle-off with Fitch, I was very relaxed — thinking that I'm either going to win and go to the Olympics, or I get to go home early. It all paid off, though. That training helped us beat the Russians.

Ed DeWitt, the 1956 NCAA champion

from Pitt and the top Freestyle wrestler at 174 pounds, offers:

The Camp shouldn't have been in Oklahoma — it was much too hot and humid. California would have been better. And we should not have had to run those stadium stairs. We could easily have slipped on the steps and gotten hurt.

I also believe we should have had Bill Smith rather than Port as our coach — or Dale Thomas would have been good. Thomas was a Freestyle advocate and helped me change from Folkstyle to Freestyle when I was stationed at Ft. Lewis. Port really didn't have any Olympic-style experience. But I did get some great training in with Blubaugh at the Camp. We had been together at West Point, so we knew one another. We'd push each other on the mats every day.

Frank Bettucci knew the rigor was sapping his strength. Others noticed it too, such as Linn Long, who remembers:

Bettucci was getting worn out and discouraged. He came to Norman in top-notch shape, but the heat and conditions were getting to be too much for him. He was older than most of us and he couldn't perform at the level that was his best.

Not all the wrestlers were available and 'in-the-room' all the time.

McCann and Shelby Wilson both spent several sick days in the University infirmary. A couple of challengers had to forfeit their matches due to injury. McCann, in fact, left camp and went back home to Tulsa at the close of the first week. Long says:

Terry was my roommate initially at the Norman camp. He got discouraged and told me that he didn't think the people there liked him. Now Blubaugh, he was something else. Doug never missed a session. He took everything they threw at him. Others could be found in the trainer's room — Doug didn't even know where that door was.

Lou Giani offers some insights on Coach Robertson and some other good memories:

Port Robertson was a gentleman and I considered him a great coach. He was an Okie and thought Oklahoma wrestlers were the greatest. I learned a lot in the training camp from Port and the Oklahoma style of wrestling.

I remember unbelievable elation when I won

Olympian Ed DeWitt, right, did not care for the Oklahoma camp environment *Photograph courtesy of Wade Schalles, from his book,* They Call It Wrestling

a spot on the team. I went running out of the field house to call my wife back home. As I got to the phone booth, I stopped and started to cry tears of joy. It was an incredible feeling — nothing like it.

Shenanigans?

IT ALL depends on whom you ask. The Eastern block — Auble, Bettucci, Farrell, Fitch, plus Russ Camilleri and Linn Long — cite specific examples where they saw favoritism play a significant role in who made the Olympic team. Others, particularly the Oklahomans, say that is baloney.

The Greco match at the final wrestle-offs between Camilleri and Rudy Williams is the one most often cited as being 'shady'. Camilleri, a tough guy from the West Coast, was the challenger. Williams, a black wrestler from Michigan, had to beat Camilleri just once to get the Olympic slot. In their first match, Camilleri won a disputed 1-0 decision with a takedown in the last 15 seconds. Two of the judges called the takedown off, but the voting was split and Camilleri was declared the winner. The second bout was a high scoring affair with Williams jumping out to an early lead on a three-point near-fall. Camilleri went ahead with a tilt and two takedowns. Towards the end of the bout Camilleri tried a lift and, according to many, fell back and landed flat on his shoulders. No call was made and the match, and Olympic berth, was awarded to Camilleri. Auble says:

The Olympic Committee guys, made up primarily of people with close Oklahoma ties, wanted Camilleri, not Williams, on the Olympic squad. Williams had Camilleri pinned — the referee and judges just wouldn't call it.

Teammate Bettucci chimes in:

Those appointed judges took the match away from Williams.

Fitch talks about the Larry Lauchle-Joe Gomes finals match at 125.5 in Greco:

Midway through the match, Gomes gets behind Lauchle while on their feet and goes to launch him over backwards. Lauchle, in defense, hooks Gomes leg with his own leg (an illegal move in Greco). Wham, Gomes falls straight to his back. Ray Swartz, the mat chairman and close friend of Lauchle's coach Rex Peery, immediately calls a fall for Lauchle — ignoring the conspicuous illegal move. It's an outrageous call. I lost all respect for Swartz, but I don't blame Lauchle one bit. He instinctively did what he had to do to avoid getting thrown.

Camilleri, competing at the time for the San Francisco Olympic Club, adds:

There were so many politics, so many trade-offs in the Trials back then. Take the Jim Burke-Shelby Wilson match. Burke had Wilson dead to rights on his back with a cradle. The ref stopped it, saying it was an illegal hold. He shouldn't have — it was legal. Burke got no points and lost.

Linn Long recalls:

I have nothing against Giani, but I believe our last matches were decided by politics. They appointed Ray Sparks as our referee and he was acquainted with Lou. During one of the key moments of our match, Sparks made me get off

Lou's leg, saying that I had an illegal hold. It wasn't illegal.

Bill Farrell adds his thoughts:

The powers-that-be didn't want me, Bettucci or Auble on the team. It was obvious to everyone but the Oklahomans. In my case, [Dan] Brand was clearly better than me, so it didn't matter. I don't recall the issues about Bettucci, but in Auble's case, he should have been on the team. The rule laid down at the start of Camp was, 'If you leave Camp you can't come back.' Well, McCann left Camp and was allowed back. When questioned about that controversial decision, Port Robertson merely said, 'That's the way it is.'

Both Auble and Bettucci feel that they deserved to be on the Olympic team, but lost out due to favoritism. Says Bettucci:

Auble took a hosing at Norman. He clearly won his second bout against McCann. The officials wanted McCann, not Auble, on the team.

Auble adds:

The officials definitely favored Shelby Wilson. Frank was so fed-up with the favoritism shown to the Oklahoma wrestlers that he forfeited his last match, handing Wilson the Olympic spot.

The Final Wrestle-offs

AFTER ten days of practices and preliminary ladder bouts, the final wrestle-offs began on Monday night, August 1. The prime events were scheduled for Monday, Wednesday and Friday, with the University of Oklahoma hosting the Monday and Friday evening matches, and action moving to the Oklahoma State University campus in Stillwater on Wednesday.

The plan was for the first of the three big sessions to be held outdoors at the football stadium — Owen Field — at 8pm Monday. However, after the initial three bouts it was obvious that the heat was a real problem. The mats became extremely slippery from all of the wrestlers' sweat and heavy dew. Hence, the matches were moved inside to the University field house. The crowds were considerable, with paid attendance in the 1,000 to 1,300 range and the fans would loudly cheer for all the Oklahoma-based wrestlers. Somewhere around ten matches a night were contested — mixed amongst Freestyle and Greco-Roman competition.

For those that were more interested in the professional wrestling scene, Dan Hodge was on the card at the Oklahoma City Stockyard Coliseum that week, seeking to retain his world junior-heavyweight title.

Three wrestle-offs stand out:

125.5 pounds Freestyle — Dave Auble vs Terry McCann

DAVE Auble was the eldest of 12 children, growing up in Ithaca, New York, the son of a construction worker. No one in Auble's family had ever attended school past the eighth grade, and even for the young Auble education was not a priority. That is, until he took up wrestling at the age of 14, where he found immediate success and latched on to Bill Layton and Jimmy Miller as his mentors.

Thanks to individual tutoring by Layton's wife and year-round training under Layton at Ithaca high school, Auble developed his academic and wrestling skills so that he was a prize college recruit by his senior year. He elected to stay local and entered Cornell University in the fall of 1956. By the time he graduated four years later, Auble amassed three EIWA crowns and two NCAA titles at 123 pounds, including winning the Outstanding Wrestler award in 1960. In the Freestyle arena, he won the gold medal at 125.5 in the 1959 Pan American Games, pinning his opponent in the round-robin finals. He entered the National AAU freestyle tournament in Oklahoma in 1959 at 125.5 and finished 2nd — to Terry McCann.

The 1960 Olympic Trials, in Auble's own words:

Coming out of the 1960 NCAAs, I was nursing an injured knee and not excited about going to the Trials. I skipped the National AAUs (won

by fellow Cornell teammate Carmen Molino at 125.5) out in San Francisco. With rest, my knee started improving, so I decided to go for it. I qualified through the New England District tryouts at Harvard and headed out to Ames in late April for the Trials.

In my first match, while favoring a bad left knee, I stretched my tendon in my right knee. I now was wrestling with two bad knees. I had a good tournament though, pinning five of the seven opponents I faced. I was trying to shorten the matches so I wouldn't have to wrestle all that long.

In the semis, I faced a long-time nemesis, Larry Lauchle. I beat him by a big score, but during the match Lauchle got a bear-hug on me and separated my ribs. There was lots of pain; I couldn't pull down, only pull up. In the finals match I went on to pin Ray Osborne. If he knew how much I was hurting he probably would have beaten me. The next day coaches Layton and Miller had to carry me out of bed and set me in a hot tub to loosen up my body just so I could walk.

After Ames, I went back to Ithaca, figuring that I pretty much had an Olympic berth waiting, since Terry McCann missed the Trials due to an injury. Later I found out that he received an exemption and was invited to the Camp even though he skipped the Qualifier. I too had a bad knee injury, but didn't realize that you could get an exemption.

It was a struggle for me through the spring and summer. I had to return to classes at Cornell so I could graduate that June and I had to keep in shape for the Finals Camp. I was depressed because of the injuries — I couldn't turn over in bed because of the pain in my knees and ribs. As the summer progressed, I healed and worked out daily under Layton's supervision.

In August, I went out to the Camp in Oklahoma with Frank Bettucci and coaches Layton and Miller. The weather was hot and miserable, and they ran an intense camp. Actually, I thrived on the work regime and the training. For McCann to quit, as tough as he was, you know it had to be rigorous. There was so much sweat pouring out from everyone, they couldn't keep the mats dry. It was kinda a bizarre experience.

At the start of Camp the coaches laid down

McCann recovered from a serious knee injury to make the 1960 Olympic team... and achieved the ultimate glory at the Games in Rome *Photograph courtesy of the late Terry McCann*

the rules for us. They made it very clear - it would be a tough. 1) If anyone leaves the Camp, they are off the team; 2) if anyone brings their family to the Camp, they are off the team; 3) and we had to live in the dorms. Not everyone played by these rules, however.

McCann left and went home at the end of the first week of Camp. I am not sure why. The coaches came and told me I now had made the final team. Several days later McCann returned, brings his wife back with him and moves into a local hotel. Then they told me I had to wrestle him for the team spot. None of this seemed fair to me. After finding out that McCann was liv-

ing in a hotel, our coaches went to the Committee and requested that we get a hotel room. They couldn't say 'no' since they gave the okay for McCann to live there, so we moved and got some comfortable nights' sleep at last.

As part of the exemption, McCann was suppose to have to wrestle and beat both the #3 and #2 guys in order to challenge me. However, #3 Osborne withdrew due to an injury and the #2 man, Lauchle, withdrew after winning the Greco spot. So, it was just McCann and me. He had to beat me twice in a row to make the team.

In the first challenge match, I came out charging. He was a lot more experienced than me, caught me coming in and pancaked me to my back for a three-point move. I took him down twice later in the bout, but he wisely stayed away from me the rest of the time and beat me. My coaches changed our match strategy for the second bout and told me to wrestle smarter, more cautiously. I did and scored a takedown with a duck-under in the first period. Terry never scored a point against me. I thought I won and had the team made. However, at the end of the match the referee raised Terry's hand as two of the judges voted for Terry, giving him a split-decision. In those days the scores were never posted during the match so you never knew the score. For some reason two of the judges awarded the match to him.

As far as I'm concerned, I won that second match and should have made the team.

In retrospect, McCann was one of the greatest wrestlers I ever saw. When I was in high school, he was winning NCAA titles and he had a god-like status with me. He was five years older, far more experienced, particularly in Freestyle, with several victories over the Russians. Wrestling him coming just a few months out of college, I was at a psychological disadvantage. Looking back at it, with his experience he probably would have done better than me at the Olympics. We'll never know.

I bear no grudges against Terry. I have great admiration for him. We became close friends and together coached an international USA team in the mid-'70s in a Pan-American tournament. But, I do have bitterness towards the Trials administrators and their politics. They took away my deserved opportunity. I think

> " I bear no grudges against Terry. I have great admiration for him... But, I do have bitterness towards the Trials administrators and their politics. They took away my deserved opportunity.
>
> — DAVE AUBLE

Terry saw some of this injustice and that was a reason why he led the charge to change the operation of the Trials over to the US Wrestling Federation and eventually USA Wrestling.

Terry McCann was the eldest of six children and raised in the tough section of northwest Chicago. His father worked in maintenance for the local library. He was always the smallest kid in the playground, weighing only 55 pounds at the age of 11. Fortunately, the local playground had a wrestling program and he picked up the sport easily. He didn't pick up studies much though. He cut so many classes as a high school freshman that he was suspended and had to start over.

He started wrestling year-round in high school, working out off-season at both the University of Illinois-Chicago and Northwestern University. He won the Chicago city high school championship three times. Even though he graduated near the bottom of his high school class, the University of Iowa accepted him as a probationary student in 1952. McCann, who later in life rose to become the Executive Director of Toastmasters International, maintained a B average and won a full scholarship after his freshman year.

McCann won two Big Ten titles and two NCAA titles while wrestling for Iowa. He also won the National AAU freestyle championship at 125.5 pounds in 1957, 1958 and 1959. He wrestled against a touring Russian team in the summer of 1958 and was the only American to record any victory at all, winning three matches and tying one.

Gray Simons was a Trials workout partner of McCann and in a recent interview had this to say about him:

I worked out with Terry a bit at the Camp

and particularly during those days leading up to the Olympics because the other guys around his weight, Lou Giani and Larry Lauchle, wanted no part of him. I could more or less stay with Terry on our feet, but he'd beat me up good down on the mat. He was a terror — a forerunner of the Brands brothers.

The 1960 Trials, in McCann's words:

I first tried out for the Olympics in 1952 and was runner-up in the Regional Trials, but didn't make the team. In 1956 I believe I would have made the team, but I couldn't go to the Trials — my college coach wasn't in favor of me going and I was married and had two kids. I needed to work in order to support my family. I couldn't take the time off from school or from work. When I graduated from the University of Iowa in February, 1957 I then started thinking ahead to the 1960 Rome Olympics.

The AAU was the US governing body for international wrestling in the '50s and '60s and they were pretty worthless. We had no international experience — we never went to the World Championships. There were only a couple of places to go in the whole country where you could get Freestyle or Greco-Roman training — primarily New York at the Athletic Club, San Francisco at the Olympic Club, and Oklahoma. Well, I got a call from the Oklahoma folks asking if I wanted to come to Tulsa and be part of the Tulsa Wrestling Club working out at the Tulsa YMCA. I accepted their invitation and moved my family to Tulsa. I found a job at a refinery there. Unfortunately, that was where I became exposed to asbestos and now I have been diagnosed with incurable cancer.

I tried to get as much international wrestling experience as I could. After winning the National AAUs in 1957, a group of us traveled to Japan. Clay Roberts of the Tulsa Y was our team coach; Doug Blubaugh and Linn Long were among my teammates on the trip. It was a great experience training and wrestling over there.

The following April the Russians came to the US and we wrestled four meets against them. I was the only American to win a match. In the spring of 1959, the great Japanese Olympic champion, Shozo Sasahara, came to the United States. During his tour he stayed with my family for two weeks. It was a fabulous experience

getting to know him and work with him on various wrestling holds and techniques. Later that summer I traveled with an All-Star US team to Russia and Eastern Europe and won all my matches against the Russians. By now, the Russians thought I was good and were eager to work out with me.

After hearing that I was invited by the Olympic Wrestling Committee to the Team Training Camp, I had my operation. By the time Camp opened in July, I had started to run, do the calisthenics, and work out on the mat. I worked out at the Tulsa Y and at Tulsa Webster high school, mostly with local high school and college kids.

It was hot in Norman but that didn't bother me. But, just coming back from my knee operation, I did have a hard time with the daily four-mile run and the stadium steps. After several days of workouts, I became completely dehydrated and fainted. I woke up in the University infirmary with IVs all over my body. I was in the infirmary for 36 hours, had lots of medication and came out of there very weak. I was discouraged, so I left Camp and drove the 90 miles to Tulsa to be with my wife and my five kids.

This was just two days before I was due to wrestle Auble. I wasn't afraid of Auble or anyone else. However, I was so weak I thought I would lose, and I just couldn't face it.

When I showed up at home, my wife [Lu McCann] was furious with me. 'Why are you here?' were the first words out of her mouth. She told me that the Committee went out of its way to give me this chance and they took a lot of criticism for doing it, and that I couldn't back out now. I didn't want to go back, but my wife had my boss — I was working at the Jaycees — summon me to his office. He gave me the ultimatum: either go back to Camp or look for a job somewhere else! After getting a good night's sleep at home, I jumped in my car and drove back to Norman.

As soon as I got back to Camp, I went to Coach Robertson, explained why I had left. I asked for reinstatement and for a few extra days postponement of my matches with Auble so I could recover. Port told me that while I did have the right to come back, postponing the challenge matches would be unfair and I had to keep to *the original schedule. So the next day Auble and I faced off.*

I really don't recall the details of the matches. I don't remember them as being that close, though one was a split-decision by the judges in my favor. You never knew the scores, they weren't posted. I know that the New York guys thought the whole thing was rigged in favor of the Oklahoma wrestlers, but I tell you, there were no shenanigans. Coach Robertson was a perfect gentleman and the most fair man to ever live. No one from the University of Oklahoma, where Port coached, made the team. There was no favoritism; everyone was treated equally.

Coach Robertson got us in the best shape. He knew that if we could wrestle in the heat in Oklahoma, we'd have an advantage in the Rome heat.

Frank Bettucci and Shelby Wilson's coach, Myron Roderick, during happier times together
Photograph courtesy of Frank Bettucci

147.5 pounds Freestyle – Frank Bettucci vs Shelby Wilson

FRANK Bettucci was another Ithaca, New York native, growing up in the backstreets of the university town. Coming from a broken home, he put his energies into athletics. He took up wrestling and was the starting halfback in football at Ithaca high school both his junior and senior years. His real talent showed on the wrestling mats, where he won several Sectional titles and Junior National honors.

In the fall of 1949, Bettucci entered Cornell University, working a myriad of part-time jobs to help earn his way through school. He continued to excel in the wrestling arena, winning the prestigious Wilkes tournament in 1950 and the Easterns as a young sophomore in 1951. Before he graduated from Cornell in 1953, Bettucci claimed three EIWA individual championships at 147 pounds and a NCAA championship in 1953, when he was selected as the Outstanding Wrestler.

After graduation, Bettucci entered the Army and continued his drive for an Olympic berth. In the 1956 Trials, he defeated his long-time nemesis, Tommy Evans, for the top spot at 147.5 on the US Olympic team. Unfortunately, three days before the Olympic

wrestling matches were scheduled to start in Melbourne, Bettucci sustained a severe knee injury in practice and he had to withdraw. He decided then and there to give it one more shot – the 1960 Olympics in Rome.

The 1960 Trials, in Bettucci's words:

I was ready for all comers at the Trials in Ames and finished 1st at 147.5. Shelby Wilson and I tied in our match, but I was the overall winner of the weight class. I beat Greg Ruth, while Wilson and Ruth tied each other – that was the difference. At the time, I thought I had made the Olympic team. No one informed me that we would have wrestle-offs in Oklahoma.

During the summer I worked out every day, same as Auble, back in Ithaca. I was in great shape when we left for the Camp. However, once we got there, things started to change. It was awfully hot and I had trouble sleeping. They put Auble and me in a room on the top floor of the dormitory. There were no fans or air-conditioners up there. I couldn't get to sleep until 2am and they woke us up at 6am to go on our four-mile run. Once, I walked into the rooms on the first floor of the dorm where the Oklahoma guys were housed. Damn, if they didn't have these big fans in their room.

It seemed to me that things were backwards

at the practices. Most all the effort was put into the running. We had to workout with our competitor — I had to work out with Shelby Wilson — and we were all reluctant to show each other our moves, thus we didn't wrestle very hard. It was not a satisfying situation. Plus, it was so hot that I had to drink a lot of water to avoid becoming dehydrated. As a result my weight started shooting up.

I could see myself going downhill. In one of the workouts I hurt my shoulder and I also cracked a rib while scrimmaging with Wilson. It was painful and I didn't know how I was going to recuperate. The energy was pouring out of me bit by bit. The routine was wearing me down and I was getting dejected.

Finally, it was time for my wrestle-off match with Wilson. It was on a Friday night in front of all the vocal Oklahoma fans and they were booing me. We both just danced around with no action. I never before felt that way in a match. I just didn't have the poop to go after him. That match ended in a 0-0 draw. [Author's note: it was officially scored as a victory for Wilson, with two judges scoring it a 1-0 decision for Wilson, giving him a point for a controversial takedown, and two judges calling it a scoreless draw.]

Wilson and I were scheduled for our second match the next morning. I was mentally torn apart and hurting a lot. I told my coach that I was not ready and was going to forfeit this match to Wilson. So, we did, thinking that I'd have one more match to see who makes the team. They sent everyone home, yet I believed that we'd go back and have another wrestle-off but no word ever came. They never sent for me.

There was a strong tight-knit contingent of Oklahoma connected people controlling the whole operation. The 'club' of sorts consisted of McCann's mentor Clay Roberts, Ray Swartz and Port Robertson — even Rex Peery. They figured ways to do favors for each other. Referee/judge Dale Thomas wanted his guy, Fritz Fivian, to make the team in Greco; the Wrestling Committee favored McCann and Wilson for the Freestyle team. Backroom deals were made. The Committee picked the judges and officials and let them know who they wanted on the team. Back at Ithaca, the Cornell Athletic Director tried to appeal my case and Auble's case to the US Olympic Committee, but it was denied.

Shelby Wilson grew up on a farm in Ponca City, Oklahoma. As a youngster he learned about fixing farm machinery and plowing the soil. He also learned how to wrestle; and in high school and college, how to be a bridesmaid.

At Ponca City high school, Wilson was undefeated in dual meets his last three years. However, in the State Tournament, he lost one match each year — twice in the finals. He went on to Oklahoma State, where he again had an undefeated career in dual meets. In his sophomore year, 1956-57, he only wrestled in one dual and won it, but was injured and was out for the rest of the year. In the following two seasons, Wilson won the Big Eight conference championship, but was upset in the finals of the NCAAs both times.

Wilson was a poster-boy for the Oklahoma State "take 'em down, let 'em up" style of wrestling. Up until 1960 under the Olympic rules, securing a takedown and releasing an opponent was of no value. Wilson didn't care for this. But the rules changed to eliminate the point for an escape; Wilson reconsidered his goals.

The 1960 Trials, in Wilson's words:

During the 1959-60 college wrestling season I was still in school, working with guys in the room as an unofficial assistant coach to Myron Roderick. I really gave no thought of competing in the Olympics, but Roderick said 'Why not try out for them? Give it a go at 136.5.'

In 1958 and 1959 I had cut to 137 pounds for the NCAAs after wrestling all year at 147. My only college defeats came at 137, so I didn't like the idea of sucking down a weight. Being a religious Christian, I prayed about things and sought higher wisdom. I knew I needed to wrestle 147.5 if I were to have a chance. It was the only time in my life I went against my coach's wishes, but I made the decision to compete at 147.5.

I had never wrestled in an international competition, but in early 1960 I began formulating a plan. I would take what I knew best and apply it to the Freestyle mode of wrestling. I would perfect my takedown ability and concentrate on defense on bottom. 'If I can take a guy down and not let him turn me, I can beat him' was my mind set.

I had no competition all year until I entered two Olympic Regional Qualifying tournaments in the spring. One was in Ponca City, my hometown, and the other in Lamar, Colorado. I won both and was on my way to Ames for the Olympic Trials.

Going into Ames, no one had much respect for me since I never was an NCAA champion nor had any international Freestyle experience. Bob Dellinger, the Hall of Fame writer from Oklahoma, helped me gain a seed. He went to the seeding meeting, spoke on my behalf and got me a decent seed so I wouldn't be thrown to the wolves right away. I ended up 2nd in Freestyle and 3rd in Greco.

Between the Ames Final Trials and the Camp in Norman, I went back to Oklahoma. The person I owe the most for preparing me for the Final Camp is Phil Kinyon, who was a finalist at 160.5. I lived with him on his farm outside Stillwater and we would work and wrestle with each other every day. We'd get up, run three miles or so, go bale the hay and then wrestle. We'd practice some moves, then go full force. We'd set the clock for 15 minutes and go after each other. I could pretty much hold my own with him. He was a great defensive wrestler on his feet, so I had to wrestle smart to get anything on him.

I had five 'go-to' takedown moves. The duck-under was my favorite, but I also regularly used the single, the double, a snap-down drag and a regular arm drag. Kinyon gave me the competition on my feet that I needed to excel. He helped me perfect my plan. Phil was good, but I'd rather wrestle him any day than Doug Blubaugh. Blubaugh was too powerful.

I came to the Camp with the flu and spent the first three days in the infirmary. I worked out the next day and recovered nicely since my body was in such good shape. After one day of practice, I entered the Greco Trials. I had to beat Ben Northrup twice in a row since he was the champion coming out of Ames. I won both matches pretty easily and I was awarded the spot on the Greco team. But I really wanted the Freestyle spot.

Hall Of Fame coach Port Robertson ran a gruelling camp in Norman, Oklahoma
Photograph courtesy of Amateur Wrestling News

My first Freestyle challenge bout was against Jim Burke from Colorado. That match was the closest I came to not making the team. For some silly reason I put the legs in on him while down. He jammed back into me crushing me to the mat and I was hurting. I threw up my hands signaling for a 'timeout'. Two judges saw it, but one didn't and scored the points for Burke. The match came down to a split-decision in my favor. I never put the legs in again.

Next up were the final matches with Bettucci. An interesting incident occurred a few nights earlier when I made the Greco team. Frank's coaches tried to convince Port Robertson, the Freestyle coach, to change the rules, arguing that I should not be allowed to try out for Freestyle since I had already won the spot in Greco. Port stood by the rules and allowed me to challenge in Freestyle. If it wasn't for Port's honor of the rules, they would have had me off the Freestyle team. Port was a most honorable and respected man.

Since I finished behind Bettucci at Ames, I had to beat him twice in a row to make the team. We wrestled evenly in the first match with *no scoring until the last minute. I was on the offense, chasing him for 12 minutes. The officials said there were to be no ties; we had to have a victor. I kept shooting and with less than a minute to go I caught him near the edge of the mat and scored a takedown. The judges had to give me a point. I held on to him to win.*

I was really fired up. We were supposed to wrestle again the next day, but Bettucci forfeited and left Camp. I don't know why he did that. What I did know was that I had made the Freestyle team at 147.5. I know he wouldn't have beaten me anyway. At that point, I felt no one could beat me.

Making the US Olympic team gave me a great feeling of gratitude for being able to represent my country. There was no big celebration. It was not something that I didn't expect. However, other than my younger brother, no one gave me a snowball's chance in hell of making the team. You weren't supposed to be able to win with the 'take 'em down, let 'em up' style in international competition. But I stuck to my plan and I did it. I retired undefeated at 147 pounds — through both college and Freestyle competition.

160.5 pounds Freestyle — Doug Blubaugh vs Phil Kinyon

DOUG Blubaugh grew up on a farm in Ponca City just few years before Shelby Wilson. Even though he was asthmatic, he took up wrestling in the ninth grade. While the canvas mat covers would hurt his nasal condition, he found that the more he trained, the better the asthma condition became. Blubaugh kept on training.

Under the guidance of his high school coaches, Melvin Clodfelter and Grady Peninger, Blubaugh developed into a strong, mature wrestler. He won the Oklahoma high school championship at 141 pounds as a senior in 1953 and was named the tournament's Outstanding Wrestler. Art Griffith recruited him to Oklahoma State University where he became an NCAA champion in 1957, after finishing 3rd and 2nd the two preceding years.

The 1960 Trials, in Blubaugh's words:

I graduated from college in 1957 and won the AAUs that year. I was part of the five man tour of Japan during the summer of '57 where I won all my matches. I saw that I could compete with them and that was a turning point. It made me shift gears to get ready to compete in the 1960 Olympics.

I joined the Army for three years. I loved the military and probably should have stayed in it for a career. They found out while I was at Ft. Knox that I had good wrestling experience and asked if I wanted to go to West Point for my duty — workout and train the plebes. I had joined to go to Germany, but this was a better opportunity for me.

Leroy Alitz was the West Point coach and I helped him train the team. Unfortunately, there was no good competition there for me except Al Rushatz. He was a tough one and a good workout partner. Bill Farrell was the NYAC coach and asked me if I would wrestle for them. 'Sure', I told him. They paid for my travel to tournaments in California, Mexico, all over the country. I was only making $72 per month as a private, but they upped it to $125 when I went Airborne.

My competition for years was Phil Kinyon. He was one year behind me in high school and at OSU. In high school, I beat him once for the conference championship. During my sophomore year in Stillwater we worked out every day together. They were very hard workouts and we exhausted each other. Phil was awfully strong. The first time I saw him in the wrestling room, he went to the chin-up bar, and with just his left hand he did seven full chin-ups; then repeated that with his right hand. I had a lot of respect for him then and still do. He could draw with anyone in the world. I don't know why he didn't turn it loose, he would have been even better.

I was the more aggressive wrestler of the two of us; Phil was the more defensive. We wrestled each other competitively eleven times; I drew with him nine times and beat him twice. At the Ames Trials, I had a tougher draw, I think, so when we ended up tying each other in the final, he was awarded 1st place due to fewer black marks. This meant that I had to beat him twice in a row at the Norman Camp to make the team.

America's triumphant trio of gold medalists received a heroes' welcome when they returned from Rome. From left: Shelby Wilson, Terry McCann, Doug Blubaugh *Photograph courtesy of* Amateur Wrestling News

I knew Port Robertson well, back from the days when he recruited me (unsuccessfully), and was ready for his hard work routine. Many others were not ready and wanted to go home. In my first three matches with Kinyon, we wrestled to a draw. It was like watching paint dry. We knew each other so well, going back to our college days and then as workout partners at Camp. After the third match, the people running the show said, 'We have to have a winner.' My reply was, 'Well just leave us out there until someone scores.' They said, 'No, we can't do it that way, but at the end of the next match we are going to declare a winner.'

We wrestled a fourth time. There was no activity as we wrestled a scoreless draw, but they declared me the winner (a split referee decision). I'm sure Phil didn't like that call. Still, I had to beat him twice. The next day they took us off to some small place on campus and had us wrestle-off again — our fifth match. I won that bout and made the team. I was very happy and was really glad to be an Olympic teammate of

my best friend, Shelby Wilson.

Phil Kinyon was born in that hotbed of amateur wrestling, Stillwater, Oklahoma. He became very proficient at wrestling while a high school student. In his junior year, 1953, Kinyon won the Oklahoma high school championship at 148 pounds. His senior year was the best — he won the championship at 168 pounds and was named the Outstanding Wrestler. His brother, Jim Kinyon, also won a state title that year at 157 pounds.

Coming out of high school, Kinyon was strongly recruited by the Oklahoma State coach, Art Griffith. Kinyon signed on and spent his freshman year at OSU. However, he admittedly was not ready for the rigors of college life and dropped out of school after one year. His local hero, Dan Hodge, had recently joined the Navy and received some notable Freestyle wrestling training, so Kinyon decided to enlist and wrestle in the Navy, too. He took up Freestyle in 1955 in San Diego at the Naval Training Center and prepared for the 1956 Olympics at UCLA, training there under Briggs Hunt. However, he was beaten by Larry TenPas and did not to make the US team.

The 1960 Trials from Phil Kinyon's view:

I was a takedown guy who loved to take people down. At Oklahoma State I learned a lot about multiple takedown setups from Myron Roderick and later, Ronnie Clinton. I didn't like to ride much, but I worked hard from underneath. I had to get out from under there. Ray Swartz helped me while I was training at the Naval Academy. He taught me a lot about how to wrestle against the Russians and Turks, especially how to avoid their lifts and throws.

In the Navy, we did a lot of weights and strength work and I worked on my stamina. I got some excellent experience wrestling against the Russians and other international men. They normally worked out four or five hours a day; in the US we usually just had two or three hour practices. I stepped up my training, receiving great instruction from Ned Blass and Doc Northrup. I wrestled against the Russians twice during their tour here in 1958 but lost both times. I also competed in the AAU's that year, finishing 2nd to TenPas, but ahead of Fritz Fivian and Blubaugh at 160.5.

When it came to the 1960 Trials, I knew

exactly what I had to do. Getting ready for the Trials and Camp, I worked a lot with Shelby Wilson. We worked hard on our strength and stamina and got used to wrestling in the Oklahoma heat.

I knew Blubaugh all too well, having wrestled against him hundreds of times in the Oklahoma State room and in tournaments. He was very strong with fabulous reactions. He couldn't see very good, but he did a lot of training and wasn't a bit afraid of hard work. We kept drawing against each other. We knew each other's moves too well. Neither of us could penetrate the other. Finally, one time he did, in our last wrestle-off at the Camp, and he beat me out for the spot on the team.

After our final match I said to him, 'Doug, I am thrilled that you have won the chance to wrestle in the Olympics. Take my energy with you. Don't be afraid.' I was tickled for him and for Shelby. I think Doug was the better of the two of us to go to Rome.

Wayne Baughman remembers those Blubaugh versus Kinyon matches and the sight of Blubaugh's bloodied face and Kinyon's eye closed shut as they slowly staggered off the mat after their final bout. "Toughest animals in the world" is how Baughman describes the two warriors.

1960 OLYMPIC TEAM MEMBERS

	FREESTYLE	GRECO-ROMAN
114.5	Gray Simons (5th)	Dick Wilson
125.5	Terry McCann (1st)	Larry Lauchle
136.5	Lou Giani	Lee Allen
147.5	Shelby Wilson (1st)	Ben Northrup
160.5	Doug Blubaugh (1st)	Fritz Fivian
174	Ed Dewitt (4th)	Russ Camilleri
191	Dan Brand (5th)	Howard George
HWT	Bill Kerslake	Dale Lewis

★ THIS was the first time since 1932 that the US won three gold medals in Freestyle. The US finished as the runner-up to Turkey in the unofficial team scoring. Pre-Olympic predictions did not anticipate anywhere near this level of success.

1960 PRESIDENTIAL ELECTION

★ LOOKING at the popular vote, the 1960 election was the closest one of the twentieth century. Nixon did not concede the election until the afternoon of Wednesday, November 9, the day after the polls closed. There were numerous charges of shenanigans at the polls, especially in the states led by prominent Democrats, Lyndon Johnson and Richard Daley.

THE SCORECARD

John F. Kennedy Lyndon B. Johnson	303 Electoral Votes 49.7% of Popular Vote
Richard M. Nixon Henry C. Lodge	216 Electoral Votes 49.5% of Popular Vote

1964
I HAVE A DREAM

> " I liked Coach Peery and thought he was a good coach. He liked me – I think because of my work ethic. He didn't care for Charlie Tribble, because of Charlie's work ethic. That happens at times with coaches. I know Coach Peery would rather have seen Lahr on the team than Tribble. I had the same thing happen against me in the World Team tryouts in '70.
>
> — Bobby Douglas, winner of the Trials at 138.5

FOR the US wrestlers, it was a mixed bag leading up to the 1964 Olympic year. People were stunned by the three Freestyle gold medals we won in Rome. Was that an anomaly, or were our best men now ready to claim gold medals on a regular basis? Thankfully, our wrestlers finally started to engage in regular international competition, as a US team competed in the World Championship Freestyle and Greco-Roman tournaments in 1961, 1962 and 1963. Toledo, Ohio hosted the '62 Worlds. And the wrestling community was thrilled when each of our eight Freestyle wrestlers brought home a 1963 Pan-American championship gold medal.

On the other hand, our 1960 Olympic gold medalists – Terry McCann, Shelby Wilson and Doug Blubaugh – all retired. In the three Freestyle World Championship tournaments from 1961-1963 we were mediocre, never finishing higher than 6th in the team standings. Nary a gold nor a silver medal winner came from the US. The best we could garner were three bronze medals, earned by Jim Ferguson, Greg Ruth and Dan Brand, over the entire three year period. In Greco, we had just two bronze medal winners – Jim Burke and Jim Raschke – during the same time-frame.

To top it all off, the Russians used their international influence at FILA, the international governing body for Olympic-style

Previoius spread: Former Cornell University teammates Carmen Molino and Dave Auble were the two top competitors for the 125.5 Freestyle spot *Photograph courtesy of Bobby Douglas*

wrestling, to have the weight classes changed in their favor. The Russians traditionally have been strongest in the heaviest weight classes and the Americans strongest in the middle weights. For 1964, and 1968, one middleweight class was dropped. 147.5 and 160.5 were combined into the 154-pound weight class, and another weight class, 213.5, was added. It looked like it was going to be impossible to repeat the success our team achieved in 1960.

In the other-than-wrestling world, the way of life for many Americans was taking some uneasy turns in 1964. We were still reeling from with the assassination of our President, John Kennedy, and didn't fully know or understand the facts behind his killing. Lyndon Johnson succeeded Kennedy and fought hard to get the 1964 Civil Rights Act passed. Despite objections from many Southerners and ultra-conservatives, Johnson signed the law, which meant that African-Americans could no longer be excluded from restaurants, hotels and other public facilities.

On the foreign front, the US was stepping up its role in the Vietnam conflict. Our troops began occupying South Vietnam in 1961 and by August, 1964, while the US Wrestling Trials were being held in New York City, the 248th American died in action. Who could foresee that more than 58,000 US soldiers would end up being killed and another 300,000 wounded in this terrible war?

The summer of '64 is remembered by Philadelphia Phillies fans as the year of their astounding season-end collapse, but most of the country was paying more attention to the upcoming Presidential election. The American people were given a clear choice. Republicans nominated for President the Arizona-based conservative, Barry Goldwater, who had voted against the Civil Rights Act of 1964 and the nuclear test-ban treaty of 1963. He called for deep cuts in the country's social programs and suggested that Social Security become voluntary.

The 1964 presidential race is said to be Hillary Clinton's first active participation in politics; she was 'a Goldwater girl'.

The Democrats held their National Convention in Atlantic City, where the delegates amused themselves watching a white horse, ridden by a little lady in a bathing suit, jump off the pier into the ocean every night. When they got down to business, the Democrats endorsed Lyndon Johnson for re-election as president. They praised his nine-month White House record which emphasized 'people, prosperity, preparedness and peace.' Johnson selected Hubert Humphrey as his running mate. Johnson and Humphrey campaigned for continued social programs and a limited involvement in Vietnam.

The economic picture remained bright for those Americans with the wisdom and money to invest in the stock market. The Dow Jones Industrial average reached 850 in September, 1964. The most active stocks in trading volume were: Chrysler, Pan American, Ford Motor, Anaconda and General Dynamics.

The Trials Process

IN THE wrestling world, the '64 US Wrestling Olympic Committee, chaired by Dr. Albert de Ferrari, tinkered a bit with the format used in '60 for selecting Olympic team members. The three level Trials process — Regional Qualifying Trials, a Final Trials tournament and the Final Team Selection Training Camp — remained in place. The difference was that the Final Camp was scheduled to immediately follow the Final Trials tournament, rather than having a three-month break between the two.

The New York World's Fair was selected as the host site for the Final Trials tournament starting August 24. This was an interesting selection. Perhaps the officials thought the wrestling would be considered as an exhibit worth seeing by the millions of tourists walking through the Fairgrounds. Actually, that was the same site, the Singer Bowl, where many of the wrestlers competed during the 1964 National AAU tournament in June.

The top two place winners from the Final Trials in both Freestyle and Greco, plus some invitees, would advance to the three-week Final Camp for training and final wrestle-offs. The Camp was scheduled to commence at the end of August in Annapolis, Maryland. The Committee named Rex Peery as the Freestyle team coach, Dean Rockwell the Greco team coach and Fendley Collins as overall team manager.

Russ Camilleri fondly remembers Rockwell, his Greco-Roman coach:

When the Greco team was selected, Coach Rockwell gathered the squad together and started out by saying, 'Do you know why I was appointed as the Greco-Roman team coach? It's because I raised more money than anyone else. I've never done this before but I'm going to give it my all.' We were a bit stunned but I admired his candor. He got us in great shape and he ended up being one of the best coaches I ever had.

I didn't know until many years later that Coach Rockwell was a Navy hero in World War II. As a young lieutenant, he won the Silver Star for his heroics at Omaha Beach on D-day. He was in charge of seven LSTs (Landing Ship Tanks) and saved them from annihilation by breaking orders of radio silence. Rockwell's war record is well documented in the books written by Stephen Ambrose, America's preeminent military historian.

From April through mid-August, wrestlers from across the country competed in 22 Olympic Regional tryout tournaments, all vying for a chance to be one of the 16 wrestlers to represent the US in the Tokyo Olympics in October. One of those competitors was Wayne Hicks, who was completing his second year at the US Naval Academy and in March had won the 137-pound EIWA title.

Hicks recalls:

I had a little bit of a background in Freestyle wrestling. While in high school, I did some fool-

ing around with Freestyle, entering the New Jersey AAUs and some other local tournaments. At the Naval Academy, Coach [Ed] Peery taught us some throws, basic turns from the top position, the rules, etc. So, when the college season was over I thought I'd give the Olympic Trials a go.

I entered the Eastern Olympic Qualifier tournament at Lehigh University in early May in the 138.5 weight class. Unfortunately, I lost to Dave Auble and Bobby Guzzo and didn't qualify for the Final Trials. I do remember putting Auble on his back briefly with a step-over move, but the ref was too shocked to call the fall.

For a couple of months in the summer, I had to attend Navy flight training in Jacksonville but was still itching to wrestle. Right after my flight training, I drove across the country with my roommate. I knew the last Regional Qualifier was being held at the Long Beach Naval Station in August. I stayed at my roommate's place out there and his sister dyed my hair blonde. I entered the tournament in the 154-pound class and remember wrestling Joe Seay to a draw. Anyway, I qualified at 154 pounds and was on my way to the Final Trials that were starting in just ten days in New York. However, Coach Peery made me dye my hair back to its normal color before he'd let me wrestle at the World's Fair competition.

The Final Trials — World's Fair, Singer Bowl, New York — August, 1964

MANY people that were there agree that the '64 Final Trials tournament was 'a real mess'. Larry Lauchle, a veteran from the 1960 team, says:

This was the most messed-up Trials I ever saw. The mats were so hot you couldn't touch them. We started wrestling outside in the Singer Bowl but they had to move the mats under the pavilion due to the heat. And the scales — that's another story. We were ready for weigh-in but the scales weren't to be found. Everyone was pissed. I remember seeing people finally taking the scales out of their carton, hastily assembling them and then weighing in everyone without

even certifying the scales.

Ron Finley and Mike Harman, both fighting for a spot at 138.5, agree with the poor conditions. Former Oregon State standout Finley recalls:

The mats were so hot that you didn't dare want to get down on the mat. As soon as I got my takedown, I'd have to let my opponent loose.

Harman remembers:

It was a great adventure going to New York to wrestle but a couple of things really bothered me — the mats were dirty and hot to touch. They never cleaned the mats. My knees got raw from the dirt and the heat on the mats. Plus, the officials showed up late for the weigh-in and everyone was pretty upset with them to start with.

Hall of Fame official Vince Zuaro recalls:

One of my boys from Freeport [Long Island] high, Sam Boone, was a top Greco wrestler. I supplied three of our school's mats for the Trials and really risked my job by arranging to sneak out our mats to allow the Trials to occur at all. The Teamsters were also upset with me because I was using non-union drivers to deliver the mats to and from the Fairgrounds.

Overall, 212 wrestlers from 28 states qualified through the Regional tournaments to compete at the Singer Bowl. The Freestyle competition was held first — there were 378 bouts contested over a three-day period. The Greco matches were held the following two days.

The Greco-Roman competition primarily consisted of Freestyle wrestlers who were trying to make the Olympic team after being eliminated in Freestyle. Just a few Greco specialists could be found. That group included a set of young twins who were starting their distinguished careers in Greco by entering the Trials at 114.5 pounds — Dave and Jim Hazewinkel from Anoka, Minnesota.

Dave tells about their introduction to Greco-Roman style wrestling and the brothers '64 Trials experience:

We both started wrestling as juniors at Anoka high school. As seniors in 1962, I wrestled at 95, Jim at 103. We then went to St. Cloud State, an NAIA school.

Ken Cox was our coach at St. Cloud. It was his first year there as well as our first year. One

The 1964 Olympic team coaches, Fendley Collins, Dean Rockwell, Rex Peery
Photographs courtesy of Amateur Wrestling News

day during the season he called us into his office. He said, 'I think you guys would be good at Greco-Roman wrestling.' We looked around the room, wondering who he was talking to. With no one else in the room we figured it must be us. I asked, 'What's Greco-Roman wrestling?'

We soon learned a few moves — like the under-arm spin and the head and arm. Coach Cox encouraged us and told us, 'I want you both to start thinking of wrestling in the Olympics'. After our freshman year we started year-round training and began going to some regional Greco tournaments.

In 1964 Jim won his second NAIA championship at 115 and we were preparing for the Olympic Trials. Coach Cox took four of us to the Trials tournament at the World's Fairgrounds. In those days there was no qualifying tournament in Greco. If you showed up you could wrestle. Both Jim and I were still light and we both entered at 114.5. We made it to the fourth round, where we met each other. We tied and that was not good. The tie gave both of us enough black marks to knock us out of the tournament.

That was the last time we ever entered a tournament at the same weight class.

The youngest competitor in the Freestyle field was 16- year-old Geoff Henson at 125.5. Henson, the son of Josiah Henson, a bronze medalist on the 1952 US Freestyle team, had just completed his junior year at The Hill School in Pottstown, Pennsylvania. Henson

recalls his youthful experience:

My first opponent was Dave Auble, who mopped the mat with me, something like 19-1. Somehow, he wasn't able to pin me and when the match was over I was relieved... but I never did figure out how I earned the one point against him. I did come back to pin some guys and ended up finishing 6th in my weight class, so I was actually quite happy with my effort.

Wayne Hicks thinks back to some of his matches:

I was wrestling up a weight class (154) and didn't expect to win the tournament but it was great fun — especially not having to watch my weight so much. My first match was with Jerry Pamp from San Francisco, who beat me in a close contest. I then went on to defeat two college guys — first, Orlando Iacovelli from Ithaca College. Next, I caught Mike Reding with a couple of my old Indian tricks and beat him. Mike had just finished as runner-up in the NCAAs for Oklahoma State at 147 pounds. Next up was Gordon Hassman, the NCAA champion at 157. I kept it close in the first period. However, towards the end of the period, Hassman realized that he could crunch me anytime he wanted to — and he did. That was it for me in the competition.

Mike Harman recalls his competition with Ron Finley, Tom Huff and Bobby Douglas:

First a little bit of background. I grew up in New Hampton, Iowa in a wrestling family. My father, Maynard Harman, was the first person from Northern Iowa to make the US Olympic wrestling team. He did it in 1932. So, the whole journey about competing for the Olympics was an important part of my life. Coming out of high school [Author's note: Harman finished 3rd and 2nd in the Iowa state tournament] I thought I was going to Iowa State. However, I received an appointment to the Naval Academy and went there instead. Imagine my surprise when I first saw a couple of Iowa natives, Leroy Alitz and Gerry Leeman, across the mat as coaches of West Point and Lehigh respectively, perennial rivals of the Naval Academy.

I graduated from the Academy in 1963 with my degree and an NCAA 3rd place medal — losing to Northern Iowa's Bill Dotson - and wanted a shot at making the Olympic team. The head of the Academy knew of my dream and arranged for me to be assigned back to Annapolis where I could train for the Olympics. I was part of the US military team that got together at West Point and entered as a team at the AAUs and the Trials.

At the World's Fair, I was wrestling well, but still had to face some tough wrestlers —Tom Huff and Ron Finley — even before I could match up with Bobby Douglas. Huff grew up in Waterloo and was a great high school wrestler there. He went on to the University of Iowa and finished ahead of me at the NCAAs. I knew Tom had a tremendous fireman's carry and I thought I was ready to defend it. Right as our match starts, he comes at me and, boom, he puts me on my back with that fireman's. I charge back with a double leg takedown, but he catches me again with his fireman's. I take him down again and it's 4-4 going into the final minute. I'm on top of Tom, get him with a bar-arm, turn him with a whizzer and put him on his back to win the match, 7-4.

My next match was with Finley. He was a little older and always one step ahead of me. Going into our match, I only had a couple of black marks and Finley had five. I knew that I needed just a tie to eliminate him and then it would be down to me and Douglas — and I'd be guaranteed a spot at the Final Camp. Now Finley was dangerous, particularly on mat tilts. He had many crazy holds. My strategy was to stay on our feet and attack with single-leg tackles. We danced around a lot. Ron's coach, Dale Thomas,

> ## I knew Tom [Huff] had a tremendous fireman's carry and I thought I was ready to defend it. Right as our match starts, he comes at me and, boom, he puts me on my back with that fireman's. I charge back with a double leg takedown, but he catches me again with his fireman's.
>
> ### – MIKE HARMAN

was screaming at the officials and at Ron. The match ended 0-0 and I was so happy — I was in 2nd place, for sure. I now had to face Douglas, who had upset three-time NCAA champion Larry Hayes in an earlier round. I lost the final match with Douglas, 4-1, but coming out of there I thought 'I can beat this guy'.

While I may have thought that, it never happened. Douglas was too good. He was a wrestler who hardly ever had black marks because he'd always pin his opponents and I couldn't. Bobby was the hardest worker on the team and a hell of a competitor.

Finley also advanced to the Final Camp by virtue of winning the Greco competition. At the Camp he beat me in the Freestyle wrestle-off. He got a point on me early in the match and for the rest of the time I chased him all over, but couldn't catch him. Ray Swartz, the former Naval Academy coach, was the referee and wouldn't call anything as he was afraid of being called for favoritism. Ron and I wrestled each other many times in our careers and became very good friends afterwards. To this day we serve together as Board members of the Oregon Hall of Fame.

Bobby Douglas was an outstanding athlete, receiving offers to play college football and baseball coming out of high school in Bridgeport, Ohio. His passion was wrestling and he set his sights and dreams on winning an Olympic gold medal. Dropping all other sports, Douglas wrestled for two years at West Liberty State in West Virginia, winning an NAIA title as a freshman and placing 2nd in the 1963 NCAAs as a sophomore.

Douglas recalls those days and his 1964

Trials experiences:

I was very disappointed to lose in the NCAA finals to Mickey Martin. I was on top of him for much of the match but didn't get as many back points as I should have. That loss made me realize that I didn't have the coaching or the competition locally to compete for an Olympic gold medal, which was my goal.

After that season I was strongly recruited by Kent State, Iowa State and Oklahoma State. I liked Harold Nichols, but I really bonded with Myron Roderick. He told me Oklahoma State had all the things that I needed in order to be an Olympian and he had a good scholarship offer. I made the decision to go there, which was a great choice.

I made the '63 US Greco team at 138.5 and traveled and wrestled all over Europe for a full month that summer. We wrestled in Bulgaria, Greece, Yugoslavia, Germany and Sweden. I did pretty well even though I ended up getting hurt. I came away from that trip with the objective of making the '64 Olympic team.

I enrolled at OSU but didn't wrestle competitively for them during the '63-'64 season. My Oklahoma State teammates became a terrific support system for me, though. You can't do it without a strong support system.

Come time for the Final Trials in the Singer Bowl, I ran into a problem. For the seven days prior to the Trials, I had no workout partner. I was in New York, but having a terrible time finding a place to workout and get down to weight. I wanted to use the NYAC but they had rules then against allowing blacks or Jews to use their facilities. A couple of wrestlers finally snuck me in there, wrapping me in a sheet. That ended up causing a lot of real bad vibes between the club's wrestlers and many of the rest of the members.

Once the tournament began, I wrestled great. It was the best I felt in my whole career. Know why? I was well rested, not having wrestled for a week before the tournament. The only match I

recall where I had some trouble was against Mike Harmon. I won 2-0. He was tough; his style was difficult for me.

There was no lack of other interesting competitions at the Trials. In the 114.5 Freestyle finals, Gray Simons met his former Granby High School teammate, Okla Johnson, who by the way, was the first Granby wrestler to win four Virginia high school titles — Simons 'only' won two. Anyway, Simons won this battle on points to finish 1st in the weight class. Dave Auble won the Freestyle 125.5 slot by beating his Cornell University and NYAC teammate Carmen Molino in the finals. At 213.5, Gerry Conine surprised everyone. Conine, a newcomer to international competition, won his Freestyle weight class with

Farm boy Larry Kristoff found success in the Big Apple Trials of '64
Photograph courtesy of Amateur Wrestling News

a first-period fall over NCAA and Pan-American champion Joe James. And, at heavyweight, Larry Kristoff and Jim Raschke traded victories. After Kristoff defeated Raschke to take the Freestyle title, two nights later Raschke, a private in the Army, pinned his adversary to win the Greco competition.

Kristoff talks about his wrestling career and events surrounding his participation in the '64 Trials:

I was a farm boy from Carbondale, Illinois. Our high school didn't have a wrestling team until January of my senior year — 1960. That's when I saw, and competed in, my first wrestling match. We had five dual meets, then the year-end tournaments. I placed 3rd in the districts at heavyweight, then I won the sectionals and a week later I made it to the state finals where I lost in double overtime. It was a tough weight class, too, as Joe James, the future Oklahoma State star, only placed 3rd.

I was an all-state fullback on the football team and heavily recruited by the big football schools — Iowa, Notre Dame, University of Alabama, etc. I asked all the recruiters, 'How about your wrestling program?', but was basically ignored by the wrestling coaches. Nobody wanted me for wrestling, not even Dave McCus-

> **The coaching staff was pretty strict with us... They'd make us go to bed before the sun went down. A couple of us would lay in bed for a while until bed-check was over, then we'd sneak out of the dorm, walk around the seawall and go into town to have a good time.**
>
> **— LARRY KRISTOFF**

• •

key at Iowa. If McCuskey had given me the time of day on my recruiting trip to Iowa, I probably would have gone there. I really wanted to wrestle in college, and that opportunity only existed at a non-big-time program, so I ended up going to Southern Illinois University-Carbondale in the fall of 1960.

I played football my first two years in college, but then stopped to concentrate on wrestling. I twice won the Division II heavyweight title and in 1963 I made it to the Division I championship finals before losing to Syracuse's Jim Nance by a riding-time point. That same year my college coach, Jim Wilkinson, raised enough funds to take three of us from SIU to the National AAU championships in San Francisco. I had a great tournament, beating Garry Stensland in the finals to win my first National AAU title.

In 1964, I was a 20-year-old college senior and anxious to give the Olympic Trials a try. Ken Kraft was among those starting up the Mayor Daley Youth Club in Chicago and he called me saying, 'we'd like you to wrestle for us'. I was happy to do so and I went to the Trials in New York as part of their team. It was my first trip ever to New York City — the farm-boy meets the Big Apple — and it was big for me. I remember staying in a hotel in the City and riding the trains out to the World's Fairgrounds — not a problem.

I entered the Trials in both Freestyle and Greco, but was really only interested in winning the Freestyle competition. I felt confident, although many people were talking about how good Bob Pickens from Wisconsin was and how he was going to beat me. Right before my match with him, I literally fell asleep on an adjoining

mat. They had to wake me up when the match was announced, so I ran out onto the mat without any warm-up. I ended up throwing Pickens to his back, pinning him, and then beating Jim Raschke to come away from the tournament in 1st place in the heavyweight division.

The Finals Camp, Annapolis, Maryland — September, 1964

THE top two place winners in Freestyle and Greco headed to Annapolis as soon as their Trials matches ended in New York. In the brief interim, the US Wrestling Olympic Committee, at their discretion, added nine wrestlers to the group, including National AAU champions Greg Ruth at 154 and Russ Camilleri at 171.5.

The 41-man squad assembled at the Academy on Monday, August 31. They were housed in a modern Navy athletic dorm and they ate in the mess halls along with the full student body of midshipmen. As opposed to 1960, there were few complaints about the conditions and training regime.

Linn Long recalls:

The Academy was a great place for us. The facilities were A#1 and I loved competing there. My only complaint was that the Navy football team was there for pre-season practice and took up all the pool tables and TV sofas.

Gray Simons adds:

Annapolis was completely different than the 1960 Camp. Yes, it was hot, but not the killer heat we experienced in Oklahoma. Our dorm was air-conditioned, so we all slept well. We had good workouts and conditioning training. Of course, I was four years older and better able to take the grind. My problem was keeping my weight down over an extended period of time. I probably should have gone at 125.5, but I thought I had a better chance for a gold medal at 114.5.

Andy Fitch remembers a dining hall ritual:

We ate our meals with the midshipmen and they made a big fuss over us wrestlers. During the first few evenings some of us would be introduced at dinner and then plebes would come over and carry us all around the dining room to

The 1964 Olympic training squad: Front row, Molino, Fitch, Simons, Wilson, Auble, Johnson, Lauchle, Kristoff. Second row, Coach Peery, Sanders, Long, Douglas, Finley, Boone, Harman, Berry. Third row, Manager Collins, Hankin, Hassman, Lahr, Pamp, Northrup, Burke, Coach Rockwell. Fourth row, Brand, Houska, Raschke, Tribble, DeWitt, Buzzard, Solowin, unidentified. Fifth row, Ruth, Conine, Baughman, Winer, Pickens, Wittenberg, Camilleri, Lovell, Kauffman, Barden. *Photograph courtesy of Amateur Wrestling News*

big cheers. That was fun.

Two-a-day practices were held in the old Navy wrestling room in McDonough Hall. After the first three days of practice, wrestle-offs began — at night in the field house. These matches were open to the public, but they weren't heavily publicized and not many people showed up to watch. Wrestlers were permitted to challenge in either Freestyle or Greco regardless of the style in which they qualified. Through a series of single-elimination bouts, a challenger emerged to earn the right to wrestle-off the 1st place man from the Final Trials. The final challenge matches were the best two-out-of-three.

Wayne Hicks didn't qualify for the Camp, but being a junior midshipman he was around the squad much of the time and would eagerly participate in the afternoon practice sessions. He recalls scrimmaging with Greg Ruth:

Every afternoon I would go over to the wrestling room for a workout and would usually end up with Greg Ruth as a partner. He was a terrific wrestler and incredibly flexible for someone

so strong. I remember he used to do pushups with his legs behind his head. Greg hated Lehigh — I think there were some year-end wrestle-off issues that didn't set well with him when he was there. But Greg impressed me as a really nice guy. After every practice he would profusely thank me for working out with him.

Larry Kristoff recalls his time at the Annapolis Camp:

Rex Peery was the head Freestyle coach, but he actually had very little international Freestyle experience. I think he got the coaching position mostly as a 'thank you' in recognition of his many years of dedicated service to wrestling. He ran the practices like a college team and would have us work on things like the chicken-wing, which is fine for college wrestling but illegal in Freestyle. Actually some of the veteran wrestlers like Dan Brand, who I greatly admired, were the ones who taught us various Freestyle techniques. We sure didn't get much of that from Coach Peery.

The coaching staff was pretty strict with us, trying to set some antiquated rules for guys in their '20s. They'd make us go to bed before the sun went down. A couple of us, I won't say exactly who, would lay in bed for a while until bed-check was over, then we'd sneak out of the dorm, walk around the seawall and go into town to have a good time. Fortunately, we never got caught.

Since I won the Trials in New York, I only had to wrestle Pickens to make the Olympic team. We wrestled twice and I pinned him both times. I didn't think he was nearly as tough as everyone said he was.

1960 Olympian Ed DeWitt went to Annapolis with hopes of making the Olympic team a second time. He recalls:

By 1964, I was caught in between weight classes — too small for 191 and too large for 171. I was selected as a special invitee to the Camp and spent a lot of time concentrating on getting down to 171. I only wrestled one match — losing to Russ Camilleri. I had to return home right after that since I was teaching school in Oregon and supporting a wife and three kids.

A problem the US wrestlers faced was trying to excel in Freestyle, while the people in charge of the AAU kept selecting Olympic coaches without Freestyle experience. It happened in 1960 and again in '64.

Still, I have some very good memories — especially ones about the progress and development of Gerry Conine, who was from Tacoma and went to Washington State. In early '64 I started working out with him. He was a taxi-driver and an unknown in Freestyle circles, never having placed in a national tournament. Getting him ready for the '64 Trials and Camp was great fun for me. He never missed a workout and kept getting better and better. He surprised everyone but himself and me when he won those Trials in New York. At the Annapolis Camp, he won easily.

That Camp was my first encounter with young Rick Sanders and he was memorable. He'd eat as much as he wanted and then sweat it off. It was not unusual for Rick to eat a full dinner, and then stay in the steam room all night long.

Bobby Douglas talks about the Annapolis environment and Coach Perry:

I wrestled very well in my matches in Annapolis — just as good as at the Singer Bowl. The workouts were hard and I was very focused on my training regime. We had a little time off and I admired the plebes and the whole Academy environment. One day we went out on a cruise — on a destroyer, I think — and I was so impressed with the quality of the men. They were A+ guys.

I liked Coach Peery and thought he was a good coach. He liked me — I think because of my work ethic. He didn't care for Charlie Tribble, because of Charlie's work ethic. That happens at times with coaches. I know Coach Peery would rather have seen Lahr on the team than Tribble. I had the same thing happen against me in the World Team tryouts in '70. Coach Bill Farrell would rather have seen Dan Gable on the team at 149.5 than me, and had us wrestle-off time and time again, but I continued to beat Dan and I eventually made the team. I am still angry about that and though Farrell and I are friends, I still jibe him about that incident.

Coaches Peery and Rockwell also instituted a strict weight-control policy: wrestlers could not be more than eight pounds over their competing weight at any time and had to be within four pounds for wrestle-offs. For several of the men pulling a lot of weight, this was a big-time hardship.

The Wrestle-Offs
125.5 pounds Greco-Roman — Larry Lauchle vs Andy Fitch

BY '64, the top US wrestlers in our lightest weights were all Eastern guys who wrestled in college in the late '50s and early '60s, and then advanced into the world of international wrestling. Dave Auble, Andy Fitch, Larry Lauchle, Carmen Molino and Gray Simons make up the group. They wrestled each other dozens, maybe hundreds, of times. They were teammates — either in college, or at the New York Athletic Club, or in the Armed Services. They were also fierce competitors and foes. Simons and Lauchle were teammates on the 1960 US Olympic team; the other three tried to make that team but lost in the Trials.

For 1964, Simons drops down to 114.5 and makes the Freestyle team handily. Auble again defeats Molino at the Camp and finally wins the 125.5 spot. That leaves the last two, Lauchle and Fitch, to fight it out for the 125.5 Greco place on the team, and while they were both highly accomplished experienced wrestlers, they could not have had more different backgrounds and persona.

Larry Lauchle grew up in the tiny, blue-collar town of Muncy, Pennsylvania – close to Williamsport, out in the middle of nowhere. He never thought about going to college until the wrestling recruiters started following him upon winning the Pennsylvania states his junior year in high school. He went to the University of Pittsburgh, wrestling for Hall-of-Fame coach Rex Peery, where he won the NCAAs in 1961 at 130 pounds. At the time of the 1964 Olympic Trials, Lauchle was serving in the US Marines.

On the other hand, Andy Fitch was raised in the leafy suburb of New Rochelle, New York. After tenth grade, he went off to boarding school in Pennsylvania. From there Fitch attended and graduated from Yale University, winning the prestigious university's first NCAA crown at 115 pounds in 1959. At the time of the 1964 Olympic Trials, Fitch was teaching French at Columbia University.

Larry Lauchle talks about the very unlikely beginnings of a championship wrestling career:

Growing up, I was scrawny and fragile, pretty much sick all the time. I had inner-ear infections and in the summers I was sent to Camp Kiwanis, which was a camp for underdeveloped kids.

When I got to the ninth grade, the high school wrestling coach, Stan Schyler, came around the classrooms looking for the smallest kids so he could fill out his 95-pound weight class. I signed up for the team not knowing anything about the sport. Well, it helped me immensely physically and I got healthier and stronger. By the time I was a sophomore, I qualified for the State Tournament and finished 2nd. I won the states my

In 1964, Larry Lauchle was unable to replicate his success at the 1960 Trials
Photograph courtesy of Amateur Wrestling News

junior year, 1956, at 112 pounds, but as a senior I lost in the semi-finals.

Before I started wrestling, I had no idea that I might go to college, but the recruiters, especially Rex Peery, started talking to me about wrestling and getting a college education. Rex was successful in his efforts, as I ended up at Pitt. I improved a lot in my four years there, especially having the opportunity to constantly work out with Rex's son, Ed. My self confidence also soared.

While still in college I made the '60 US Olympic team in Greco, even though I didn't really know a whole lot about that style. For Americans, Greco was tough to learn and it was tougher for us then than it is today. A lot of time was spent on the mat and the Europeans were very experienced at that. Once they changed the rules taking the par-terre out, then it wasn't as bad for us Americans.

After graduating from Pitt in 1961, I joined the Marines and continued to wrestle and prepare for the '64 Olympics. I was stationed at Camp Pendleton in California and worked out a lot with Larry Hayes. In May of 1963 I was part of a US Armed Forces team that won an international competition in Cairo, Egypt. We had some good wrestlers on that team, such as Simons, Ruth and Camilleri.

The competition was always close between Auble, Fitch, Molino and me. It looked 'iffy' for my chances to make the '64 team. I decided to enter the Trials in New York in Freestyle and Greco, knowing that Fitch would just be wrestling Greco and Auble just Freestyle. I needed to be in the top two in either style to get to the Finals Camp. I was in pretty good shape in the Freestyle portion – Auble had defeated Molino for 1st place and I had to wrestle Carmen for the runner-up spot. In our match I got ahead of Carmen, taking him down three times. Then, Carmen hit a foot-sweep and boom, he pins me. I ended up 3rd, so I had to make weight again and go into the Greco Trials. There, I lost to Fitch and drew with Clem Crow, but was awarded 2nd place due to fewer black marks.

Andy Fitch, left, took time off from teaching French at Columbia University in New York to win a spot on the 1964 Greco team *Photograph courtesy of Bobby Douglas*

When I arrived in Annapolis, Coach Peery told me to tryout for Freestyle as well as Greco. Unfortunately, shortly after the start of Camp I got blood poisoning and had to be admitted to the hospital for several days. I missed the chance to challenge Molino and Auble in Freestyle. I was ready for the Greco matches, though, and came out strong in my first match, beating Molino. However, in the finals against Fitch, I lost. He headlocked me and that was it.

That was some great competition amongst us guys. I still see Carmen a lot. We go together to the NCAAs each year and enjoy our family reunions. A few years ago my daughter married his son.

Andy Fitch grew up in a very different environment from Lauchle:

I first wrestled in tenth grade at New Rochelle High School before asking my parents to send me to The Hill School, then one of the best wrestling schools. I learned to wrestle from Hill Coach Frank Bissell. During Christmas break back in 1952 and 1953 he would take me and a couple of my teammates out to Mepham High on Long Island to learn and drill under the great 'Sprig' Gardner. Bissell had wrestled for the New York Athletic Club, so some of us started going there for workouts and tournaments. That's where I got my first taste of Freestyle wrestling.

I continued to wrestle Freestyle plus a little Greco at the NYAC after winning the NCAAs in 1959, my senior year at Yale. Gray Simons, twice NCAA Outstanding Wrestler, won his first title the year after I won mine. I was three or four years older than Simons and could do alright with him in Freestyle while he was still in college and when we were at the 1960 Finals Camp. However, I wrestled the worst match of my life in our single elimination match there; Gray beat me handily to make the US team at 114.5.

After winning the Pan-Ams in 1963, I began to concentrate on Greco-Roman style since by now Gray was toying with me in Freestyle. I made the US World Championships Greco team that year at 114.5, in the absence of Dick Wilson, who'd been to the '56 and '60 Olympics. He was really the only US Greco wrestler who knew what he was doing, and was virtually unbeatable in the style. After I substituted for an injured Simons at the Freestyle Worlds in Bulgaria [finishing 6th], we wrestled the Greco championships in Sweden. While not placing, I got some excellent training and experience that year, including a draw with the eventual world champion from Yugoslavia.

For the '64 Trials, I decided to go 125.5 in Greco. Why? Well, I couldn't beat Wilson in Greco at 114.5; and, like everyone else, couldn't beat Simons in Freestyle. Gray even won the National AAUs at 125.5 that year. Dave Auble, who some thought should have made the team over gold-medal winner Terry McCann in 1960, had a lock on 125.5 Freestyle. Larry Lauchle, 1960 Olympian and NCAA champ, and Carmen Molino were the competition at 125.5 in Greco; in the Trials at the Singer Bowl, I'd already wrestled the former to a draw, and beaten Molino — so some decent odds, anyway.

The '64 Olympic Camp was at Annapolis, with great facilities and normal practices, not like the horrific ones in Norman in '60. However, I did have my problems with Freestyle Coach Rex Peery, who was looking for a way to get Lauchle, his wrestler from Pitt, on the team.

Peery didn't like me. I was an abrasive wise guy and had a mustache — in those days an act of rebellion and a red flag for the Service Academy guys who wave the flag and that stuff. I'm not sure that he knew about my active protesting against the Vietnam War in 1963, but that wouldn't have helped. Anyway, one day we had to get yellow fever shots. At afternoon practice Peery was demonstrating on me and intentionally gave me a hard squeeze where I was really sore from the big needle, which made some of the guys laugh. Thank God for Dean Rockwell, the Greco coach, who stood up for me and came to my rescue after an incident in Los Angeles en

route to Tokyo.

In the finals, after Lauchle had beaten Molino, I had to wrestle him two-out-of-three to make the team. In the first match we were on our feet and Larry got behind me. He was a strong guy with several effective moves. As he went to suplay me over the top I got an adrenalin rush and countered him by switching my legs, coming chest-to-chest and landing on top of him. That gave me a three or four point lead and I easily won the first match.

I heard from teammates before the second match that the coaches wanted the larger Lauchle to just keep pushing me and they'd see if they could get me stalled out. And when I arrived at the mat to wrestle, who's sitting as a mat judge? Coach Peery's son, Ed, the Naval Academy coach and three-time NCAA Champ for Pitt.

Well, Larry came out pushing and there was lots of huffing and puffing, and sure enough I received one or two stalling calls. At one point, right in front of Peery, Lauchle hooked his leg around mine to gain leverage — blatantly illegal in Greco. I looked down and said, 'For God's sake, Ed,' but no call was made. Finally, as Lauchle leaned hard into me, I threw my favorite move — a headlock — and he went over like a sack of bricks. Once he realized where he was [on his back], Larry tried reflexively to take me over, but it was too late. I won and felt an enormous relief. I was on my way to the Tokyo Olympics.

171.5 pounds Freestyle — Charlie Tribble vs Dean Lahr

THIS was arguably one of the toughest Trials weight classes ever. There were eight men entered in Freestyle who had been either NCAA or National AAU champions, some of them multiple times.

One of the top contestants, though, had just two years of junior college experience — Charlie Tribble from San Bernardino, California. He tells his story:

I didn't start wrestling until the 11th grade after being cut from the basketball team at San Bernardino high school. I immediately was successful at the sport, losing only once my junior

Olympians Charlie Tribble and Dan Brand were formidable workout partners
Photograph courtesy of Bobby Douglas

> **Coach Peery was a little difficult. I never thought he liked me; I couldn't do anything right in his eyes. He never complimented me and kept telling me that my moves would never work in real competition. At one time I thought it might be racist, but he idolized Bobby Douglas, who was in Camp with me, so I guess it was just me.**
>
> **– CHARLIE TRIBBLE**

• •

year and then winning the CIF my senior year, 1960.

After high school, I joined the California National Guard and entered San Bernardino Junior College, where I wrestled and also played football for them. In 1961 I was the California JC champ but I took the next year off to go on active duty. When I came back to school the following year, I again won the state JC championship. I left there with a career record of 54 wins, 0 losses, and 52 pins.

To tell you the truth, I never paid a lot of attention early on to wrestling or heavy training. If I hadn't been naturally so good, I probably would have quit.

When I went on active duty I started wrestling Freestyle — at Ft. Lewis, Washington. They had a wrestling team there and I went over to see how you could get on the team. The coach, can't remember his name, said, 'You gotta beat me — right now'. I didn't have any equipment, but he found me some shoes, so I went out there and pinned his ass. He said, 'OK, Tribble, you're on the squad'.

In 1962, I traveled with Jim Ferguson, the National AAU champ that year, to a Far West tournament. It was my first Freestyle tournament. Ferguson was tough, but I beat him. People started telling me, 'Hey, if you can beat Ferguson, you ought to try to make the Olympic team.' That's when I first started to think about the Olympics.

I entered the National AAUs in New York in '64 and finished 2nd to Len Kauffman. My only loss was to the 3rd place guy — Steve Combs. I had beaten him before and since, but not that day. I

also beat Ferguson, but five minutes later I had to wrestle Combs and lost on what I thought was a bad call. I was a rather young guy at the time compared to veterans like Ed DeWitt, Russ Camilleri, and Ferguson. But I was strong and if I got in on a leg, it was mine.

After the AAUs I went back to San Bernardino and worked out with ten guys at the San Bernardino YMCA; I went from one to the other. But my biggest problem was getting my weight down. I normally weighed around 200 pounds. It was an ordeal for me to make 171.5.

I returned to New York with my coach Bob Smith for the Trials in August. Again I beat Ferguson, DeWitt and Camillari, but lost to Dean Lahr by two points. There were multiple national champs in the weight and I think I wrestled seven of them and beat all of them but Lahr. Pinned most of them, actually. Yet, I was about the only one with no international wrestling experience.

At the Annapolis Camp, I wrestled and beat Kauffman and then had to wrestle Lahr, best two-out-of-three. In the first match, I beat him badly. In the second match, I thought I had beaten him again the same decisive way, but the officials awarded the match to him on a judges' decision. I couldn't believe that he really beat me. The next day, Lahr came up to me and said, 'Good luck. You've won, I'm going home.' However, they made us start the round-robin over. I don't know why. I wrestled and beat Ferguson again and then pinned Kauffman to win the place on the team.

Lahr was the smartest of all the guys I wrestled. He knew exactly what he needed and wanted to do, and he did it. Camilleri was the toughest. He beat me four times before '64, but I beat him the last six times we wrestled. He was ten years older than me and much more experienced. He had a great amount of fight in him.

I remember the Annapolis Camp — Coach Peery was a little difficult. I never thought he liked me; I couldn't do anything right in his eyes. He never complimented me and kept telling me that my moves would never work in real competition. At one time I thought it might be racist, but he idolized Bobby Douglas, who was in Camp with me, so I guess it was just me.

Douglas was a good friend to me. He really helped me one day as I was having weight problems. Coach Peery's rule was that no one could be more than eight pounds over their weight class, meaning I couldn't be over 179.5. Well, I was usually 15 pounds over during Camp. One day around 5pm, Douglas hurries over to me and says, 'They're having a secret weigh-in tonight at 11pm.' He knew I was well over the limit, so he worked with me the next several hours, running and working out. At 11pm, Coach Peery came around the dorms and woke us up for weigh-in. When we were assembled, he said 'Tribble, you're first!' I got on the scale and it read 178. He almost choked. He couldn't believe I made the weight. He was ready to send me home.

The next day we got our uniforms and our pictures taken and there's Coach Peery shaking hands with me. I received a lot of support from Douglas and our manager Fendley Collins. Collins kept reassuring me, 'You'll be okay, Charlie, just hang in there.'

The University of Colorado's Dean Lahr was voted the Outstanding Wrestler at both the 1964 NCAA wrestling championships and the Final Olympic Trials at the World's Fairgrounds. First, his college coach, Linn Long, and then Lahr himself, talk about his career and his challenges at the Trials.

Coach Long recalls:

I recruited Dean from North Denver high school. He was a state wrestling champ at 167 as a senior, yet went to Colorado on a football scholarship. He was an all-city and all-state quarterback and ran the hurdles in track. What a great athlete and person.

Lahr wasn't eligible to wrestle college matches as a freshman but I took him to tournaments to gain some experience. In the Rocky Mountain AAUs he wrestled Jack Flasche (the 1962 NCAA champion at 157) from Northern Colorado. Dean tore him up. In '62, Dean's sophomore year, he reported late for wrestling since CU went to a bowl game. That season, he lost three times to Oklahoma State's two-time NCAA champion Bob Johnson — in the dual 13-12, in the Big Eights and in the finals of the NCAAs. Those were his only college losses.

In '63, Lahr won the NCAAs and defeated veteran Freestyle wrestlers Jim Ferguson and Ed DeWitt to win the National AAUs. From there he went to the World Championships in Bulgaria

where he finished in 4th place. For his senior year at Colorado Lahr finally decided to give up football to concentrate on wrestling. He was rewarded with another NCAA title and the Outstanding Wrestler award.

Dean was a proud and determined individual. Without a doubt, his standards were way above what anyone would ever believe.

Dean Lahr fondly remembers his wrestling days:

Coach Long always tried to get me the best experiences he could. When I was a freshman we went to the National AAUs in Toledo as my first exposure to Freestyle wrestling. I won a couple bouts and found that there was not much of a difference wrestling against these people who primarily had a college wrestling background.

When I made the US World team in 1963 and competed in Bulgaria, it was my first experience wrestling against guys who really knew what they were doing in Freestyle. That wasn't the only change — their mats were different, more like a mattress with a rough canvas cover. The Europeans were accustomed to this, but we Americans had to worry about snagging our feet and it hurt all of us. It really cut down on our quickness advantage. I had just turned 21 and went up against the defending Olympic champion, losing 3-1 and ended up placing 4th.

1964 started out as a good year as I won the NCAAs and was named Outstanding Wrestler. However, in June on my 22nd birthday, I severely hurt my knee while practicing takedowns with CU heavyweight Richard Redd. Redd was going for a lateral drop and he put all his weight, 235 pounds, and my weight, 175 pounds, on my right leg. Something snapped. I didn't know what happened and doctors weren't sure either. I could no longer workout, though. There were ligament problems and the trainers would put ice and heat on it so I could finally run. I did run daily — even up those Boulder stadium steps — but I couldn't wrestle at all until the week before the Trials.

At the Trials in New York, my knee was constantly swelling, but it really didn't bother me too much when I was out on the mats. There were 41 guys at my weight — numerous former national champions, a really stacked weight class. Leonard Kauffman, a college junior from Oregon State, was the one we all were most concerned about.

However, he was easier for me to beat than Charlie Tribble. Kauffman was a pinner. He was great on throws when you came in on his legs. He would pull you up onto his hips and execute a front wizard throw. That was a Dale Thomas trademark move. Kauffman and I wrestled each other often, so I knew what to avoid — I never came up inside him. I attacked from the side and was able to beat him.

My toughest bouts were against Tribble. Tribble was stronger than me by far, but not in as good condition. He also was cutting an awful lot of weight. At the Singer Bowl I wrestled him smart, though, as I just sparred with him evenly until the last minutes of the match when he started wearing down. Then I got my points. I beat him 3-1 in the finals match.

At the Olympic Camp in Annapolis, we practiced twice a day and my knee had a tough time handling the rigor. I went back to Boulder briefly to the Medical Clinic there, had the knee drained and returned to Annapolis for my wrestle-off matches with Tribble. In the first match, I thought I could tear him up from the start. I wanted to whip him straightaway. That was the wrong strategy. I should have made him just move around for six or seven minutes, wear him down, and then go for my points. He beat me pretty good, 5-1. In the second match, I took the more cautious approach,

like I did in New York, and won the match on a close judges' decision.

By now my knee was ballooning up to the size of a basketball. I realized that the way I was feeling I would not be able to properly represent the US in the Olympics. I withdrew from the tournament the night before my final challenge bout. Coach Long was disappointed but he supported me, saying, 'Dean, you are not at the level you have been. I have no problem with your decision. If this is the way it is, it's okay with me.' Two weeks later I was back in Colorado on the operating table; Charlie Tribble was with the US team in Tokyo.

One last story from Mike Harman:

On the final night at Camp after the last of the wrestle-offs, Bobby Douglas and I decided to go out for the evening and I drove to the outskirts of Annapolis. Now, I didn't have much awareness of the black/white racial thing so it didn't mean anything to me to be walking into a tavern with a black man. Anyway, we go into the tavern and I ask for a couple of beers. The bartender tells me, 'I can give you one, but not your friend. We don't serve black people here.' Well, that infuriated me and I grabbed this guy and was about to whomp him. However, Douglas quickly pulled me away saying, 'Mike, I have a lot to lose if you cause a scene. Let's get out of here.' We left.

1964 OLYMPIC TEAM MEMBERS

	FREESTYLE	GRECO-ROMAN
114.5	Gray Simons	Dick Wilson (4th)
125.5	Dave Auble (4th)	Andy Fitch
138.5	Bobby Douglas (4th)	Ron Finley (4th)
154	Greg Ruth (6th)	Jim Burke
171.5	Charlie Tribble	Russ Camilleri
191.5	Dan Brand (3rd)	Wayne Baughman
213.5	Gerry Conine (6th)	Pat Lovell
HWT	Larry Kristoff	Bob Pickens (6th)

★ *Bobby Douglas and Charlie Tribble became the first African-American Freestyle wrestlers to represent the US in the Olympics. Bringing home only one medal, a bronze, was disappointing, especially in light of the 1960 Freestyle team's success.*

1964 PRESIDENTIAL ELECTION

★ *The election was nothing but a landslide for the Democratic Party. Goldwater could only carry a handful of Southern states as his extremist conservative views were not accepted by many, even senior members of the Republican Party.*

THE SCORECARD

Lyndon B. Johnson Hubert H. Humphrey	486 Electoral Votes 61.1% of Popular Vote
Barry M. Goldwater William E. Miller	52 Electoral Votes 38.5% of Popular Vote

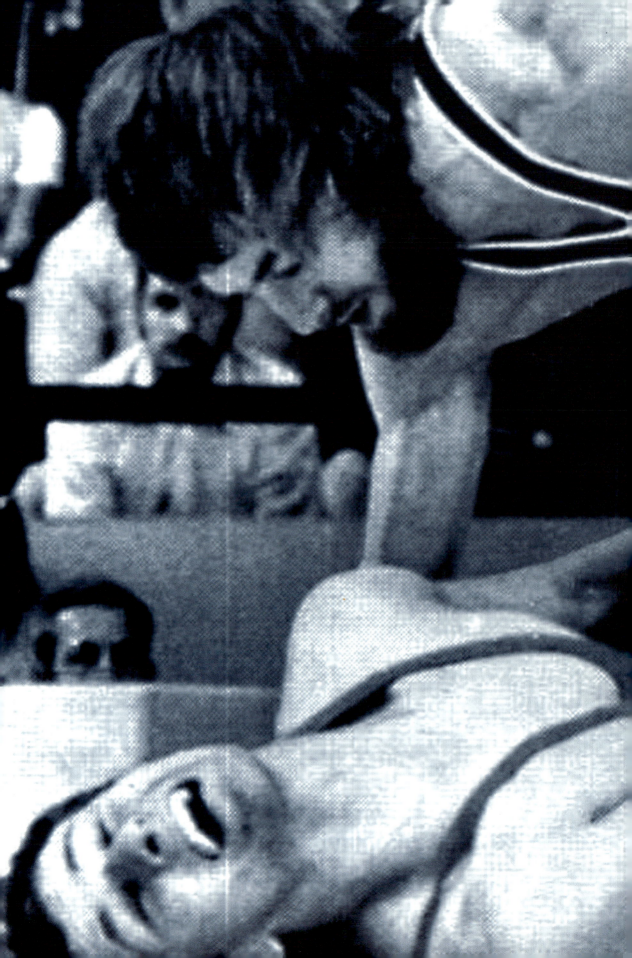

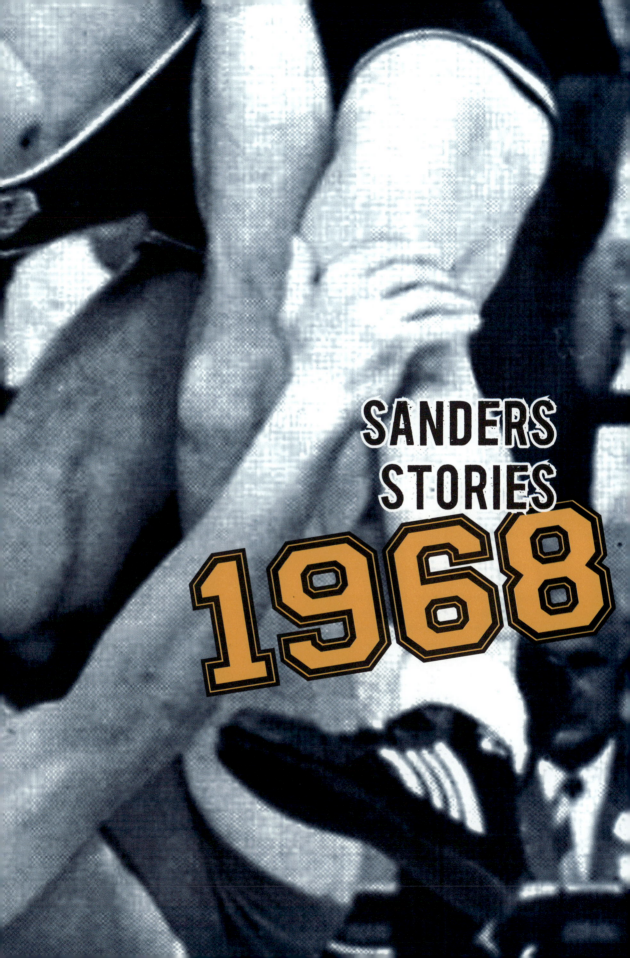

SANDERS
STORIES
1968

> **That Trials Camp in 1968 did me wonders. Coach [Tommy] Evans was really good for me. If I take that Camp away, I would never have been the same wrestler or coach that I turned out to be.**
>
> **— Dan Gable, who was invited to participate as a workout partner at Alamosa**

FROM 1964 to 1968, the US wrestling community doggedly fought to increase the exposure of Olympic-style wrestling both nationally and internationally. Stunned by a dearth of wrestling medals brought home from the '64 Olympics, wrestling leaders sought a) an increase in the number of Olympic-style wrestling clubs around the country, and b) more competition in major international Freestyle and Greco events, not just the World Championships. People such as Joe Scalzo, Dean Rockwell, Josiah Henson and Terry McCann (who was the organizing chairman of the upstart United States Wrestling Federation) headed the charge, but not always at the same pace nor in the same direction.

Some significant results were achieved. Through the determination of Scalzo as Chairman of the National AAU Wrestling Committee, in 1966 the United States hosted the FILA World Freestyle Wrestling Championships. To top it off, the US team, under the tutelage of Bill Smith, placed 3rd in the world — our highest finish up to that time. Seven wrestlers placed in the top five in their weight class, with Bobby Douglas and Larry Kristoff winning silver medals.

In 1968 a couple of new stars emerged from the college wrestling ranks — Dan Gable and Wayne Wells. Both won their first NCAA titles in March of '68. Just a few weeks later they embarked upon their international Freestyle careers. Another collegian, Rick Sand-

ers, was already a veteran in international Freestyle competition. Sanders lost his bid to win his third NCAA Division I championship in '68 when he was upset in the finals by Oklahoma State sophomore Dwayne Keller. Gable, Wells and Sanders went on to play key roles in the '68 Trials.

Wrestling may have been on an upswing, but generally it was very troubling times for Americans in 1968, both at home and abroad. The Vietnam War continued to claim the lives of thousands of American troops, Vietnamese soldiers and innocent civilians. Pictures of American soldiers from Charlie Company invading the hamlet of My Lai and killing two hundred civilians in March of '68 served as a reminder of the atrocities that were taking place in this senseless conflict. For many, this war had already lost its meaning.

It was no better back on American soil. On April 4, one week before the National AAU wrestling championships, Dr. Martin Luther King was gunned down by a sniper in Memphis, Tennessee. In the ensuing days, race riots in Washington, DC claimed the lives of 13 people while thousands of others were injured.

On May 11, speaking to a crowd just before the Nebraska primary election, presidential candidate Robert Kennedy made the following remarks:

We recognize squarely that this is a seriously troubled time in America's history. American people must have a change in the national spirit to help stop the mindless orgy of violent destruction on big city streets. It is up to the Democrats to take the lead in bringing about a reversal of the trend that is marked by consistent advances in the GNP while the social tide of this country deteriorates.

Previous spread: Rick Sanders was arguably the most eccentric and talented lightweight in the annals of US amateur wrestling
Photograph courtesy of Bobby Douglas

Three days later the voters in the Nebraska primary spoke. For the Democrats, Kennedy received 53% of the vote, Eugene McCarthy won 31%, Hubert Humphrey just 9%. On the Republican side, Richard Nixon garnered an overwhelming 70%; Ronald Reagan trailed with 23% of the vote.

Less than one month later, on June 5, Senator Robert Kennedy was shot to death in a Los Angeles hotel, just hours after winning the California Democratic primary.

The Republicans held their National Convention in Miami Beach in early August. Richard Nixon handily won a first-ballot nomination and surprised the nation by choosing Maryland Governor Spiro Agnew as his running mate. The Democrat National Convention in Chicago in late August was tumultuous. Anti-war protesters, led by Abbie Hoffman and Tom Hayden, clashed with police and National Guard troops. TV coverage brought the street violence into the living rooms of many Americans.

Minnesota Senator Eugene McCarthy put forth a decidedly anti-war campaign in the primaries, calling for the immediate withdrawal of American troops from Vietnam. The Democrats eventually nominated Vice-President Hubert H. Humphrey, who sought a policy more in line with President Johnson's. Humphrey named Maine's Edmund Muskie as his vice-presidential candidate. George Wallace, who was best known for opposing school integration in his home state of Alabama, ran as a third-party candidate for the presidency on his own American Independent Party ticket.

The most positive news for many Americans came from the financial and sports pages. The Dow moved up past the 900 mark in the summer of 1968. The stocks with the highest trading volume included INA Corporation, Occidental Petroleum, AT&T, Hooker Chemical and Pan American. On the playing fields, Catfish Hunter and Arthur Ashe made history. Hunter artfully twirled a masterpiece for the Oakland As on May 8 to become the first pitcher in the American League to throw a perfect game during the regular season. In early September on the tennis courts of Forest Hills, New York, Ashe became the first African-American to win the US Open Men's Singles title.

Olympic-style wrestling received little attention by ·the sports media outside of Oklahoma and Iowa, but there were bursts of activity happening in the wrestling world in preparation for the Trials and the upcoming Olympics, slated to be held in Mexico City in October.

The Trials Process

IN 1967, the US Olympic Wrestling Committee, led by Capt. Josiah Henson, named Bill Smith as the coach of the US Olympic Freestyle team. Smith had a remarkable wrestling resumé: a two-time NCAA champion at the University of Northern Iowa; a three-time National AAU champion; and a gold medal winner in the 1952 Olympics. As a coach, Smith headed the Olympic Club of San Francisco team for 10 years, winning three National AAU team titles in Freestyle and four in Greco-Roman. He also coached the US contingent at the FILA World Championships in 1965, 1966 and in 1967.

However, Smith was having some personal financial difficulties as the Olympic Club started to de-emphasize wrestling. Smith left his coaching post there in late '67. The Canadian Olympic Committee, buoyed by a generous government subsidy, asked Smith to coach their 1968 Olympic wrestling team. Smith couldn't turn down the financial opportunity. In February, 1968, Smith accepted the Canadian offer and sent his resignation to Henson.

A month or so later Smith had second thoughts about his move to Canada. He asked the Canadians to release him from his commitment and he requested Henson to withdraw his prior resignation from the US team coaching position. The US Olympic Wrestling Committee wouldn't hear of it. They voted to recommend Oklahoma's Tommy Evans as the head Freestyle coach and accepted Smith's resignation. Evans had earlier been named coach of the Greco

Qualifers for Final United States

114.5-POUNDS

Earl Bourguardez, Tampa, Florida
Greg Bruestle, Minneapolis, Minn.
John Burke, West Chicago, Ill.
Mike Cachero, Phoenix, Ariz.
Bruce Canfield, Bronx, New York
Arthur Chavez, San Francisco, Cal.
Herb Cosme, Oildale, Cal.
Jim Craig, St. Petersburg, Fla.
Mario Criscione, Bronx, New York
Terr Finn, Norman, Oklahoma
Marc N. Galperin, Springfield, Mass.
Sergio Gonzales, Los Angeles, Cal.
Tommy Green, Stillwater, Okla.
David Grinderd, River Falls, Wisc.
Grant Hanjyoji, Portland, Oregon
Jack Hornbuckle, Norman, Okla.
David Keller, Toledo, Ohio
Danny Keith Kida, San Diego, Cal.
Jon Kinateder, River Falls, Wisc.
Steve Lampe, Ames, Iowa
Paul A. Lanoue, Lowell, Mass.
Joe Larocca, Lansing, Mich.
Wiley Lodge, Rochester, Minn.
Ken Melchoir, Lock Haven, Pa.
John S. Miller, Portland, Ore.
Charles Palmer, Colorado Springs, Colo.
Cowan Range, Toledo, Ohio
Walter L. Rawles, Norfolk, Va.
Richard Sanders, Portland, Oregon
J. Chris Sones, Fountain Valley, Cal.
Rene Francois Apanu, Norfolk, Va.
Jim Squier, Battle Creek, Mich.
Ray Stapp, Stillwater, Okla.
Gary Svendsen, Coon Rapids, Minn.
Randy Stewart, Colorado Springs, Colo.
Richard Tamble, Alamosa, Colo.
Terry Tancil, Spring Valley, Cal.
David Unik, Athens, Ohio
Norm Wilkerson, Ames, Iowa
Dan York, Portland, Oregon
Greg Zuidema, Evanston, Ill.

125.5-POUNDS

Bruce Henke, Dickinson, North Dakota
William Hickman, Minneapolis, Minn.
Gregory Johnson, Lansing, Mich.
Ronald Junko, Toledo, Ohio
Dwayne Keller, Stillwater, Okla.
Frank Kinateder, River Falls, Wisc.
Lyle Laird, Humboldt, Iowa
Joseph Lemmo, South Plainfield, N. J.
Forrest Lewis, Alamosa, Colo.
Larry Marchionda, River Falls, Wisc.
Henry Marsh, Rye, New Hampshire
Dave McGuire, Norman, Okla.
John Morley, Moorhead, Minn.
Doug Neuharth, Aberdeen, So. Dakota
Larry Owings, Hubbard, Oregon
Bob Paiz, San Bruno, Cal.
Mark Piven, Mineola, New York
Amos Sanchez, Greeley, Colo.
Ramiro Sandoval, San Diego, Cal.
Dan Sato, Sterling, Colo.
Gary Schuler, St. Petersburg, Fla.
Bill Schwarz, Wayne, Nebr.
Bill Seabourn, Bakersfield, Cal.
Richard Sofman, West Orange, N. J.
Craig Swenson, River Falls, Wisc.
Ron Thrasher, Norman, Okla.
Dick Tressler, Superior, Wisc.
Alvin Turner, Chicago, Ill.
Rick Vaughn, Grand Rapids, Mich.
Steve Weisman, North Miami, Fla.
Joseph Zychowicz, Toledo, Ohio

138.5-POUNDS

Dale Anderson, East Lansing, Mich.
Larry R. Becht, San Diego, Cal.
Bob Bergen, Canby, Oregon
Thomas Best, Allentown, Pa.
B. Ned Bushong, East Stroudsburg, Pa.
Pete Campbell, Rock Island, Ill.
Michael Clark, Oregon, Ohio
Charles Coffee, Minneapolis, Minn.
Russ Crowley, Lusk, Wyo.
Gene Davis, Stillwater, Okla.
Daniel Dean, Garden Grove, Cal.
Mike Doody, Joliet, Ill.

Fumiki Nakamura, New York, New York
Frank Nichols, Minneapolis, Minn.
Bob Olson, River Falls, Wisc.
Norm Parker, Chicago, Ill.
Anthony C. Pierannunzi, Providence, R.I.
Steward Pruzansky, Passaic, N. J.
Albert Rivera, Santa Ana, Cal.
Jose B. Rivera, Santa Maria, Cal.
Ronald Russo, Bloomsburg, Pa.
William Saye, Middlebury Hgts., Ohio
Gary Sherman, North Miami, Fla.
Mike Sidoff, River Falls, Wisc.
Butch Socha, Satellite Beach, Fla.
Mike Stanley, Alamosa, Colo.
Richard Stuyvesant, Moorhead, Minn.
Gayle Tollifson, Phoenix, Ariz.
Pete Vanderlofske, Annapolis, Maryland
Ed Wells, Pendelton, Oregon
Jerry Wells, Dickinson, No. Dakota
James Woodward, Gilroy, Calif.
Mike Young, Provo, Utah

154-POUNDS

Randy Ault, Phoenix, Ariz.
Dale Bahr, Ames, Iowa
Jerry Bell, New York, N. Y.
Len Borchers, Stanford, Cal.
Lester Wayne Bright, Chesapeake, Va.
Richard Casey, West Chicago, Ill.
Lt. David A. Clery, Warrington, Fla.
Dan Direnzo, Weehawken, N. J.
Joseph Dyser, Zanesville, Ohio
Bobby Douglas, Bridgeport, Ohio
John Eagleston, Oklahoma City, Okla.
Lee Ehrler, San Francisco, Cal.
James M. Ellis, Indianapolis, Ind.
Ralph Gambin, Phoenix, Ariz.
Joe Gerst, Bloomsburg, Pa.
Donald Hartsberg, St. Cloud, Minn.
Terrell L. Hays, Tempe, Ariz.
Don Hein, Ames, Iowa
Larry Hilderman, Jamestown, No. Dakota
John Hollman, Fargo, No. Dakota
Werner Holzer, Des Plaines, Ill.
Orlando Iacavelli, Ithaca, New York

team, so now the Committee needed to find a replacement for Evans. In May they chose veteran Henry Wittenberg, a Freestyle gold medalist in the 1948 Olympics and silver medalist in the 1952 Games.

Wrestlers across the country began their quest to make the '68 Olympic team as early as January, 1968. The US Olympic Wrestling Committee organized a series of 20 Regional Qualifying tournaments whereby Freestyle wrestlers would qualify for the Final Trials by finishing 1st or 2nd in their Regional tournament. Then, the top two in each weight class at the Final Trials, plus some special-case invitees, would advance to the Final Camp at Adams State College in remote Alamosa, Colorado for intensive training and final challenge matches.

pic Wrestling T

191.5-POUNDS

nt, N. J.
eld, Cal.
, Oregon
Falls, Wisc.
mosa, Colo.
na, Ohio
n, Okla.
wa
Aurora, Colo.
ing, Mich.

OUNDS

ankato, Minn.
Santa Monica, Cal.
nosa, Colo.
nd Park, N. Y.
III.
rick, N. Y.
Lansing, Mich.
ers, Ipswich, Mass.
a, Ariz.
field, III.
ng, Mich.
ssa, Colo.
easant, Mich.
endale, No. Dakota
ille, Fla.
Philadelphia, Pa.
no, Cal.
Annapolis, Md.
oledo, Ohio
Tucson, Ariz.
sh, North Carolina
antain View, Cal.
der, Colo.
argo, No. Dakota
Vaukegan, III.
lk, Va.
adelphia, Pa.
kins, Minn.
orman, Okla.
Ellensburg, Wash.
olden, Colo.
rtland, Oregon
Weymouth, Mass.

Charles Arnold, Evanston, III.
Forrest E. Badmington, Dracut, Mass.
Lt. Wayne Baughman, US Air Force
 Academy, Colo.
Geoffrey Baum, Allentown, Pa.
Bob Buehler, Fremont, Cal.
Russ Camilleri, San Francisco, Cal.
Nick Carollo, Alamosa, Colo.
Fletcher Carr, Erie, Pa.
Howard T. Chatterton, Cambridge, Mass.
Anthony Chris Christ, Williamsburg, Va.
Victor Ciaccia, Johnstown, N. Y.
Gary Cook, East Stroudsburg, Pa.
Ben Cooper, Carbondale, III.
Bruce L. Crile, Phoenix, Ariz.
Glenn Engle, Alamosa, Colo.
Pat Flaherty, St. Paul, Minn.
Randall Forrest, Bronx, N. Y.
Fred Fozzard, Norman, Okla.
Dave Friedenbach, Mandan, No. Dakota
Dwight Fritz, Alamosa, Colo.
Robert Grimes, San Diego, Cal.
Alvin Fred Heany, Washington, D. C.
William Hoge, Bismark, No. Dakota
Chuck Jean, Ames, Iowa
Tom Kline, San Luis Obispo, Cal.
Mike Latimer, Des Moines, Washington
John Lightner, Garden City, Kan.
Charles McBean, Parma, Ohio
Bill McDaniel, Norman, Okla.
Verl Miller, Burns, Oregon
Ralph D. Orr, Los Angeles, Cal.
William Parenteau, Anoka, Minn.
Lawrence Paull, Moses Lake, Wash.
Tom Peckham, Ames, Iowa
Ben Peterson, River Falls, Wisc.
Alex Porter, Valley Stream, N. Y.
Claude M. Potts, Riverside, Cal.
George Radman, West Point, N. Y.
Mike Rybak, St. Cloud, Minn.
Denny Scorbeck, River Falls, Wisc.
Darren Sipe, Issaquah, Wash.
Veryn Strellner, Iowa City, Iowa
Richard Sullivan, Cambridge, Mass.
L. Keith Tennant, Gainesville, Fla.
Chester Willia Hall....

From the official program of the 1968 Olympic Trials in Ames, Iowa *Courtesy of Jay Hammond*

The Committee reversed its 1964 decision to hold the Final Camp immediately after the Final Trials tournament. Seeing the success that the 1960 team enjoyed with a summer break in formal training, the Committee voted to have a four-month layoff between the Final Trials and the Camp. The Final Camp did not commence until mid-September.

The Final Trials — The Armory, Ames, Iowa, May 9-14, 1968

APPROXIMATELY 350 wrestlers qualified to wrestle in eight weight classes at the Final Trials. The majority entered in Freestyle, about 100 in Greco-Roman, and a couple dozen or so wrestlers chose to compete in both styles. Using the black mark system, in each Freestyle weight class there were five or six elimination rounds and then a round-robin involving the three wrestlers with the least amount of black marks.

A couple of weight classes were particularly loaded, such as 138.5 and 191.5. At 138.5 Bobby Douglas, a veteran from the 1964 squad, was the clear favorite. His competition included the fearsome Iowan Tom Huff, NCAA champions Dan Gable and Gene Davis, plus a pair of highly touted high school prodigies — Larry Owings from Hubbard, Oregon, and the youngest competitor, Charles Holmes, a junior at Carl Albert high school in Midwest City, Oklahoma. The 191.5 weight class was probably the deepest. Wayne Baughman, Jeff Baum, Russ Camilleri, Bill Harlow, Chuck Jean, Tom Peckham and Charlie Tribble were amongst the entries. Each was a national champion and/or Olympic team member at one time or another in their career.

There was also a high school senior from River Falls, Wisconsin, entered at 191.5. He had just finished as runner-up (his highest placing ever) at the Wisconsin State Tournament. He decided to enter Olympic Trials through the local Regional Qualifier. He was fortunate that there were no wrestlers at his weight class with previous Freestyle experience. He won all his matches and thus won the right to advance to the Final Trials.

Once at Ames, his high school coach, Jack Walsh, introduced him to the Iowa State coaching staff and the next day he was introduced to highly-skilled Freestyle wrestlers on the mat. He was pinned in his first match. He then had to go up against Chuck Jean, a tough Iowa State wrestler who would be the NCAA champion in 1969 and 1970. The high-school wrestler went out and took Jean down and put him on his back. For the rest of the bout, though, Jean took command and ended up thrashing the youngster.

That first takedown was a defining moment. Two weeks later, Coach Harold Nichols phoned the youngster and offered him a partial scholarship to wrestle at Iowa State. Nichols liked the kid's aggressiveness and the way he went after Jean. If not for that one takedown, in all probability Ben Peterson would never have gone to Iowa State University, never have been a teammate of Dan Gable and never have taken home an Olympic gold medal.

Numerous other fine wrestlers did not win the Trials, but their experiences in Ames remain firmly entrenched in their mind. 125.5-pounder Mark Piven was a protégé of two of the most acclaimed high school coaches in America, 'Sprig' Gardner and Lou Giani. He also went on to become a Hall of Fame wrestling official. Piven tells his story about the '68 Trials and the events leading up to it:

I grew up in Merrick, New York, the home of Mepham high school. I wrestled varsity starting in tenth grade, Gardner's final year coaching there. I practiced with the Mepham team in ninth grade, so I had two full years under him. I ended up being Coach Ken Hunte's first County champion.

I figured that I would go to college either at Lehigh or Penn State. Gardner encouraged me to go to Penn State. I had a decent but not great career there. The highlight was finishing 3rd in the NCAAs in 1964 at 130 pounds. I beat Mike Young of BYU in the first round, then lost to Yojiro Uetake. I took him down to start which pissed him off and he promptly pinned me. While I did never place in the Easterns, in those 1964 NCAAs I placed ahead of all four EIWA 130-pound medal winners.

Finishing 3rd in the NCAAs gave me an automatic bid to go to the 1964 Trials at the Singer Bowl. I wrestled at 138.5 and didn't know anything at all about Freestyle, but the tournament was in my backyard so I went just to experience the competition. I got killed.

> **Fortunately for me, one of my workout partners was Rick Sanders. He was the one who made it possible for me to wrestle in the Final Trials. One day Rick walked into the gym and to my surprise handed me a round-trip plane ticket to Iowa. He told me not to ask any questions, just be there.**
>
> **– LARRY OWINGS**

I went on to earn a Masters degree and started teaching at Farmingdale high school back on Long Island. I regularly entered AAU tournaments and when '68 came around I had a lot more Freestyle experience. I worked out religiously with Lou Giani at the Freeport Recreation Center and worked a lot of clinics and camps with him. I then won the Eastern Regional at 125.5 and qualified for Ames.

I traveled to Ames with the NYAC but was not a true club member. Chick Murano was my personal coach and a great guy. We went out early to Ames to get acclimated to the environment. I vividly remember one day going into the steam room and seeing Bobby Douglas in there. I couldn't get over how muscular he was — quite a chiseled specimen.

I won all my matches to get into the final three-way round-robin with Don Behm and Rich Sofman. I first wrestled Behm and he pinned me. Next I had to wrestle Sofman, who officially wrestled for NYAC. I had never beaten him before. I got an early takedown and was in the lead when we went off the mat in a weird position. I tore a hamstring muscle and couldn't continue. I felt terrible and had to default to Sofman, giving the #1 position to him. I went home on crutches and never wrestled again in competition. It was very, very frustrating to have advanced that far and then lose by injury default.

Moving on up to the 138.5 weight class, the wrestling gods brought together Messrs. Larry Owings and Tom Huff to wrestle the man with whom they will forever be yoked to the same plow — Dan Gable. All three remem-

Bobby Douglas was too much for all competitors at 138.5, even Iowa State sophomore, Dan Gable
Photograph courtesy of Bobby Douglas

ber clearly the events from those couple of days in May back in the Ames Armory.

Larry Owings recalls:

I wrestled for Camby high school and was a two-time Oregon high school champion. I was the last of four brothers, all good wrestlers. Altogether we won six individual state titles.

In high school, I tried to enter every wrestling tournament I could — Folkstyle, Freestyle or Greco-Roman, it didn't matter. During my senior year, I remember going to the Tri-Cities tournament and having to wrestle Gene Davis. He just pounded on me and I lost by something like 29-2. That was the worst beating of my life. After the season I continued to work out and entered the Regional Qualifier tournament in Portland. There I wrestled a lot of college guys and beat them. I won in the semi-finals but I

badly hurt my ankle and was on crutches after the match. I didn't know if I could wrestle in the finals. The match was against my high school teammate, Bob Bergen. I eventually did go out there and, with a lot of determination, beat him 4-3 to win. We both qualified for Ames as high school seniors.

In preparing for the Trials, I worked out at home and at the Multnomah Club in Portland. But I had a problem. I wasn't sure that I was going to be able to go to Ames since I had no money to get there. Fortunately for me, one of my workout partners was Rick Sanders. He was the one who made it possible for me to wrestle in the Final Trials. One day Rick walked into the gym and to my surprise handed me a round-trip plane ticket to Iowa. He told me not to ask any questions, just be there.

At Ames, I had a tough time. For my first match I drew Dan Gable, the current NCAA champion. He beat me all right, but I don't believe it was all that bad: 13-4, I think. I had Dan on his back once, nearly pinning him, but I couldn't hold him there and eventually lost. My next match was with Tom Huff. I also had him briefly on his back, but he was too good for me and I lost my second match in a row. That was it. I returned home to Oregon with my tail between my legs, even though, who knows, I may have been the 4th best wrestler at 138.5 — we'll never know. I did gain a greater appreciation for nationally ranked wrestlers, though. And, I really thought I could beat Gable if we ever wrestled again.

The next time I wrestled Gable was in the 1970 NCAA finals match when I was a college sophomore and he was a senior.

Tom Huff talks about his wrestling career up to and including the '68 Trials:

I was from Waterloo, Iowa and grew up in a wrestling family. Bob Siddens was the high school coach at Waterloo West where my three brothers also wrestled. In my ninth-grade year my older brother won the State Tournament at 95 pounds. The following year I won at 95 and he won at 112. I graduated in 1959 as a three-time Iowa high school champion.

Upon graduation, I went to the University of Iowa. As a sophomore, I made the team but didn't place in the NCAAs. The next two years I placed 3rd and 2nd, losing to Bill Dotson in overtime my senior year. Bill was also from Waterloo but he went to Waterloo East high school.

I stayed at Iowa City and enrolled in Dental school there. After earning my Dental degree I joined the Air Force. In '68 I was stationed in Colorado Springs, working out and wrestling for the Air Force team, and becoming good friends with Wayne Baughman.

In the spring of '68 I won the Regional Qualifier in Colorado and was preparing for the Final Trials in Ames. The 138.5 weight class was a tough one — particularly Douglas, Gable, and Dave Pruzansky. Gable had just won his first NCAA title. Gable and I both wrestled Larry Owings in the initial two rounds and we both won to eliminate him. Owings was really strong. Before I wrestled Gable, Owings came up to me

and said, 'I wish I were in your shoes right now.' 'Why's that?' I asked. Owings replied, 'Well, I really want to beat that guy and now I know I can do it.' I ended the conversation with something like, 'It's not going to be easy.'

Pruzansky was very tough. Gable tied him and I beat him by a decision. I remember him as being very good.

The final round-robin came down to Douglas, Gable and me. I first had to wrestle Douglas. We had become good friends over the years, ever since we wrestled back in '63 trying out for the World team. He had a fabulous gut-wrench. In our match I remember taking Bobby down right away with my fireman's carry and it was a close match. However, twice I was penalized for stalling. Actually, I was trying very hard to resist his gut-wrench. What happened was that he'd let go of it while I was resisting him, and I just continued to lay there on the mat... and receive a penalty point against me for stalling. At the very end of the match I caught Bobby again with my fireman's. However, time ran out as I dropped him onto the mat and I didn't get the points that would have won it for me.

Next I had to wrestle Gable for the chance to finish 2nd and be invited to the Alamosa Camp. Now this was more than just another match — both of us being from Waterloo and all. For years Iowa fans were asking, 'Wonder who would win a Huff-Gable match?' We were both big deals in our careers at Waterloo West and then in college, even though I never won the NCAAs. Anyway, I was about six years Dan's senior and my pride wouldn't let me lose to an up-and-coming guy who was just a college sophomore. I took Dan down with my fireman's in the opening seconds and had him on his back but we went off the mat. Back up on our feet, I took him down again — this time in the center of the mat — and put him straight on his back. His body got locked with his shoulders pinned and he didn't have a chance to bridge or turn. I didn't even have time to put in a half-nelson. He was pinned in just over a minute into the match. I had earned a trip to the Finals Camp in Alamosa.

Dan Gable talks about his experience:

Much of my coaching was based on what the 1970 NCAA loss to Larry Owings did for me.

Even Tom Huff couldn't spoil Bobby Douglas's dream of wrestling in the Olympics
Photograph courtesy of Bobby Douglas

But the '68 Trials, now that you've brought it up, were a big factor, too. The '68 Trials experience is kind of a story never told, as to how it affected the way I coached.

By 1968, I was a good wrestler and headed in the direction of being a great wrestler. But if my career had ended in 1968 with one NCAA title as a sophomore, I would soon be forgotten.

I was a freshman at Iowa State in 1967 and couldn't compete for the team, though I did wrestle in the National AAUs for the first time [Author's note: placing 3rd at 125.5 behind Rick Sanders and Masaaki Hatta.] In 1968, I went undefeated for Iowa State and won the NCAAs at 130 pounds. That was a peaking event for me. My last major Folkstyle event had been in March of 1966 when I won the Iowa state high school tournament. So, with this two year hiatus, I was very focused on winning those NCAAs.

After the NCAAs I needed a break — and took one. I had hardly taken a breath all season long. The Trials were being held just a month or so after the NCAAs and I actually didn't know if I was going to compete until I went to the weigh-in. I was having a good time letting my hair down and I don't exactly know what finally made me go. I probably just needed to wrestle. However, I wasn't terribly focused — same as at the 1970 NCAAs where I was cooperating too much with everyone, especially the media.

Wrestling at the Trials was an unbelievable experience. My first match was with a high school kid from Oregon — Larry Owings. I didn't give him much credit, him just being a high schooler and I beat him fairly handily. I tied Dave Pruzansky whom I had never heard of before, but he was a pretty fine wrestler and afterwards we became good friends.

I really didn't know much when it came down to the final round-robin with Tom Huff, Bobby Douglas and me. Against Douglas I went in with a lot of confidence. However, he technically took me apart. It was the first time I ever felt that I really had my butt kicked. He hit me with a headlock and also got one good bear hug on me. He whipped me by a good ten points.

I then had to wrestle Huff who was also from Waterloo West. I didn't think I would lose to him. I knew he had a great fireman's carry but I didn't think that would matter. I never wrestled anyone who had a fireman's like his — he hit it on me from the outside and pinned me just like that. I really didn't get a chance to wrestle.

I took 3rd, which was not good enough to qualify for the Camp. The Ames tournament opened my eyes about the skills I needed to acquire to compete successfully at that level. And the focus I needed to have.

A couple of veteran contestants, Wayne Baughman and Russ Camilleri, were amongst the pack trying to make the Olympic team at 191.5 pounds. Many would argue that Baughman and Camilleri were our two toughest light-heavyweights in the '60s and through the early '70s. They usually wrestled at either 171.5 or 191.5, bouncing back and forth at will.

Baughman, a native of Oklahoma City, won an NCAA crown at 191 pounds in 1962. He won fourteen AAU and USWF National championships — five in Freestyle and nine in Greco-Roman — and represented the US in the 1964, 1968 and 1972 Olympics as a competitor and twice afterwards as a coach. Camilleri, a Californian who wrestled at San Jose State University, amassed eleven National AAU championship titles — six in Freestyle and five in Greco Roman — between 1960 and 1971. He was named the Outstanding Wrestler in six of those championships. Camilleri wrestled for the US in the 1960 and 1964 Olympic Games. No one seems to know how many times Baughman and Camilleri wrestled each other.

Russ Camilleri recalls:

After competing in the AAUs in 1966, I took some time off and didn't wrestle much for a year and a half. The exception was the '67 AAUs. My coach, Bill Smith, told me I had to go to the National AAUs. I said, 'That's crazy, I haven't been working out.' Smith says, 'Don't work out. Your first time out, you are fine, then you go downhill for ten days or so, then after three weeks you are okay. You don't have three weeks, so just go at 191 without working out and see what happens'.

So, I went ahead and wrestled in the '67 AAUs without any training. I really couldn't move; I was so stiff and sore the final day. I had to wrestle Wayne Baughman, who beat me 1-0. Then Bill Harlow beat the living crap out of me. He cut apart the whole inside of my mouth from his cross-faces and I lost something like 8-0 to

> ❝ **Harlow somehow hurts his arm and defaults to Baughman. Harlow is eliminated and Baughman gets no black-mark points. They made a deal, I know it, and it knocked me out of 1st place.**
>
> **– RUSS CAMILLERI**

him. Myron Roderick didn't get along with me — that was the early days of the feud between the AAU and the new Federation — and he kept yelling at his wrestler, Harlow, to destroy me.

That incident was the motivation I needed to train so hard for the '68 Olympics. I wanted to go back and get Harlow. I thought Baughman was a gentleman, but not Harlow. Since the Olympic Club was in the process of de-emphasizing wrestling, I trained mostly at San Francisco State, starting a couple of months before wrestling season. I went with six guys from the Olympic Club to the National AAUs and won at 191.5, defeating Harlow along the way and Tom Peckham in the finals. That was the first time I ever wrestled Tom.

It was the Greco portion of the AAUs that upset me. I should have finished 1st. The top three wrestlers at 191.5 were Baughman, Harlow and me. In an early match, I beat Harlow by a point. Harlow and Baughman then had to wrestle. With 15 seconds left in their scoreless bout, Harlow somehow hurts his arm and defaults to Baughman. Harlow is eliminated and Baughman gets no black-mark points. They made a deal, I know it, and it knocked me out of 1st place.

At Ames, I was injured and not in good condition. I hurt my back during training and couldn't work out. It never got better. I lost to both Harlow and Peckham. I did get a last laugh though when Harlow and Peckham traded first period takedowns, as agreed upon earlier, to eliminate Baughman.

Wayne Baughman tells his story:

I was at my prime wrestling-wise in 1968. Leading up to those Trials I was stationed at the Air Force Academy Prep School in Colorado. Then I went to Athens, Ohio for a month to work out with Harry Houska, who was the NCAA champion in 1964 and a very tough wrestler.

Right before the Trials, Houska and I drove from Athens to Ames. We spent a night on the road in a motel. That night Houska had a severe asthma attack. It was a tough, tough ordeal for him but he made it through.

At the Trials, Houska did manage to wrestle while still having his attacks. However, he did not place in the top two. People were saying 'He's not in shape,' but I knew better. We worked out together and he was in as good a shape as I was. I believe he could have beaten out Jess Lewis for the team if it weren't for those asthma attacks. If I had been smarter I would not have allowed Houska to compete. I should have petitioned for an injury deferral and a special invitation to the Finals Camp for him.

There was a lot happening at Ames. I remember just before the Huff-Gable match, I was back in the warm-up area. Gable's coaches were talking with him. This included Harold Nichols and Les Anderson from Iowa State and Bob Siddens, Gable's and Huff's high school coach. Anderson was trying to show Gable how to counter Huff's infamous fireman's carry. Siddens looked at Anderson and said, 'I don't think Dan can counter it, so he better figure a way to score more points than Huff.'

As for my own situation, I had to wrestle both Peckham and Harlow in the Freestyle round-robin. I wrestled too conservatively, wrestling 'not to lose.' I tied them both, with no offensive scoring in either match, just a couple of passivity points. Then Peckham and Harlow had to wrestle each other. I'm thinking that I'm going to the Finals Camp, because one of these guys is going to lose. Just before the match a young high school kid comes up to me and says he was in the warm-up area and heard Peckham and Harlow talking. The kid said that they agreed to trade offensive points in the first period and then have no score thereafter; that way they would tie, eliminate me, and both of them would advance to the Camp. That's exactly what happened.

I went to Tournament Director Henson but he was not impressed. He said 'that's a good story but there is no way to prove it.' I was very disappointed that I couldn't compete in Freestyle and wrestle for Tommy Evans, who was my college coach. I did make it there in Greco, though.

The Finals Camp, Adams State College, Alamosa, Colorado – September, 1968

COMING out of Ames, only the finalists in each Freestyle and Greco weight class qualified for the Finals Camp. The US Olympic Wrestling Committee also voted to invite five Freestyle wrestlers, each of whom was unable to participate at the Final Trials due to prior injuries. These five were Rick Sanders, James Hansen, Mike Young, Wayne Wells and Pat Kelly. Several other wrestlers, including Dan Gable and members of the Adams State team, were invited for the purpose of providing additional competition, but they could not compete in the challenge matches.

The invited wrestlers started as the third person on the ladder and had to win two matches against the second place man to advance to the final round. The Ames Trials champion had to be defeated twice in a row in the finals to lose his spot on the team.

Most everyone gave high marks to the Alamosa site and the coaching staff for having the team well-trained and prepared for the Mexico City Olympics.

Tom Huff offers a few comments on the Camp experience:

Alamosa was a tough Camp. We had an excellent coach in Tommy Evans. I had some problems with herpes on my head and had to take some time off. That didn't help me and when I went to wrestle-off with Douglas I had a groin muscle pull so I was not at my best. He beat me pretty decisively.

I usually worked out with Douglas, but also with guys up a weight and down a weight. Gable was there as a volunteer workout partner and would often work with Wayne Wells. Dan was so intense and relentless. In one of the drills I remember all of a sudden Dan must have gotten a little too relentless for Wells and Wayne gives him a punch. The startled Gable says something like, 'Hey, I'm just wrestling the way I always work out.'

Wayne Baughman recalls:

Don Behm (back) was a two-time runner-up in the World Championships and won a silver medal in the 1968 Olympics in Mexico City *Photograph courtesy of Wade Schalles*

I've got to say, at Alamosa there were no distractions. There was nothing else around. We had good dorms, two guys to a room. No negatives really, other than it was such an isolated place. We had some very tough workouts. Coaches Evans and Wittenberg tried to outdo each other.

Actually, when I heard that Henry Wittenberg was to be our Greco coach I was upset. I thought this was a lot of crap. What did he know about Greco-Roman style wrestling? He never wrestled the style. I was upset about the whole thing. However, soon after Camp started I became a big fan of his — and hated him at the same time.

He worked our butts off. He taught us how

to be ready to compete. He would take us to the sand dunes outside Alamosa and make us run to the top. We competed against the Freestyle team, and if we didn't beat the Freestylers in the 'dunes run' we had to run them again. I remember beating my guy to the finish line and we didn't have to re-run those dunes. Wittenberg became one of my favorite people ever — as a person and as a coach.

There were some tight matches there. Probably the most controversial matches were between Don Behm and Mike Young at 125.5. Young was the Pan-Am Games champion at 138.5 in 1967 and placed 3rd in the World Championships at 138.5 the same year. He decided to drop down to 125.5 because he knew he couldn't beat Bobby

Douglas. In the Behm-Young matches there were numerous controversial calls. I think the coaches favored Behm to be on the team because they were afraid that Young might not be able to make and hold the weight.

125.5 pounds Freestyle - Mike Young vs Don Behm vs Rich Sofman

MIKE Young offers these thoughts:

I started my wrestling career at Idaho Falls high school and then wrestled at Brigham Young University. In my junior year, 1965, Fred Davis came in as our coach and that was a turnaround for me. I went to the NCAAs that year seeded 6th but lost to Gene Davis in the quarters. Though I was undefeated as a senior, I was ineligible to go to the NCAAs because I had wrestled as a freshman.

1967 was a great wrestling year for me. I entered the Great Plains Freestyle tournament and won it, beating NCAA champion Davis along the way. I earned the spot on our Pan-American team and won the gold medal at those Games. I then took a 3rd in the FILA World Freestyle Championships. As an international wrestler, I considered myself good on my feet but not so good on the mat — a bit like Shelby Wilson.

However, come 1968, it was questionable whether I could try out for the Olympics. I had damaged some cartilage while working out and had to undergo knee surgery. I couldn't compete at the Ames Trials, but received a special invitation to the Finals Camp in Colorado.

Don Behm remembers:

I started wrestling in ninth grade at New Trier high school. That's the same school where Princeton graduates Donald Rumsfeld and Brad Glass both wrestled. We had a great coach, Al Hurley, from Oklahoma. I finished 2nd in the Illinois states as sophomore and won at 120 pounds as a junior and a senior.

I'll tell you now the key to my success. Every Wednesday night I'd go over to the Northwestern wrestling room run by Ken Kraft. I got to work out with lots of good wrestlers, lots of college guys. One night I wrestled with Terry McCann. I had no idea who he was. He kicked my ass badly. This was a whole new league of wrestling for me. I was exposed to it early on, thanks to coaches Hurley and Kraft.

My senior year I went on a recruiting visit to Oklahoma State. I received a scholarship offer from the OSU coaches, but due to an oversight in the admissions office, the school didn't accept me. It all was resolved later but in the meantime I had already accepted an offer from Grady Peninger at Michigan State, who was a good friend of Coach Hurley.

At Michigan State my best NCAA finishes were 3rd in 1965 and 2nd in 1967. After graduating in '67 I stayed around East Lansing, finishing up some courses. I started working out with MSU volunteer assistant coach Dave Auble. If not for Auble I would never have made the US Olympic team. Auble told me in the fall of 1967, 'Behm, I am going to fine-tune you'. He did just that and he made a big difference in my Freestyle wrestling career. I used some of Auble's techniques all through my Freestyle days.

I was looking forward to trying out for the '68 Olympics. I had always felt that the secret to success was working hard. I never felt any pressure because I knew I always worked hard at wrestling. I kept thinking about my idols — to be as tough as Terry McCann and as slick as Gray Simons.

In April of '68 I finished 4th at 125.5 in the National AAUs in Lincoln, behind Rich Sofman, Massaki Hatta and Jim Hansen. I lost badly to Sofman in the last round. He was difficult for me to wrestle — he was so small, only about four feet tall. I knew then that I had to train even harder.

The next month I went with a large contingent from the Mayor Daley Club to the Final Trials at Ames. I remember pinning a couple guys to start and then facing Ted Parker, another native Illinois wrestler. Parker, in his senior year of high school, had beaten my high school co-captain Peter Diltz in the Illinois state finals. I wanted revenge and got it; I defeating Parker in a close match. That felt good.

I made the final round-robin along with Mark Piven and Sofman. I pinned Piven and then drew with Sofman, 1-1. My hard training was paying off as I was closing the gap between us. I would finish 1st as long as Sofman didn't pin Piven. But Piven, while ahead in the match, gets hurt and has to injury default, so I ended up 2nd. However, I had my invitation to the Finals Camp.

Rich Sofman thinks back on his career and the '68 Trials:

I never wrestled at all until I went to college. In the fall of 1961, I enrolled at the University of Pennsylvania. I was quite small and the freshman crew coach recruited me to be the coxswain for the eight-man Penn freshman boat. The stroke on the boat was also on the wrestling team and he told me to 'come on out for wrestling, too.'

I went over to the wrestling room and met Coach Don Frey. I started learning the sport and took to it. I learned a lot, especially throws, pancakes, and headlocks. The headlock was really my bread and butter move. By my senior year I had improved considerably. At the EIWA tournament, I lost to the top-seed at 123 by one point in the semi-finals and finished 4th.

After graduating from Penn in 1965, I started working out at the NYAC, particularly with Chick Murano and Andy Fitch. They were great partners for me and I continued to improve. In April of 1966 I won the National AAUs at 125.5 [Author's note: defeating an impressive field that included Rick Sanders, Fred Powell and Jim Hazewinkel.]

As the '68 Olympic year rolled around I picked up my training pace at the NYAC and entered the AAUs feeling great. I pinned most of my opponents in the early rounds, then killed Behm 9-1 and defeated Hatta to take the 125.5 title. I didn't know it then but I had hit my peak — too early.

At Ames, I wrestled well, pinning just about everyone. I met Behm in the final round-robin and we drew, but I had fewer black-mark points so I won the top seed for the Finals Camp.

Mike Young recalls:

To get ready for the Camp, I spent a lot of time in the summer of '68 with Rick Sanders and Bobby Douglas. The three of us became very close as we worked out together in Portland and Boise. During the summer and at the start of the Camp, I was expecting to challenge at 138.5, the same weight class as Douglas and Huff. I normally weighed around 150 and didn't think I

Former Ivy League wrestler Rich Sofman peaked too early in his attempt to make the 1968 Olympic team *Photograph courtesy of Wade Schalles*

could pull down to 125.5. Plus, there was only a three-pound weight allowance for the challenge matches.

Four or five days before the challenge matches, Sanders and Douglas took me aside. They told me that I should go down to 125.5 so that the three of us could be Olympians. I was dubious. 138.5 was my comfortable competing weight and I only had a few days to make 125.5.

Well, they talked me into it. I remember staying up all night sweating it out in a rubber suit. Sanders and Douglas stayed up all night with me. It was miserable — a major mistake on my part. I made weight finally and had to wrestle and defeat Don Behm twice to advance to the finals. The first match went well and I won. For our next match I was really feeling horrible and lost on a headlock move of Behm's. I just couldn't muster up the strength to go after him hard and I lost, 2-1.

While I was upset that I didn't get to go to the Olympics, I believe that Behm was the right man to go. He was a terrific competitor. And, Douglas was really an excellent wrestler and I don't know if I could have beaten him had I stayed at my normal weight class.

Don Behm says:

I was ready for the Finals Camp. Actually, I worked harder to get there than while I was

> ❝ **He definitely had the edge on me in the next two bouts and defeated me both times to win the weight class. I was blown away. I have never been so devastated in my life. I went home crying in my soup. However, Don Behm earned it – I can't say I could have done as good a job as he did in Mexico City.**
>
> **– RICH SOFMAN**

••••••••••••••••••••••••••••••

there. I was in great shape and knew that no one was doing what I was doing. The key to my success in Colorado was my understanding about the high altitude and my personal training for it. I knew from experience that you had to adapt quickly to the environment. As soon as I got off the plane I went and worked out. My body quickly started adjusting to the need for more oxygen.

While there I would run 25 wind sprints of 75 yards each, and then go run three miles across the sand dunes. I started working out three times a day and then increased it to four. I was in the best shape of my life. Rick Sanders was my usual workout partner and we pushed each other very hard.

My first opponent was Mike Young. I knew he was cutting a huge amount of weight and he had to beat me twice in a row. Didn't happen. He beat me decisively in the first match, but I knew that he couldn't keep up with me the second day, and my conditioning paid off. I beat him and now had to wrestle Rich Sofman. We drew in our first match, but then I beat him twice and won the Olympic spot. All my training paid off for me.

I was elated. All I could think of was, 'I did it'. I called my wife back home and everyone in my family was so happy.

Rich Sofman remembers his own crushing disappointment:

At the Finals Camp, I wasn't in 'the zone'. For some reason I wasn't feeling great. One day out there, a manager or someone gave me an Olympic uniform. That was bad – I believe it jinxed me.

As the challenge matches started, I watched Behm and Young wrestle each other. I was sure that Young would win and that psyched me up. Young and I had never wrestled each other. I would have much rather wrestled him than Don. Until you wrestle me, because I am so short, it's difficult to figure me out.

However, Behm beat Young, so Don was my Finals challenger. I just had to beat him once. In our first match, he shot in on me and I threw him on his back to take the lead. However, Don came back to tie me 2-2. He definitely had the edge on me in the next two bouts and defeated me both times to win the weight class.

I was blown away. I have never been so devastated in my life. I went home crying in my soup. However, Don Behm earned it – I can't say I could have done as good a job as he did in Mexico City.

154 Freestyle – Werner Holzer vs Wayne Wells vs Fred Lett

WERNER Holzer recalls his wrestling days: I started wrestling at the Chicago City Park & Recreation Department in 1948. I was a scrapper and I was good enough to stimulate my interest. In high school I was a teammate of Terry McCann. Terry was a senior when I was a freshman. We both won state titles for Chicago Schurz high school.

Both my parents were immigrants and there were no plans for me to go to college. However, winning the Illinois State Tournament in 1955 gave me a chance at a scholarship and I chose to go to the University of Illinois.

In college I was undefeated my sophomore year in dual meets. At the NCAAs, I lost to Ron Gray in the semi-finals and ended up 3rd at 147 pounds. My junior and senior years I competed, but I had severe shoulder problems which limited me. I placed in the Big Ten tournament but not in the Nationals.

After graduating in 1959, I went into the Army and I missed the '60 Trials. I was stationed in California and wrestled for several years, first

Wayne Wells captured an Olympics spot in his first serious attempt at Freestyle competition
Photograph courtesy of Wade Schalles

with the Los Angeles Y, then the San Francisco Olympic Club. I did well, but was never number one in my class. I tried out unsuccessfully for the 1964 Olympic team.

I moved back to Chicago and in 1965 Steve Combs, Brad Glass and I founded the Mayor Daley Club. We were new kids on the block, yet we won the National AAU team title in both 1966 and 1967. I was the National AAU champion at 154 in '66 and 2nd [to Bobby Douglas] in '67. I wrestled my first international match in the FILA World Championships in 1966, finishing 4th in the world.

In the 1968 Trials in Ames, I entered both Freestyle and Greco. I was having a good Freestyle tournament and had the least black marks entering the final round-robin match. I faced Fred Lett, to whom I had never lost before. Somehow, that day he beat me so I ended up finishing 2nd. I did win the Greco tournament, beating Bill Berry.

I was able to compete at the Finals Camp in both Freestyle and Greco.

In the challenge matches, I lost my opening Freestyle match to Wayne Wells, then tied him, then lost again to him. He got me on a duck-under, which was my best move. Wayne was tough to get to and I didn't have the zip as I did when I was 25. I had a good headlock which helped me with my Greco-Roman style. I beat Berry again to make the Greco Olympic team.

Some thoughts about the coaching situation — Bill Smith resigned as Freestyle coach at the start of '68. He was my coach at the Olympic Club and was very knowledgeable in international Freestyle. Tommy Evans didn't know nearly as much, but I had no problem with him. His integrity was impeccable. He was extremely fair and had all the basics, but not all the techniques that Bill had. Evans pushed the Freestyle guys hard. I don't think Henry Wittenberg really knew much about Greco and was a little too easy on us. We pushed ourselves. Overall, I thought the conditions were great at Alamosa and I was not short-changed

What I am most proud of is the participation

of the wrestlers from the Mayor Daley Club. We placed five men on the US Olympic wrestling team – Don Behm, Steve Combs, Larry Kristoff, Bob Roop and me. Two other members came close, Bill Harlow and Pat Kelly. We made a tremendous impact right off the bat.

The University of Oklahoma's NCAA Champion Wayne Wells talks about events leading up to the 1968 Trials:

I wrestled at John Marshall high school in Oklahoma City, coached by Virgil Milliron. That's the same school Wayne Baughman went to, only I came along a couple years later.

I won two state titles and was recruited by Tommy Evans to the University of Oklahoma in the fall of 1964. As a freshman I competed three times that year: two duals against the Oklahoma State freshmen, plus the state AAUs. For those matches, we never called it Freestyle or Olympic style – it was 'AAU style'.

I was fascinated by the 'AAU style', but didn't get to do it much. I remember wrestling and beating Ron Finley, an old experienced hand who was wrestling up a weight class or two. That gave me the confidence that I could do this. Later in 1965, Evans took us to the National AAUs in Omaha. Three matches and I was out. That's the last AAU Tournament I wrestled until I went to the Olympic Training Camp in Alamosa in '68.

In the fall of 1967, my senior year, I injured the cartilage in my knee. I didn't want an operation then; I was afraid it would put me behind in my quest for an NCAA title. I did win the NCAAs and had the knee operated on after the season and after the East-West match was completed. It was a significant operation. In those days they opened it up all the way. Today it would have been more simple arthroscopic surgery.

So, I couldn't go to the Trials which were held in May. That was probably a blessing. I very well might not have won them. I would have received too many black marks that hurt you in a tournament situation.

I was very inexperienced in Freestyle tournament wrestling as opposed to veteran guys like Werner Holzer and Fred Lett. I could do okay on top, but getting a takedown in those days was brutal. The experienced guys had their strategy. They could just stand there the whole match just looking at you, waiting for you to make a mistake. They knew how to wrestle for a draw and how to work the black-mark system – it's a whole different mind-set from what I was used to.

Thanks to the influence of Port Robertson and Tommy Evans, I got an invitation to the Alamosa Camp. I was definitely a dark horse. I had never wrestled or even seen an international match. The closest was watching some films from Shozo Sasahara during his trip to America.

At Alamosa, I had to win all my matches... first against Holzer, then Lett, if I was to make the team. It was tough for me to get down to 154, especially at the high altitude and with a slim weight allowance. I found it very difficult to sweat and I had to make weight four days in a row for my matches.

I beat Holzer in two really close contests. He was extremely hard to score on. We tied once and I won the other two matches, 1-0 and 2-1.

My parents drove to Alamosa from Houston to watch me wrestle, arriving there for my two final matches against Lett. Our first match I hardly remember; I think I won by a pin.

In our second match, Lett went ahead of me by one or two points – that's like ten points against a veteran such as Lett. It's extremely difficult to catch-up at this level. He was running from me – just like I would have done if the situation were reversed. He'd jump out-of-bounds whenever I got near him. I was losing with less than one minute left in the bout and I was panicking trying to figure out something. Back in the center, I jerked him down to his knees. As he came up, I closed my eyes and went for it... I leapt at him with a pancake and flipped him over. He went right to his back and I pinned him with just seconds to go. If not for that one desperate move, he would have gone to the Olympics instead of me. I was fortunate and lucky.

Looking back at the training camp – I think Evans was trying to outdo Port's 1960 regime. We worked and worked and worked. Three-a-day practices sometimes. Altitude was a source of problems for many of the wrestlers. Everyone's skin was like parchment paper. We were all flatlanders up in the hills for an extended

The Freestyle Olympic team with coaches Gorrigan and Evans *Courtesy of* Amateur Wrestling News

The Greco Olympic team with coaches Wittenberg and Torio *Courtesy of* Amateur Wrestling News

> Evans barks, 'Get up Sanders or go home.' Sanders continues to lie there but then barely lifts his head and rolls it around to face his coach and then lashes out, 'Just blow the whistle, coach.' Evans blows his whistle, and Sanders bolts up and off he goes sprinting as fast as he can... Rick Sanders was, by far, the toughest guy on that team.
>
> — WAYNE WELLS

● ●

six-week period. Tommy kept pounding us. I was used to this since I had wrestled for him at OU. Others were always asking me, 'What's he up to today?' I never was sure.

To those that knew him, Rick Sanders' combination of true talent and unorthodox character were unsurpassed. His eccentricities of behavior are legendary. There are numerous Rick Sanders stories out there. Here are two that Wayne Wells tells about Sanders from the 1968 Finals Camp in Alamosa.

Sanders story #1

Sanders had an injury deal like me but came to Camp angry that he had to start at the bottom of ladder and win all four of his matches. The first night in the dorms, Sanders found a pile of acoustical ceiling tiles that some contractors had left behind. He got some duct tape and took all the tiles to his dorm room where he completely covered his closet — inside the door, the walls, floor, ceiling, everything. We asked him what he was doing. He replied, 'Well, I'm probably going to be staying up most of the nights while I'm here and I don't want to bother you guys with my loud stereo music.' Sure enough, around midnight when the rest of us went to bed, Sanders would close himself in the closet and blast his stereo for hours-on-end. He never did disturb us.

Sanders story #2

Rick and Coach Evans would go round-n-round. Coach called him 'Snipe' because he was always carrying around this bag with all sorts of stuff in it. Evans told him he must be out 'Snipe hunting' and the name 'Snipe' stuck.

Sanders had this habit of always being late for practice. One day at a pre-practice meeting, Sanders walked into the practice room a little after Evans had started talking to the wrestlers. Evans asks for an explanation and Sanders starts to give some lame excuse. Evans blares out, 'I don't want to hear any more of your shit. Don't be late again.'

The next day Sanders arrives late for practice once again. Evans says nothing. Everyone looks at me as if to say, 'what's up with the coach?'. We are all thinking that Sanders has finally worn down Evans, who was a pretty easy-going guy off the mat. Well, at the end of that morning practice, Evans leads us out to the football field — it is high-noon at the high altitude and Evans tells us that now we are going to run 100-yard sprints. We start running the sprints. It gets up to 8, then 10, and we're still going. As we get to 12, I realize that Evans is going to make us run a mile — 17 sprints — and that's exactly what he does. Everyone by now is getting exhausted and stripping down to their shorts. All except one of us — Sanders. He's running with a couple pair of sweat suits on with his hood up around his head.

After the 17th wind sprint, we all literally fall on the ground in the end zone, puking and feeling like each of us is dying. Evans slowly walks all the way down the field to us. We all sit up to look and listen to him. But not Sanders. He continues to lie on the ground — face down. Doesn't move a muscle. Evans goes over to him and with his toe nudges Sanders in the ribs and tells him to get up. Still nothing. We are wondering if he has completely passed out. Evans barks, 'Get up Sanders or go home'. Sanders continues to lie there but then barely lifts his head and rolls it around to face his coach and then lashes out, 'Just blow the whistle, coach'. Evans blows his whistle, and Sanders bolts up and off he goes sprinting as fast as he can down the field. Evans makes him run seven more sprints which Sanders does. He was not late again.

Wells concludes:

Rick Sanders was, by far, the toughest guy on that team.

Dan Gable adds one more story:

My idol at the time was Tom Peckham, also a member of the Cyclone Club. Tom was an NCAA champion at Iowa State and a leading contender for an Olympic team berth at 191.5. After he won the Ames Trials tournament, he needed a workout training partner and it turned out to be me. He had this job refurbishing wrestling mats. I joined him during that summer of '68, traveling all over Iowa and Minnesota, living in motels and working out at local high schools.

Tom didn't care that I was 60 pounds lighter. I was a good partner for him. He'd beat me to a pulp but I'd keep fighting back. He'd get a heck of a workout from me.

We ended up going to Alamosa together. I decided that I was going to take a quarter off from school just so I could participate in the Camp. That was a good decision. I worked out with many of the guys and actually did pretty well against them.

The Camp built up my confidence to a higher level. I wrestled Huff a lot and didn't do too badly. I usually wrestled Douglas, Wells, Holzer, Combs and did okay. I also wrestled a bit with Sanders. I learned his arm-bar series and a lot about the weight-loss techniques that he used.

Back to Peckham — he was my roommate, too. I was a lot more into the Camp than he was. Yet, I couldn't compete and he could. He was seeded #1 and was challenged by Harlow. Harlow whipped him in the first wrestle-off match. After the bout, Peckham was laying on a bench in the practice area feeling terrible. He said to me, 'Gable, pack your bags, I am heading home'.

Well, I lose my cool with Tom. He still had one more bout to wrestle and win the trip to Mexico City. I am now his coach. I had been working and training with him for four months. So, I start chewing on him. He could have told me to go away. But, I told him very forcefully that we have come this far, we are not pulling out now. He listened to me and went out on the mat and wrestled Harlow the second time. Tom defeated him, winning the Olympic berth.

That was my very first coaching experience!

1968 OLYMPIC TEAM MEMBERS

	FREESTYLE	GRECO-ROMAN
114.5	Rick Sanders (2nd)	Richard Tramble
125.5	Don Behm (2nd)	Dave Hazewinkel
138.5	Bobby Douglas	Jim Hazewinkel
154	Wayne Wells (4th)	Werner Holzer (6th)
171.5	Steve Combs	Larry Lyden
191.5	Tom Peckham (4th)	Wayne Baughman (5th)
213.5	Jess Lewis (6th)	Henk Schenk
HWT	Larry Kristoff (5th)	Bob Roop

★ *JAPAN, led by Oklahoma State grad Yojiro Uetake, won three golds in the '68 Olympics. Turkey and the Soviet Union each earned two Freestyle gold medals. The US was hindered by injuries, particularly the one to team captain Bobby Douglas, who was forced to withdraw from the Games.*

1968 PRESIDENTIAL ELECTION

★ *In a race initially considered a toss-up, Richard Nixon became only the second Republican in 40 years to win the presidency. Hubert Humphrey suffered from his close association with President Johnson's Vietnam War policies. George Wallace was a strong third party candidate, but did not necessarily swing the election either way.*

THE SCORECARD

Richard M. Nixon Spiro Agnew	301 Electoral Votes 43.4% of Popular Vote
Hubert Humphrey Ed Muskie	191 Electoral Votes 42.7% of Popular Vote
George Wallace Curtis Lemay	46 Electoral Votes 13.5% of Popular Vote

LYMPIC PICTORIAL

WRESTLING

Armory
IOWA STATE UNIVERSITY

May 9-14, 1968

Price - 50 cents

1968
United States
Olympic
Team Trials

THE PRIME
OF MISTER
DAN GABLE

1972

> 66 **Gable really helped the '72 team. At the Finals Camp, we'd schedule two workouts a day, but Dan would take the Peterson brothers aside and do three. John really got good; he was improving, not by the week or by the day – but by the minute.**
>
> — **Bill Farrell, 1972 Olympic Freestyle Coach**

BY 1972, the AAU was hearing footsteps. They were coming from the newly created US Wrestling Federation (USWF). The feud between the AAU and the USWF had begun and wouldn't be resolved for over a decade.

A little background is essential. Since its founding in 1912, FILA, the international governing body for the Olympic styles of wrestling, had recognized the AAU as the sole national governing body for Olympic-style wrestling in the United States. However in the late '60s, a group of men, dissatisfied with the AAU's role in promoting our Freestyle and Greco wrestling competition, formed a competing group – the USWF. The NCAA, fed up with its squabbles with the AAU over the years, backed the upstart group. Shortly thereafter, FILA recognized both organizations and urged them to come together. That never happened.

Beginning in 1969, both the AAU and the USWF held their own 'National' Freestyle and Greco tournaments. At the youth through the senior level both organizations conducted clinics and tournaments and sponsored trips abroad for the wrestlers. While the USWF organized the Team Trials for the 1971 World Games, FILA awarded to the AAU the responsibility for organizing the '72 US Olympic Wrestling Trials.

Leading up to the Trials, feelings of animosity ran strong and deep between the leaders of the two competing groups. While

Previous spread: Dan Gable dominated his competition in the 1972 Trials and Olympic Games in Munich *Photograph © Bettmann/CORBIS*

there was more, and probably better, wrestling competition with both groups active, the situation was confusing for many and raised the potential for partiality among coaches and officials. Wrestlers and coaches were forced to pick sides as politics clouded the sport of Olympic-style wrestling in the US throughout the decade of the '70s and into the early '80s.

Not all the news was negative. The best news for the wrestlers was the 1969 FILA decision to expand international competition from eight to ten weight classes for World tournaments and the Olympics. A 105.5 pound weight class was introduced and other weights were shifted so that an additional middleweight class was added.

In the intervening years after the 1968 Olympics, the US enjoyed greater success than ever before in the international Freestyle events. In 1969 and 1970, we finished 2nd in the World Freestyle tournament, though we fell back to a disappointing 6th place in 1971.

Most encouragingly we crowned our first individual World Champions – Fred Fozzard and Rick Sanders in 1969, Wayne Wells in 1970, and Dan Gable in 1971. Other Freestylers that finished in the top three in the world between 1969 and 1971 included Don Behm (2nd twice), Mike Young, Bobby Douglas, Bill Harlow, Russ Hellickson, Henk Schenk and Larry Kristoff. Plus, Dave Hazewinkel placed 2nd in the world in Greco in 1970 – the highest place ever achieved by a US wrestler in 14 years of international Greco-Roman competition.

Looking beyond the arena of amateur wrestling, things for Americans looked a little calmer than four years earlier, but looks may have been deceiving. President Richard

Nixon was completing his first term of office and was an overwhelming favorite to be re-elected. Then, on June 17 — less than a week before the Olympic Trials kicked off — five men were arrested for breaking into the Democratic National Committee headquarters in Washington's Watergate Hotel. President Nixon's response was that he 'deplored the incident and no lieutenant of his was involved.'

In regards to Vietnam, while the fighting was still devastating there came a sense that the end was finally nearing. Troop withdrawals were being announced monthly. There were just 50,000 draft calls in 1972 in contrast with 300,000 three years earlier. Henry Kissinger was heavily involved in the Paris Peace talks during the summer of '72 and in August the US Senate voted to end the war in four months.

At the Democratic National Convention, anti-war candidate Senator George McGovern received the delegates' votes as the presidential nominee. McGovern named Missouri Senator Thomas Eagleton as his vice-presidential running mate. It was soon revealed that Eagleton had received electroshock therapy for depression during the 1960s. The resulting negative attention prompted McGovern to drop Eagleton from the ticket, replacing him with Sargent Shriver. This occurred just a few days after McGovern had stated publicly he was still "behind Eagleton 1000 percent."

On June 23, 1972 Congress passed the Title IX law that states: "No person in the United States shall, on the basis of sex, be excluded from participation in, be denied the benefits of, or be subjected to discrimination under any education program or activity receiving Federal financial assistance." There were unintended consequences for wrestlers and coaches. Wrestling teams that finished in the top 25 in the '72 NCAAs included Washington (4th), Idaho State, Arizona, Illinois State, Toledo, Slippery Rock, New Mexico and Brigham Young — these are just a few of the 400-plus men's college wrestling programs that were eliminated in the years following the enactment of Title IX.

The stock market hovered around the 950 mark in the summer of 1972. On November 14, for the first time ever, the Dow Industrials closed above 1000, but the '70s bear market was about to begin. It would take more than ten years for the Dow to pass the 1100 level.

An unusual event caught the world's sports headlines — the "Match of the Century" for the World Chess Title in Reykjavik between Russia's Boris Spassky and America's Bobby Fischer. The American had never defeated Spassky, but he was ready for this challenge. In a 21-match contest that lasted from July 11 to September 1, Fischer emerged the winner, 12.5 to 8.5. His victory ended 24 years of Soviet domination of the World Chess Title.

Back in the US, hundreds of American wrestlers were preparing themselves for the hope of facing the Russians and other world wrestling powers on the Olympic mats in Munich in late August and early September. One of those hopefuls made the following headline in the *Daily Oklahoman*, *"Some Lawyers Can Twist Arms"* — referring to the official announcement on the last day of the Finals Camp wrestle-offs that Wayne Wells was one of 108 applicants to pass the Oklahoma bar exam.

The Trials Process

MOST everyone was thrilled that the US Olympic Wrestling Committee, headed by Wesley Brown, named Bill Farrell from the NYAC and Allen Rice from the Minnesota Wrestling Club as the Freestyle and Greco head coaches respectively. Both gentlemen had served as head coaches of the successful US teams in the World Championships in 1969 and 1970. Russ Houk and Steve Archer were named managers, and Farrell asked Jim Peckham and Bill Weick to be his Freestyle assistant coaches.

Twenty-four Regional Qualifying tournaments were held across the US in the spring. In May, Coach Farrell organized a four-day Olympic development camp at St. Andrews, Tennessee. More than 60 top Olympic prospects attended the camp. Farrell and others contend that it provided invaluable experience in Olympic-style techniques for everyone.

Qualifiers from the Regional Trials and some designated national tournaments were eligible to compete in the Final Freestyle Trials. These matches were scheduled to be held in Anoka, Minnesota on June 22-24. The Final Greco-Roman tournament was scheduled for Anoka on June 26-27 and was open to anyone who showed up.

After a one-month hiatus, the top place winners at the Trials advanced to the final round of wrestle-offs in Minneapolis to determine the 20 wrestlers who would represent the two 1972 US Olympic wrestling teams in Munich.

The Final Olympic Team Trials, Anoka, Minnesota, June 22-27, 1972

MORE than 400 wrestlers entered the Final Trials held at the high school gymnasium in Anoka, a suburban town about 20 miles northwest of Minneapolis. There were 294 Freestyle entries and 139 in Greco-Roman style in ten weight classes. Distinguished University of Minnesota coach Wally Johnson directed the tournament.

Jim Duschen, a competitor in both Freestyle and Greco, remembers the tournament well:

The facility at Anoka was pretty good. There was a nice size gym and the crowds, as I recall, were large. Like me, a bunch of the wrestlers competed in both Freestyle and Greco, especially since you didn't have to pre-qualify to enter the Greco tournament.

Most of our best Greco wrestlers were from Minnesota. Alan Rice was regarded as the premier Greco instructor in the country and he and his Greco club wrestlers had a strong following in the area. That clearly helped boost the attendance.

Alan Rice and Wayne Baughman – two of the US Greco-Roman icons of the '60s and '70s
Photograph courtesy of Amateur Wrestling News

Dave and Jim Hazewinkel wrestled for and graduated from the host Anoka high school in the mid-'60s. The twin brothers are recognized as our two best Greco-Roman wrestlers coming out of the '60s. Each was a two-time medalist in the World Games between 1966 and 1970. Dave was the first American to win a Greco silver medal in the World Championships, and Jim was the first to make the Greco World team at three different weight classes.

Jim Hazewinkel recalls:

It was a real thrill to have the Olympic Trials in our hometown and to wrestle back in our high school gym in front of a lot of friends and family. One of our best friends was Chuck Coffee who was a few years older than us. Chuck took up Greco after college and was good enough to make the US World team in 1966 and 1967. In the '68 Trials, we both competed at 136 and I beat him to make the Olympic team.

Well, in 1972, Chuck decides to drop down to the 125.5 pound weight class. This time Dave beats him to make the Olympic team. I know Chuck figures if it weren't for the two of us Hazewinkels that he'd be an Olympian.

Leo Kocher, then a junior at Northwestern University, talks about his experiences at the tournament:

I was just a so-so wrestler at Northwestern, known more for my looks as a bearded, long-hair-type guy. But I wanted to give the Trials a try, so I qualified and went to the Minnesota tournament. It was a huge thing for me.

I started out strong and beat a Big Ten Conference champion and then a NYAC wrestler. I think it was Jerry Bell, a veteran who had been on the US Pan-Am team. Those matches that I did win gave me a huge boost of confidence.

In the fourth round I came up against Jeff Callard of Oklahoma. Early in the match, he hits me with an under-arm spin and catches me in an arm bar and is hurting my shoulder something awful. I am grimacing in pain but the referee won't stop the match. He was probably an AAU ref who saw Ken Kraft (a USWF supporter) in my corner and didn't show us any mercy. Anyway, Callard keeps cranking on me and sure enough pins me and I am eliminated. I guess you could say that was my introduction to the 'I would just as soon break your neck as pin you' school of wrestling.

In the early rounds Wells beat Wells... and Hicks beat Hicks. That is, Oklahoma star Wayne Wells dominated Joe Wells of the Mayor Daley Club, 21-3. Greg Hicks of Athletes-In-Action downed Wayne Hicks of Navy, 7-2.

And in a featured match at 149.5, Dan Gable overran Larry Owings, 7-1.

Owings recalls his 1972 experience:

I didn't realize the magnitude of what I had done in beating Gable in the 1970 NCAA finals. I was basically a country bumpkin not accustomed to any celebrity status. Anyway, in the fall of 1970 I got married and soon after my wife became pregnant. It was a rocky marriage and she didn't want me leaving home to go wrestle.

Consequently, I no longer practiced like I should have. I lost my focus and it took away my fine edge. And, I was really tired of everyone coming up and asking me about this Gable thing.

All along I was planning to tryout for the Olympics at 136.5 pounds. Despite my wife's objections I went to the tournament, but missed

" **I do think that if I had the drive that I had as a high school senior in 1968, I would have made that '72 team.**

— LARRY OWINGS

weight by a pound or two and was forced up to 149.5. I knew that Gable was looking for me. He was out to get me, no doubt. I gave him a reason to beat me and he did. I was the only person to score a point on him, though.

[Author's note: Gable dominated everyone. He won by pin (2.55), pin (4.33), 21-0, 27-0, 7-1, pin (2:48) and a 13-0 victory over Joe Seay in the finals.]

Owens continues:

I remember a couple other incidents. Lloyd Keaser, the Navy wrestler, came up to me in the shower early in the tournament and told me that if we met each other on the mat, he would pound on me. Well, we did meet in a late round, but I pounded on him — bad. I had him crying on the mat. His earlier remarks gave me the needed incentive to win.

I then had to wrestle Joe Seay and he beat me. I just didn't have the necessary edge in that match. I ended up finishing 3rd behind Gable and Seay which entitled me to go to the Finals Camp. However, I didn't go; too much pressure from home, a loss of drive, a number of things.

I do think that if I had the drive that I had as a high school senior in 1968, I would have made that '72 team.

Two brothers from Wisconsin, John and Ben Peterson, emerged on the international wrestling scene in the early '70s to vie for spots on the '72 Olympic team. They embarked on divergent routes during their college careers, but hooked on to Dan Gable in the homestretch leading up to the Trials.

John Peterson talks about his wrestling days and the '72 Trials:

My oldest brother, Phil was a great athlete — an all Big Ten right guard at the University of Wisconsin. He was probably the best athlete ever to come out of our local school, Cumberland High. The next brother, Tom, was a year behind. He was trying to be different from his basketball playing brother, so he went out for wrestling despite mom's objections. She only knew about the Pro Wrestling on TV. Dad got excited about the sport once he saw it and subsequently got me and my younger brother Ben involved.

As a high school freshman, I hurt my knee playing football, so I couldn't wrestle. I started competing as a sophomore, and did okay, but I never qualified for the State Tournament. In my senior year, I realistically thought I could be a state champion. However, I ended up 3rd in the Sectionals and only the top two guys qualified for states.

At the time, I didn't think I could wrestle competitively in college. I took the summer off — no workouts for the first time in awhile and I believed my wrestling career was over. I wanted a degree in Industrial Education, so I enrolled at the University of Wisconsin at Stout, an NAIA school, in the fall of '67. Once there, I was anxious to wrestle so I asked the coach if I could tryout for the team. He said, 'Sure, we don't offer scholarships; everyone is welcome to come out.'

I enjoyed a decent, but not great, college wrestling career. My highest national placing was as a senior, finishing 5th in the 1971 NAIA championships. I lost in both the semi-finals and in the consolation wrestle-backs.

Freestyle was much more to my liking. My first exposure to Freestyle was back in 1967 at Coon Rapids at the Pan-Am Trials. Ben and I watched that tournament and liked that style instantly. Wrestling on my feet was my strong point — I had a good double leg drop. Shortly after that we attended a clinic at River Falls with Coach Al Rice. That was our first practice with Freestyle and Greco techniques.

I entered the 1968 Regional Olympic Trials and lost to the Big Ten champion from Michigan State, so I didn't qualify. Brother Ben won the Regionals as a high school senior and advanced to the Ames Final Trials tournament. That's how he got his scholarship to Iowa State.

In December of '70 I entered the Midlands tournament at 167 pounds, finishing 2nd. I lost to Jim Tanniehill in overtime. However, I beat an Iowa State guy in the semis and took great pride in that. After the finals, I talked with Dan

Gable a bit and he encouraged me, saying that I 'had some potential.'

In the summer of '71, Ben was invited to the Pan-Am training camp in Florida. He asked Coach Doug Blubaugh if I could come along. Blubaugh said, 'If he works as hard as you, he can come.' I owe Blubaugh an awful lot. I trained under him for six weeks that summer and improved enormously. I was now wrestling at a more comfortable weight — 180.5. I was runner-up to Bob Anderson in those Pan-Am Trials.

The week before the '71 World Team tryouts in August, there was a qualifying tournament. I wrestled and lost to J Robinson in Freestyle and didn't qualify. The next day, I wrestled in the Greco portion — up at 220 pounds — and finished 2nd, which earned me an invitation to the final tryout tournament.

Then some good fortune came my way. Neither Anderson nor Robinson tried out for the Freestyle World team at 180.5. I was in the right place at the right time. I beat a couple guys in the final round-robin to make the US World team going to Sofia, Bulgaria. Once there I lost both my matches and didn't place. However, I came back thinking positively about making the Olympic team the following year.

After that experience, Gable invited me to Ames to workout and train for the Olympics during the '71-'72 school year. I took him up on that offer. In December I won the Midlands tournament. I was gaining a lot of ground working out in the ISU wrestling room.

In the spring of '72, my brother Ben and I wrestled in the USWF National championship in Stillwater. We both took 4th place and we both felt terrible. I lost by 15-1 to Steve Combs. I kept going for my double leg takedown and Combs kept throwing me with a counter toss. After that I went to an intensive training camp in Tennessee. That was a huge boost for me. Gable showed me how to correct my mistakes on my takedowns so that I wouldn't get thrown to my back. I kept getting better every day.

The Olympic Trials tournament was in Anoka, just 90 minutes from my hometown. I had some more good fortune. Fred Fozzard, 1969 World Champion and winner at the USWF tournament 180.5 didn't come to the Trials. I won the rematch against Combs. This time the

Ben Peterson thrived under the tutelage of Dan Gable to win the Trials at 198 pounds
Photograph courtesy of Wade Schalles

score was lopsided in my favor. Gable's drills were paying off big time!!! I ended up beating Ed Vatch to win the Trials at 180.5. It was time to prepare for the Finals Camp.

Brother Ben Peterson tells his wrestling story:

I started learning a little about wrestling in grade school and I did some intramural wrestling in junior high. Then, I made the Cumberland high school team my freshman year. I wrestled seven varsity matches and lost them all by pin. In my senior year, I was undefeated until the finals of the Wisconsin State Tournament. I got beat and I never did become a state champion.

I received a partial scholarship to Iowa State and enrolled there in the fall of 1968. Dan Gable had a big influence on me during my years at

Ames. By my senior year in college I had already attended two World team camps because of Gable. The first one was in 1970 at Superior, Wisconsin. I went for two weeks. We were supposed to pay for our room and board. However, the head coach there, Bill Farrell, never asked me for it, saying, 'Aw, you don't need to pay, the AAU will take care of it. Keep on training hard, you are doing good.' That was a big confidence builder for me.

The next year the Pan-Am training camp was in Florida and the World team tryouts and camp were in Annapolis — pretty much back-to-back. My brother and I spent the summer at both places. John earned a World team berth but Russ Hellickson won at my weight class, 198 pounds.

Back in Ames for my senior year and the 1971-72 wrestling season, I was trying to con-

> **I go over and ask him, 'John, how did you do?' A grin slowly comes across his whole face. 'I beat [Combs], 7-0.' Now he knows he would probably go to the Olympics.**
>
> **— BEN PETERSON**

centrate on defending my NCAA crown plus preparing myself for the Olympic Trials. It was not easy.

At the time, Gable was a graduate assistant at ISU. My brother John came down there to train and he shared an apartment with Dan. I was still a senior working to get my degree. We practiced every day. After the regular team practice we stayed around the mats with Gable and a few others and got in some extra Freestyle practice time. Others in our group, as I recall, were Rich Binek and our big heavyweight, Chris Taylor. Working with Taylor was a key factor in my favor. I learned how to handle the extra weight and power that Hellickson would have on me.

Gable told me, 'You have got to keep your focus on being an NCAA champion. First things first; put things in the right perspective.' Gable had the right mindset — he was the spark plug — but not the only one. I was also receiving great coaching and encouragement from ISU Coaches Nichols and Anderson as well. I went on to win my second NCAA crown in March.

A couple of weeks later the USWF Freestyle Nationals were held in Stillwater and were disappointing for both John and me. We both lost badly and ended up 4th in our weight classes. I got whipped 9-0 by Bill Harlow. I couldn't defend his high-crotch move. After my lopsided loss I questioned whether I could really do this."

[Author's note: Ben didn't realize it at the time, but he was about to receive a big break. The slick-wrestling Harlow reportedly was in a poor financial position and his wife was about to have a baby. He ended up not entering the Trials.]

Ben continues:

After the Stillwater tournament, John was ready to pack it in and go back home. 'I am wasting my time; I have no money', he told me.

However, the Iowa State people found him a job helping to setup the baseball fields in the spring. Even though that took away one of his practices, it kept him around Gable and me in the Iowa State room.

John's loss to Combs was because he was getting beat with the same move — a hip-toss counter to John's double-leg. Gable told him what to do differently — change from a 'double and lift' move to 'circle and chop the knee' attack. John practiced that religiously from April until the Final Trials in June.

John got his chance to wrestle Combs again at Anoka. I am wrestling on another mat the same time John is facing Combs. I finish my match and ask my coaches, 'Where is John?' Well, he's across the gym, sitting in a chair catching his breath. He has a fatigued look, almost expressionless. I go over and ask him, 'John, how did you do?' A grin slowly comes across his whole face. 'I beat him, 7-0.' Now he knows he would probably go to the Olympics.

Anyway, back to my story and my intense competition with Russ Hellickson. Our rivalry goes back to the '69 Midlands. I didn't know much about him then. Now I know he is good natured and a friend of everyone. Anyway, Russ beats me 6-2. He rode the living daylights out of me. I was totally outmanned. The following year at Midlands, Russ edged me in the finals by a point. A few months later Russ beat me 4-1 to make the '71 World team. In my senior year I finally defeated him at the Southern Open finals in November. At the Midlands, Russ and I go into overtime and I win the title by referee decision. He still insists that the officials gave it to me. In April of '72 Russ wins the 1972 USWF Nationals, beating Harlow in the finals.

At the Anoka Trials, Russ and I meet in the final round. In the first period we are going at it tooth and nail. I get a bear hug on him coming up from a double leg shot. In this move I try to get it tighter, always trying to reposition myself so I don't lose my balance. We are in the bear hug a good 30 seconds when suddenly I lose my balance. He loses his as well. We both fall to the mat — I am on my behind, he's on all fours. All he has to do is put his right arm across my chest and I'm done. I explode in panic and come up trying to catch my balance. We both go scram-

bling across the whole mat and suddenly he's on his back and I am on top of him. I pin him to win the weight class.

Russ was becoming the master of the single-leg. I got in on him instead. He was a position wrestler. He wanted certain positions. I was more of a scrambler. When he fell to the mat, he was lost. I was uncomfortable there, but not 'lost'. That was the difference that day.

The Finals Camp – University of Minnesota, July 25 – August 15, 1972

THE top three place winners in Anoka automatically qualified for the Camp. Now, a new wrinkle to the Trials was introduced. The 4th, 5th and 6th place winners from Anoka, plus the injury hardship invitees, qualified for a pre-camp tournament. The winner of the pre-camp tournament then went into the challenge round in 4th place. All challenge matches were two-out-of-three, except that in the finals the Anoka champion received credit for an earlier victory over the challenger if they had met in Anoka. Draw bouts were not counted.

Seven wrestlers that couldn't compete in Anoka were invited to the tournament as injury hardship cases. The list included 1971 World Team member Jimmy Carr, and Buck Deadrich, a former National AAU champion. Both eventually made the '72 Olympic team.

Coach Farrell recalls some particular moments:

The challenge matches were held during the first week of the Camp, so that the wrestlers going on to the Olympics could focus on training from that point forward.

I was 43 or 44 years old at the time, but I still worked out with the bigger guys. I worked some with Chris Taylor, but not too much. Ben Peterson could go with him, though. It was hard for Taylor to get in shape since he had very few workout partners. He was such a nice guy. For intensity, the Wells-Gable scrimmages were something to see. Those two were exceptional and very serious when scrimmaging each other.

Fortunately, I had two great assistant

coaches. Bill Weick was a better technician than me. He's a superior coach, as is Jim Peckham. I was best as the organizer. You had to know the six-black-mark point system — there was considerable strategy involved with it and you had to know what to do in certain situations. I spent a lot of my time instructing the wrestlers on this aspect.

The facilities at the University were disappointing. The University had just built a beautiful new athletic building which included a spectacular training area for wrestlers. However, there was a workers' strike on campus and no one could move into the building. We were forced to use the old Williams Arena where the workout area was really too small for us. Alan Rice had the Greco guys training on an ice rink upstairs.

Missoula native Gene Davis was a four-time Montana high school champion and an NCAA champion in 1966. Competing for Athletes-In-Action, Davis downed fellow Oklahoma State alumnus Darrell Keller to win the Trials at 136.5. He comments about Coach Farrell:

Farrell was a great organizer and promoter. He wouldn't teach that much himself, but he'd

Coach Bill Farrell received high marks from members of the 1972 Freestyle team
Photograph courtesy of Amateur Wrestling News

bring in good talent for us. He'd want Peckham and Weick to show us stuff and he got guys like Sanders and Wells to demonstrate their techniques to the rest of the squad.

Once the wrestle-offs were over, it was hard, tough training but we had some fun times, too. I remember once the coaches took us out to Verne Gagne's place on one of the nearby lakes. I think the coaches got a little nervous watching us water-skiing. However, we all survived.

In a 1984 interview in *Amateur Wrestling News*, Wayne Wells pays tribute to coaches Farrell and Weick:

Bill Farrell... from '69 to '72, when he was the coach, held our (US) program together. He had faith in himself and us. I know he was responsible for me not quitting. I was going to quit because of money reasons and some other personal reasons, and he just wouldn't let me. He kept calling until I said, 'Okay! I'll do it.'

And Bill Weick... Bill was a great wrestler in his day, but no one knows how much time he gave in coaching and being an assistant coach.

Gold medallist Wells was admitted to the Oklahoma bar on the eve of the 1972 Trials
Courtesy of Tom Fortunato

> **Owings didn't come to the Camp. So I had to wrestle Seay, who had beaten me badly in the Trials. This time I beat him – twice in a row in fact. Then I had to wrestle Gable. That was an experience of a lifetime – a surreal situation. Whatever I did, he would put me on my back. The score ended 22-0.**
>
> **– 'BUTCH' KEASER**

We had a very close rapport and relationship in '72.

Lloyd 'Butch' Keaser, the 149.5 Freestyle competitor from Navy, recalls his wrestling experiences leading up to and including the '72 Trials:

I grew up in Pumphrey, Maryland where I wrestled with some pretty good success through high school. I applied for a commission to the Naval Academy and my dream came true – they accepted me. I enrolled at the Academy in 1968 and had a good, though sometimes frustrating, wrestling career there. I was a three-time EIWA champion but the Nationals were different.

As a sophomore I lost my first match at the NCAAs and was done. My junior year I lost to Darrell Keller on a referee decision in overtime in the semi-finals and finished 4th. That hurt. My senior year, '71-'72, I broke my hand early in the season but I returned in time to win the EIWAs. At Nationals, I lost to Tom Milkovich 3-2 in the semis on his takedown with 11 seconds left. I managed to come back and place 3rd at 142 pounds.

After graduation in '72, I decided to tryout for the Olympics. That style of wrestling was very new to me. I got a crash course in Freestyle as Wayne Hicks and I trained together. I tried to get down to 136.5 pounds but I hurt my knee. Since I couldn't wrestle much, I didn't lose the necessary weight so I entered the Trials at 149.5.

At Anoka, I took my lumps. I wrestled Joe Seay and he hit me with a beautiful headlock. It was too late for me to react. I came down on my head and blacked out. Then, Larry Owings whooped up on me with something like a can-opener move. I was in pain the whole match. I wanted another shot at him, but that never happened.

I finished in 7th place, but one of the contestants didn't show up for the final weigh-in, thus I just barely qualified to go to the pre-camp ladder tournament. Well, I won the mini-tournament which meant I was in the top four along with Gable, Owings and Seay.

Owings didn't come to the Camp. So I had to wrestle Seay, who had beaten me badly in the Trials. This time I beat him — twice in a row in fact. Then I had to wrestle Gable. That was an experience of a lifetime — a surreal situation. Whatever I did, he would put me on my back. The score ended 22-0. Then I had to wrestle him again. This time it was closer. I felt pretty good about that, actually. It showed some improvement on my part and I could see that Gable was human since he got tired just like me. He is the only guy I've ever wrestled whom I didn't think that I could beat the next time we met.

The coaches asked me if I could hang around the Camp and train with the team. I said 'yes' and that gave me the opportunity to wrestle with the best. I learned more in those following weeks than ever before. I came away from the Camp physically bruised, but met many guys who became lifelong friends.

Bill Farrell was 'bigger than life' to me. He was a very good communicator, big on conditioning. I have a great deal of respect for that man.

I often think about how I might have done if I had gone at 136.5. Gene Davis was a great technician. I think even if I were there he would have won the spot. I am glad it worked out the way it did. I was tired of cutting weight and actually I could perform better when I was eating regularly to make 149. Davis deserved to be on that Olympic team.

Joe Seay, a high school wrestling coach in California in 1972, recalls competing at 149.5 in both styles at the Camp:

I knew ahead of time that my best chance to make the team was in Greco, so that's what I concentrated on in my training. I had tried out for the '64 and '68 teams but never made it.

The gold medal winner wrestled a total of 21 matches in the Trials and the Olympics. Only one point was scored against him.
Courtesy of Tom Fortunato

In '72 I made it to the Finals Camp, but Lloyd Keaser beat me in the Freestyle wrestle-off, so I focused on the Greco challenge matches at 149.5.

The Camp environment was very grueling. All these guys were such good wrestlers. Everything was intense and on the Greco side, all the matches were close. This wasn't so on the Freestyle side as Gable clobbered everyone — beating Keaser in the 149.5 finals by 22-0 and 11-0.

For me, the emotional side was even tougher than the physical side — everyone was trying to accomplish their lifelong hope and dream of making an Olympic team. It was difficult getting your mental thoughts together each time, knowing that one false move could end things for you.

There were lots of Greco matches during the Camp — I had seven of them, five ending in ties. I tied Werner Holzer four times before the Committee awarded me the match. Then I had to wrestle Phil Frey from Oregon. We tied once, but then I got hurt and he beat me twice to advance. Once again, I missed making the Olympic team. I was disappointed and I retired then from active training and competition to concentrate on coaching.

Dan Gable talks about his preparation for the Trials and his run to the Olympic gold medal:

Going into the '72 Trials, I was the defending World Champion. I was getting a lot of press and was the pre-favorite to win the gold medal before even making the '72 US team. Dealing with that pressure was all part of my training and eventually led to my becoming a more successful wrestling coach.

I also had to deal with an injury that I received two months before the Trials. While rolling around with one of the smaller guys in the room, which was a bit unusual as I more often go with the larger guys, I hurt my left knee badly. I had injured it before but nothing like this. I went to the doctors and they told me it needed repair and that I wouldn't make it back on the mats for three months. That wouldn't work for me — I didn't have three months to give up. I decided to wrestle with the bad knee.

Shortly after hurting my knee, I was supposed to wrestle a match against the Russians at Lehigh University. However, it was so bad that two days before the match I had to phone the people at Lehigh and cancel. It was a painful call for me. I had never missed a match before — in high school, college or international. I heard that the Russian wrestler was dismayed when I didn't show up at the weigh-in, asking, 'Where's Gable? Where's Gable?' He figured he'd get an easy bout now against my backup. However, there was a three-kilo weight allowance, so Wayne Wells dropped down a weight class to face him. Needless to say, the Russian didn't win.

Leading up to the Trials I was living in Ames. It was spring-time, or rather party-time. That environment was not the best for my training routine, so I decided to move back to my hometown of Waterloo where I could concentrate on my wrestling regime. I brought the Peterson brothers and Dave Pruzansky as workout part-

ners. We set up wrestling mats all over town to workout — one or two garages, a basement, even a car dealership. Plus, we could use my old high school training facilities at Waterloo West.

While working out in Waterloo, we set a demanding schedule. We'd usually have three or four workouts a day — one before breakfast, one later in the morning, one in the afternoon and sometimes one right before dinner. Mom took care of all the cooking for us, and was amazed at how much the Petersons could put down. We would use our evenings to relax, watch some TV and recover for the next day.

We'd break up the routine occasionally with some crazy things like going over to Black Hawk creek in the afternoons and do a little river rafting or fishing. We'd go down to the river bank with our fishing poles, try our luck, then wrestle on the muddy river banks. I remember one day taking the Waterloo West high school heavyweight, Bob Fouts, down to the river with us. I was wrestling with him there and he got me with his headlock, threw me to the ground and really banged my head. Luckily it was pretty soft ground or else I would have been in serious trouble.

Because of my bad knee, I was having severe problems when on my feet and finishing my leg tackle takedowns. I couldn't put any pressure on the knee coming up from underneath. I had to learn other means of taking guys down. Bobby Douglas taught me some excellent counter moves and moves off the front-headlock. I was learning a new way to wrestle

By the time the Regional Trials were held in Iowa City my knee was holding up better. My counter offense was working well which actually made my attack more effective. I was better off in the long run having to diversify my style.

While I was going through the Trials I didn't look at the combined results. I was just focusing on each match. But later I realized that I won something like 21 matches in a row, 15 to make the team and then 6 in the Olympics. Only one person scored a single point on me — and that was Larry Owings. As much as I tried to prepare myself for facing Owings, I never got our 1970 match out of my head. I kept thinking while I was out there, 'I got to get this match over and done with'.

> The Finals Camp wrestle-offs in Greco were very exacting. First of all, Alexander did not attend – he was recovering from a gunshot wound... The story goes that Gary was working as a manager in a grocery store. After getting off work he went over to his girlfriend's place. He found another guy there. A scuffle broke out and the guy shot Gary through the jaw... So, I started out on top of the ladder instead of #2.
>
> **– BOB BUZZARD**

As I looked back on that Trials match with Owings from a coaching point of view, I understood that the college match we had greatly affected me and something shut down in our follow-up. You think you are prepared but you can always be better prepared. I realized how much of this sport is mental. And that is what we are trying to work on right now with our wrestlers at Iowa."

Bob Buzzard, also a 149.5 Greco competitor, tells his story:

I started wrestling in the fourth grade in Waterloo, Iowa. I didn't have great success immediately and didn't like it all that much. But, I got better as I got older. I ended up winning two Iowa high school state titles and was the runner-up once.

Here's a little Dan Gable story for you. My dad was instrumental in getting Dan into wrestling. Dan was going to be a swimmer. However, my dad had a hunting club and Dan would come up there as a little guy. Dad didn't like the idea of someone not wrestling. He told Dan that he ought to get into a real sport – like wrestling. He said something like, 'Let me take you over to the junior high and let you try their wrestling program. I want to excite you about wrestling.' Dan took right to it.

Originally, Dan was thinking of going to college at the University of Northern Iowa, but my dad helped influence him to go to Iowa State.

I went to ISU five years ahead of Gable. I wrestled in the NCAAs twice but they were never my deal. Cutting weight wore me down. In both '64 and '65 I was seeded 1st at 137 pounds, but the best I could do was a 3rd and a 4th.

After college, I moved to Michigan and started my Freestyle career at the Michigan Wrestling Club, working out mainly with Dave Auble and Bobby Douglas. I was green to Freestyle. In college I was better on the mat than on my feet, so I had to change from my Granby-roll-around style of wrestling. I worked hard at it and in 1967 I won the National AAU Freestyle title at 138.5 pounds.

After that I could no longer make 138.5. My wife was a nurse and too good a cook, so I had to move up a weigh. In the ensuing years I saw myself in the same weight class as Gable, so I started focusing more of my training in Greco.

I was hoping to wrestle in the '68 Olympic Trials but I missed them due to an appendicitis attack.

I then got a job teaching at Libertyville high school outside of Chicago. I joined the Mayor Daley Club when Terry McCann was a coach there. He was a super human being who worked us very hard, really pushed us. He meant so much to all the guys at Mayor Daley. He never took a dime from the organization. Mayor Daley is where I learned to compete at a high level. Steve Combs and Werner Holzer were great workout partners for me.

Come 1972 I was tuning myself to make the Greco team at 149.5. I wrestled in the USWF Greco Nationals in Eugene, Oregon in April and finished 2nd to Dave Hazewinkel. Along the way, I beat Gary Alexander, a top Greco wrestler from Minnesota.

Next up were the Olympic Trials in Anoka. Alexander won my Greco weight class though I don't think I wrestled him. I did wrestle Phil Frey and Joe Seay and beat them both to finish 2nd.

The Finals Camp wrestle-offs in Greco were very exacting. First of all, Alexander did not attend – he was recovering from a gunshot wound he received two weeks before the Camp. The story goes that Gary was working as a manager in a grocery store. After getting off work he went over to his girlfriend's place. He found another guy there. A scuffle broke out and the guy shot Gary through the jaw, disabling him and keeping him from the Camp.

So, I started out on top of the ladder instead of #2. Seay defeated Holzer and then Frey beat Seay, which set up a final showdown between me and Frey. Since I had defeated him at Anoka, I only had to beat Frey one time. He had to beat me twice.

Now Frey was a good defensive wrestler. He'd catch you on your mistake and could block my arm-spin well. In our first match, he beat me by one point. Wayne Baughman watched the match and told me afterwards, 'That was the worst officiating I ever saw. You won't lose this next one.' Well, that was good encouragement for me. There actually were a lot of my throws that never did get scored. Anyway, Phil pulled his groin muscle in our second match and defaulted to me. I made the Greco Olympic team in my last chance!

John Peterson gives an account of his Camp memories:

At the Camp, others had to wrestle-off to get to me. In the final round I faced Geoff Baum from Oklahoma State. He was my brother Ben's #1 rival in college. I beat him twice by a couple of points to make the Olympic team. Those were the only two times I ever wrestled him. After the last match, Baum went up to my folks and told them, 'I wish you never had any kids.'

The Camp itself was very hot — sweat dripping off you all the time. We worked out in the Williams Arena which was right across from the football stadium. Coach Farrell had us run those stadium steps and tortured us with the Real Runner machine. He was a great motivator. Once a week he'd get the ten Freestyle team members together and tell us very sincerely that we were the best Freestyle team that the US ever had. After the Olympics, he confided to Ben and me that he actually had some doubts about us two, but he never let us know that the whole time leading up to the Games.

I remember Rick Sanders as a very hard worker. He trained harder than most of us. He taught me all types of single-leg counters. His lifestyle wasn't the best but he did have a more serious side. We had some good talks about the Bible and he had some genuine interest in that area. My brother wasn't real happy with him,

though, especially the loud boom-box that he carried around. Ben would go over and turn it down, or off; minutes later, Rick, with this little smirk of a smile on his face, would turn it right back up again.

Heavyweight Greg Wojciechowski talks about missing his opportunity to be an Olympian in '72:

I believe I got screwed out of a chance to be the heavyweight on the '72 Greco team. Up until that year, a wrestler could only make our Olympic team in one style, even though you could tryout for both. Well, they changed the rule for Chris Taylor. He beat me pretty decisively in Freestyle, but it was close between us in the Greco finals. We tied twice and then he beat me by a point or two. I had defeated him on other occasions even though he had over a 200-pound weight advantage on me. However, Alan Rice loved Taylor and he pushed the Committee to make an exception. They took Chris in both styles and left me home. They haven't allowed anyone else compete in both Freestyle and Greco since then.

The Final Wrestle-offs
114.5 pounds Freestyle — Jimmy Carr
vs John Morley

IF YOU were a lightweight champion-caliber wrestler, chances are you came from 'back east' during the decades of the '60s, '70s and '80s. So it was in 1972 in the 114.5 pound Freestyle division. The two best were from Pennsylvania and New York — one a young phenom, just a junior in high school; the other an NAIA college graduate who gained notoriety in the wrestling world by winning three National AAU titles while competing for the NYAC.

Jimmy Carr recalls:

I started wrestling in Tom Canavan's garage in Erie, Pennsylvania. I came from a wrestling family. I liked to go watch my older brother Fletcher wrestle. He was seven years older than me. He passed down a few pointers. After a year or two he told our mom it was time for me to stop watching and to get out on the mat and wrestle.

Canavan got me to work out on his mat in

Jimmy Carr, the phenom from Erie, survived a serious knee injury suffered while working out with Rick Sanders, and won the Trials as a 17-year-old *Photograph courtesy of Wade Schalles*

his garage. There were some tough young kids in the area at my weight class. Tom Turnbull was a good one. I started going to youth tournaments and always placed 2nd or 3rd behind wrestlers on my own team. I knew I could beat these guys, but hadn't put my mind to it yet — I was just 10-11 years old.

Canavan stuck with me and as I increased my intensity I started winning. I began to wrestle year-round, going to Freestyle tournaments in the summer. I started beating the people I had previously lost to, and winning some open tournaments against guys much older.

In 1970 I went to the Junior Nationals out in Iowa and won them, beating another black kid in the finals.

In 1971 they were holding tryouts for the Pan-American games. Canavan and I drove out to Oklahoma for the tryouts. I tried to go down to 105.5 but couldn't make it. Wrestling at 114.5, Randy Miller beat me. I didn't do well at all. I told Canavan, 'If you had let me wrestle 114.5 to start with I could have beaten all those guys.'

Later that year, I went to Annapolis trying to make the US World team. I figured to

go at 114.5. Once there I told Canavan, 'Heck with trying to make weight, let's just make this a vacation.' He said, 'No way, son.' I realized then that I couldn't let him down, so I went ahead and gave it my best shot. I made weight. I was seeded something like 9th, but I won all my matches against these older guys. I wrestled Randy Miller again and wiped him off the mat. I made the team and wrestled for the US in the 1971 FILA World Championships at Sofia, Bulgaria at the age of 16.

I knew then that I had a good shot at making the US Olympic team the following year. My training intensified. My workout schedule included lots of running — sometimes ten miles a day. My best workout partner was my brother Joe. He was a 163-pounder and we'd go at it hard. We'd especially work on takedowns and bounce each other off the walls, never stopping until one or the other of us got the takedown.

Canavan brought in Rick Sanders a couple of times to work out with me — still in Canavan's garage. Rick gave me many valuable pointers and I considered him a good friend. He also gave me a bad injury.

It was in March of '72 and I was working

out with Rick. I could usually take him down with my best move − a duck-under to a suplay. Sanders told me that if I did that move on him one more time that he was going to hurt me. Of course, a few minutes later I took him down with it. And sure enough, Rick gets my leg, twists my knee and I end up with stretched ligaments and in a cast. Sanders said, 'I warned you. I told you not to do that move on me again.'

Well, I couldn't wrestle in the National AAUs or in the Olympic Trials in Anoka as I was still in a cast at the start of the Trials. However, I received an exemption and was invited to the late-July training Camp.

The doctor had told me and my mother that I'd probably be in the cast for six months. I had started working out and was not going to miss the opportunity to try to make the team. So, one day, I took off the cast myself and made up this story. I told my Mom that the doctor said the knee had healed and there was no further need to have the cast and that I was on my way to the Finals Camp. It wasn't until I got to the Camp − and it was too late − that my mom compared notes with the doctor and found out that he never did give me permission to take off the cast.

At the Camp I started at the bottom of the ladder. There were six guys ahead of me. I won the mini-tournament, so then there were just four of us left at 114.5 − John Morley, Terry Hall, Dan Sherman and me. Morley had won the National AAUs and the Trials tournament, so he was the favorite and it came down to the two of us in the final round.

Morley had a reputation as a tough wrestler and he had hurt more than one wrestler in their matches. At the weigh-in for the final round, he stared at me and said something like, 'Hey kid, I'm going to hurt you out there on the mat today.' I just smiled back at him.

In our first match, I got a single-leg take-down early in the match. It was closely fought, with lots of shots and counter after counter. There was no further scoring though and I won by virtue of that one-point takedown. We then tied each other a couple of times.

In our last match, I got ahead of Morley with a single-leg takedown. Again there was intense action, but no scoring. Then in the last period

with about one minute to go, I had a whizzer in on him as we went off the mat. After the ref blew the whistle, Morley takes my arm and twists it over my head, hurting my elbow and wrenching my shoulder. I started going after him I was so mad. Rick Sanders, who was in my corner, immediately stops me and says 'Forget it, you win. The ref has disqualified him.'

As I thought about it years later, that was a smart move on Morley's part. He saw that he was losing to me and wasn't going to make the Olympic team. However, if I was injured, he was the first alternate and would go in my place.

As a matter of fact, they kept Morley around Camp for awhile after the competition was over just to see if I would recover and be able to compete in the Olympics. I was hurting pretty badly. Coach Farrell helped me out considerably by finding some new technology that helped heal my shoulder rather quickly. Within a week I was back working out and doing okay, but I had to convince the coaches that I was able and prepared to go to Munich.

Bill Weick, assistant Freestyle coach in '72, comments on the Carr-Morley rivalry:
I think Morley should have made the team, not Carr. It was a shame that Farrell was both Morley's coach at the NYAC and was our head Freestyle coach. He was in a bind. If he had stood up for Morley, he would have been accused of favoritism.

John Morley tells his story:
Just before my sophomore year in high school I moved from Brooklyn to Nassau County, Long Island and enrolled at Oceanside high school. Although my mother was against the idea, I went out for wrestling and started learning the fundamentals from Coach Jack Hay. He was from the Sprig Gardner school of 'drill, drill, drill.'

By my senior year I was becoming a pretty decent wrestler, finishing 2nd to top-seeded Johnny Harris in the County finals. I was also wrestling some Freestyle then. I won the Metropolitan Juniors and was named Outstanding Wrestler. But when I tried the Metropolitan Seniors, I faced Hiroaki Aoki and he got me in a bear hug, threw me to the mat and knocked me out.

> **Was Carr better than Morley? I don't think so. Morley was far more experienced. I don't think it was necessarily a conspiracy, but Jimmy was the sentimental favorite... I stayed out of it, but I thought the team would have been better represented in Munich with Morley on it.**
>
> **— BILL FARRELL**

● ●

As a 16-year-old senior I ended up being recruited by Hofstra, Cornell and Minnesota State-Morehead. After going to watch the NCAAs at Ithaca in 1964, I decided Morehead was the best place for me. It was an NAIA school and I could compete as a freshman. At the end of my first season I advanced to the semi-finals of the NAIA Nationals and drew Richard Sanders. He was so much beyond me. I got pinned, but finished 4th, which I didn't consider as too bad.

In my senior year I finally qualified to compete in the Division I NCAAs and I took 5th. Sergio Gonzales and Terry Hall beat me, but I would get back at both later on in my career.

After graduation I returned home to New York. I wanted to wrestle at the NYAC. I earned a spot on the NYAC team at 114.5 and went to the 1969 National AAUs out in Iowa. I ran up against Yasuo Katsamura from the Nebraska AC and he does a number on me. I ended up taking 3rd, drawing with John Miller, the NCAA champ from Oregon.

I now have a wife and daughter and am teaching at East Rockaway high school. I show up for the first fall practice at the NYAC and who is in the room but Katsumara. He beats me in a local tournament but I feel that I am gaining on him. In the spring, at the National AAUs, I meet Katsumara in the finals at 114.5. I beat him 4-2 for my first National title; I am on top of the world.

After some tough tryout matches with John Miller, I made the US World team in '70 and ended up taking 5th in the Edmonton World Championships. I also won the National AAUs

in '71 and '72, beating Sergio Gonzales in the finals at 114.5.

I was in top shape going into the Trials for the '72 Olympics. I was working out regularly at the NYAC with Don Fay and Andy Fitch. They really pushed me. I sailed through the Trials tournament in Anoka — I pinned Terry Hall in the final match and went unscored upon in the tournament.

At the Finals Camp I had the wrestle-off matches with Jimmy Carr. In our first match, he takes me down and then I can't catch him. He beats me 2-1. Our next two matches were draws. He was running the whole time. I must have shot 50 takedowns, but Carr was always off the mat.

In our fourth match Carr gets an early takedown and the same thing happens. I keep shooting but he's always backing up. My face is all beat up from so many head-butts. Finally, I under-hook him and he limp-arms it. He gets hurt; the referee signals that the match is over due to an illegal move on my part. I lose my chance to wrestle in Munich.

Yes, I was terribly disappointed, but I later realized it just wasn't meant to be. I needed to move on. I never blamed anyone — that's life. God gave me a talent and I did the best I could with it.

There were lots of politics but I did put it aside. Bill Farrell was a tremendous mentor. He's an incredible person, someone I always look up to as a man.

Bill Farrell talks about the Carr-Morley competition:

Morley hurt Carr. It was declared an illegal move. Jimmy's bench people — Russ Camilleri was one — told Jimmy that he shouldn't go back out on the mat, that he had won. I couldn't say anything on behalf of Morley since I was the team coach, even though John was representing my NYAC team.

Some people thought Jimmy was faking the injury. I'm not sure. Was Carr better than Morley? I don't think so. Morley was far more experienced. I don't think it was necessarily a conspiracy, but Jimmy was the sentimental favorite — and a favorite of the media. He was a young kid, just 17, and a black kid. His making the team was good for newsprint. I stayed out of it, but I thought the team would have been better represented in Munich with Morley on it.

198 pounds Greco — Willie Williams vs Wayne Baughman

IT TOOK 54 minutes of wrestling between these two decorated wrestlers to decide which one would go to Munich. Willie Williams relates his story:

I didn't start to wrestle until my junior year of high school in Chicago Heights. I never qualified for the Illinois State Tournament, but the coach at Illinois State saw me wrestle and offered me a partial scholarship to compete there. I made the team and as a senior I won the Division II championship and placed 5th at the Division I NCAAs.

After college I joined the workouts at the Mayor Daley Club where I latched onto Terry McCann. He became my educator and my guiding force. I didn't know the ropes of competing at a high level, but he kept putting things out there for me. In 1970 I won the spot on the US Greco World team. Terry led me. I really hadn't understood what Greco-Roman wrestling was, but Terry taught me what I needed to know.

Just being around Terry was very exciting for me. He transcended himself into a whole life activity. All this was not just a wrestling philosophy; it was a life philosophy for me to follow.

Back to the wrestling. I knew Wayne Baughman was going to be my main competitor for the '72 Greco team. The first time I ever wrestled him, I think it was in 1968 in Freestyle, he completely dominated me. He was older and one of the toughest competitors I ever encountered. In 1970 and 1971 we were teammates on the US Greco team — I was at 220 and Baughman was at 198. In '71, I won the USWF Greco title at 198 and he won it the following year.

At the Trials tournament in Anoka, I beat him in the finals, so I had a leg up on him. At the training Camp, Baughman made it through to the finals and needed to beat me twice. He won the first bout by a point. Then we wrestled a couple of draws. In the end we had a marathon match. It seemed like it went on forever. The officials decided we needed to go sudden

death, and he finally got a point on me to win.

I felt very dejected and went home. I really didn't feel like sticking around the Camp. I thought that was the end of my career but subsequently I came back to be the US National Greco champion five more times.

Wayne Baughman remembers the marathon match:

Willie Williams and I had a memorable Greco bout in the Finals. I had finished 3rd in the Anoka tournament in Freestyle and was runner-up to Willie in Greco. I think that was the first time he beat me. Then in the final Freestyle challenge matches, Hellickson beat me twice, so my last chance to go to the '72 Olympics was in Greco at 198.

I beat Willie by one point in our first bout; then we probably wrestled the longest bout in US Olympic Trials history. In the 54th minute of a very grueling match I finally scored a sudden death point to win, 3-2. This all occurred within just over a one-hour time frame. We had already wrestled to a draw in two nine-minute matches, and then three more three-minute overtime periods. The judges finally decided that we should go back out on the mat until someone scored the next point. Obviously, we were both exhausted. Somehow, 27 minutes of wrestling later, I got the takedown to win my third straight trip to the Olympics.

198 pounds Freestyle — Russ Hellickson vs Ben Peterson

VYING for the right to wrestle for the US at 198 pounds were two light-heavyweights, who hailed from similar small towns in Wisconsin dairy country. Russ Hellickson tells his story:

I grew up on a dairy farm in Cottage Grove, Wisconsin and played three sports in high school — football, wrestling and baseball. I started wrestling in tenth grade at Stoughton High which earned a strong wrestling tradition in the state after Coach Vern Pieper took over the program in the early '60s.

From there I stayed close to home and went

to the University of Wisconsin. I lettered in football as a sophomore. However, as a 6ft 200-pound nose guard I was undersized, so I decided to concentrate on wrestling.

I didn't achieve what I wanted to in college wrestling. I never became an All-American. Since I wasn't on scholarship, I had to work full-time to support myself so I never had the extra time to devote to wrestling.

After graduation I was back working on the family farm when Duane Kleven, the new Wisconsin wrestling coach, came to see me to ask if I would be one of his assistants. He offered to pay me $600 a year for this part-time work. The campus was just seven miles from the farm so I took the job. I saw it as an opportunity to keep on wrestling and training.

I trained for the Midlands that season (1970) and won them. After that Werner Holzer from the Mayor Daley Club sent me a letter inviting me to come and practice with them. It was a two-hour trip each way to Chicago but I wrote back saying, 'Yes, I'd like to pursue an opportunity to try Olympic-style wrestling.'

We practiced at various venues in and around Chicago: Harper Junior College, Navy Pier, and Northwestern University. Terry McCann was the coach and he reminded me of my dad. He created a very disciplined environment. Terry had a dominating voice and had a powerful presence. My first time at a Mayor Daley practice I got beat up all day. Terry came up to me afterwards saying, 'I like your fight but you need work on your technique. I can help you be whatever you want to be.' I believed everything he ever told me.

Terry worked with me quite a bit and taught me his under-hook techniques. He then told me that I ought to go see Doug Blubaugh who was an assistant coach at Michigan State, so I went over to East Lansing for a while to work with Doug. He really helped me, especially with the single-leg takedowns.

I was influenced so much by McCann and Blubaugh. They were totally dedicated men. They set up a great work environment and I had some excellent workout partners. By 1972, I got the feeling that I was going to be an Olympic

Coach Farrell called the matches between Sanders and Behm the hardest fought of all the bouts at the Trials Photograph courtesy of Bobby Douglas

1976
BATTLES AT BROCKPORT

> " In the spring of '76 I got a call from "Sports Illustrated". They were cross-checking with me on a story they were going to run on Wade Schalles. Sure enough they had some things wrong and I told the reporter he needed to do more research. The writer then goes on to tell me that the reason for the story was that Schalles was the most likely US wrestler to win a gold medal at the Montreal Olympics. I saw that as a real slap in the face – not just to me but to all our other competitors. I told the guy, 'Print what you want, it doesn't matter to me.' The reporter asked me, 'Why doesn't it matter?' I tell him, 'Schalles is not even going to make the team.' And then I hung up on him.
>
> **– Stan Dziedzic, Schalles's main rival at the 1976 Trials**

U S WRESTLERS didn't fare too well in international competition between 1973 and 1976. In Greco, the US was still not competitive with the rest of the world. We scored a combined total of four team-points in the '73, '74 and '75 World Championships; no US wrestler came close to vying for a medal.

Jimmy Carr, Gene Davis and the Peterson brothers were the only holdovers from the successful 1972 Olympic Freestyle team. Yes, Lloyd Keaser won a gold medal at the 1973 World Championships in Iran, and that was remarkable. Otherwise we were very mediocre. The only other Freestyle medalist in the three World Championship tournaments between '73 and '76 was Ben Peterson, who placed 3rd in '73. The bottom fell out in '74 when we scored only three points and finished 13th. We rebounded to finish 5th in '75, but still no medalists. In the Pan-American Games, which the US normally dominates, only half of the 1975 team won gold

Previous spread: Third seed Stan Dziedzic defeated Wisconsin sophomore Lee Kemp for the right to face Wade Schalles in the final wrestle-off at Brockport *Photograph by Chris Poff, courtesy of Scholastic Wrestling News*

– our worst showing ever. Hopes for bringing home Olympic medals from Montreal were dim.

The brightest light on the Freestyle horizon was the 1972 and 1973 NCAA champion from Clarion, Pennsylvania, 163-pounder Wade Schalles. He had built a considerable reputation as an exciting, unorthodox wrestler and as a pinner. Schalles backed up his reputation by winning the prestigious Tbilisi tournament in Russia, pinning five of his six opponents. Nevertheless, back home he faced stern competition for a spot on the US team from Carl Adams and Stan Dziedzic.

Speaking of stern competition, that's what the Democrats were hoping to give the Republicans in their quest to return to the White House in the 1976 presidential election.

Like the US wrestlers, President Nixon didn't fare particularly well either between 1973 and 1976 – or at least not during the first 20 months of his second term in office. Faced with certain impeachment for his role in covering up the Watergate affair, Nixon resigned as president on August 8, 1974 and Vice-President Gerald Ford assumed leadership of the country.

Ford sought re-election as president in 1976 and fought off a strong challenge by former movie star Ronald Reagan for the Republican nomination. The Democrats changed their pace from nominating Mid-westerners such as McGovern and Humphrey. They found a Southerner, Jimmy Carter, the former Navy officer and peanut farmer, to head the Democratic ticket.

Everyone was predicting a close election.

With the Vietnam War behind them, Americans saw domestic issues as their primary concern. A Gallup poll in May, 1976 identified the three top issues facing the nation: 1) the high cost of living; 2) unemployment; 3) dissatisfaction with government. The cost of living in the US from 1972-1976 increased about 8% annually, compared to under 3% annual growth from 1960-1972.

The stock market was no help to the economic strain of most Americans. The Dow Jones Industrial average swayed back and forth between 950 and 1,000 during the summer of 1976, not much higher than it was four years earlier.

In the sports world, the nation's folk hero of the summer of '76 was a 21-year-old rookie pitcher for the Detroit Tigers who talked to the ball before he threw it to home plate. Mark 'The Bird' Fidyrich captivated the state of Michigan along with much of the country with his unorthodox style and ability to get batters out. He won 19 games during his magical baseball season – yet only 10 more the rest of his big league career.

In Olympic sports news, the first boycott of the Olympic Games since the 1932 Berlin Olympics was brewing. The governments of 25 African nations were making plans to withdraw their athletes from the Games at the Opening Ceremony. They were acting in protest of the International Olympic Committee's decision to allow New Zealand, whose national rugby team was touring the apartheid nation of South Africa, to compete in the Olympics.

And, from a back page *Associated Press* story in July, an article pointed out, "The Russians promise Coca-Cola, fried chicken, an open-door policy and good weather for the 1980 Olympic Games."

Jimmy Carter's people must have missed reading that one.

The Trials Process

STRETCHING from Othello, Washington to Jacksonville, Florida, 20 Regional qualifying tournaments were scheduled to be held in the spring. Qualifying wrestlers were invited to a 30-day training camp in Iowa City prior to competing in the Final Olympic Trials tournament at Cleveland, Ohio in mid-May.

After Cleveland, the eight place winners in each weight class, plus a few selected others, were then invited to an Olympic Training Camp in DeKalb, Illinois for another 30-day intensive training session. From there, the elite wrestlers moved to Brockport, New York for the Final Camp and wrestle-offs. The first three place-winners in each style from Cleveland automatically qualified for Brockport. The other five place-winners competed in a two-day tournament to determine the fourth qualifier. The winner from Cleveland had the luxury of sitting back and waiting for the survivor of all the other wrestle-offs to meet him. The final wrestle-offs were best-of-three series.

The US Olympic Wrestling Committee, chaired by Russ Houk of Bloomsburg, Pennsylvania, made some controversial choices for the head coaching positions of our Olympic teams – Jim Peckham in Greco and Wayne Baughman in Freestyle. Peckham was the US Greco coach of our '74 and '75 World teams and Baughman coached our '73, '74 and '75 Freestyle squads. Those teams did not perform up to expectations. Both Peckham and Baughman admit to having some problems.

The Coaches

PECKHAM, who placed 7th as a member of the 1952 US Greco Olympic team, recalls his wrestling background and personal experiences as coach of the US team:

I learned to wrestle at the YMCA in Boston as a young teenager. My high school didn't have a wrestling team and I didn't go to college. All my wrestling was done at the club level.

In 1964, Emerson College hired me as their wrestling coach and later as their Athletic Director. I was active at the national level and assisted the Freestyle and Greco coaches train our teams for the '72 Games. I thought our '72 Freestyle team was our best ever. They took on the Russians when their best wrestlers were receiving all of their funding from the Soviet government.

I had my problems with a number of our Greco wrestlers in '76. There was a lot of dissention on the Greco team. Some of the Minnesota guys, in particular, were disruptive to team unity. Several of them did not accept me as their coach — they thought they knew more than anyone else in the country. They created more dissention than Carter had liver pills with their poor attitude. For instance, I would tell them to climb the rope. A few did, but others would just hang around the back of the line saying, 'Aw, we don't need to do that.'

I never saw that attitude on the Freestyle side.

The 90-day training camp was probably a good idea, but for the Greco wrestlers it was less effective than it could have been due to the attitudinal problems that transcended everything. The atmosphere was not conducive to a positive training environment. And, in the end, we got no Olympic medals. I think we could have increased our chances for success if the guys were more open to suggestions.

Mind you, not everyone was a problem. Mike Farina was a great little guy. Brad Reinghans, oh, he was an outstanding competitor. Tough and reliable, on and off the mat. They don't make them any better than Brad Reinghans. I wish I could have had a whole team of people like him.

Wayne Baughman, a three-time Olympian, was named '76 Olympic Freestyle coach in March, 1975. Other nominees were Doug Blubaugh, Larry Kristoff, Jim Peckham and Bill Weick. Baughman tells his story:

It all started back in 1973 when the AAU named me the head coach of our World team that competed in Iran. That was my first year as a National coach. Well, the AAU wanted Wade Schalles, not Stan Dziedzic, on the World team at

> **"The 90-day training camp was probably a good idea, but for the Greco wrestlers it was less effective than it could have been due to the attitudinal problems that transcended everything. The atmosphere was not conducive to a positive training environment. And, in the end, we got no Olympic medals.**
>
> **— JIM PECKHAM**

163 pounds. I told them that Stan won the spot on the team through a fair wrestle-off process; if we didn't take Dziedzic, they'd have to get rid of me. I won that battle.

The AAU indicated to me later in '73 that I could be the next Olympic Freestyle coach. 'Why me?' I asked. 'I only ever made the Greco team.' They said, 'We're losing matches because we can't control tie-ups and the upper body. You've won the Freestyle and Greco Nationals plus the Pan-Am Games and you know how to combine the two styles. You had the power to control your opponent's upper-body and are doing it as well as anybody in the US. We are tired of losing matches because the competition controls us with their upper-body tie-ups and they often get our wrestlers cautioned out.'

I knew we had to control tie-ups so we wouldn't get shoved around. I started teaching guys on the World team how to use the basic under-hook for their tie-up. Pretty soon I started to get some criticism that I'm trying to make them all Greco guys. I began to back down.

Things came to a head in '75. We had a terrible World tournament. No medalists, although we placed seven men in the top six. Jim Humphrey and Ben Peterson were way ahead in their matches and got pinned with upper-body throws, as did Greg Hicks. Butch Keaser was ahead 12-0 when in the closing seconds he got thrown and pinned. I was disappointed in myself that I had backed off from more upper-body wrestling.

Everyone came down on me. The AAU was really on my case. Some of the guys went behind my back to get me removed as head coach. They

John Peterson and Gene Davis repeated as Trials champions at Brockport
Photographs by Pete Hausrath, courtesy of Amateur Wrestling News

would have preferred Bill Weick and/or Jim Peckham. A group of athletes circulated a petition to get rid of me. However, I stopped it, saying that I would finish the job I was given, my way, whether you like it or not. I was not afraid to make enemies; I kept the job.

The Final Olympic Team Trials, Cleveland, Ohio, May 13-17, 1976

HISTORIC Public Auditorium in downtown Cleveland hosted 320 Freestyle and 146 Greco wrestlers for the 1976 Final Trials tournament. The entrants included an impressive list of high school wrestlers — Mike DeAnna, Mike Farina, Dave Schultz and Bobby Weaver to name a few. At the other end of the spectrum, Shelby Wilson, an Olympic Freestyle gold medal winner from 1960, remarkably came out of 16 years of retirement

to win the Regionals and advance to Cleveland. The coaches and officials wouldn't let Shelby compete though; he was no longer considered an amateur, having taken a salary during his coaching years.

There were some other unique situations that occurred in Cleveland. Reminiscent of 1960 where 'Doc' Northrup and his son qualified for the Final Trials, a father and son combination qualified for the '76 Final Trials. Russ Camilleri competed in his fifth Final Trials, while his 19-year-old son, Joe, qualified for the first time.

The senior Camilleri recalls:

I coached Joe in high school out in San Francisco. We wrestled in a lot of open tournaments together. I'd make sure we were at different weight classes so we didn't have to wrestle each other. We both qualified for the Final Trials tournament, me at 180 and Joe at 163 and we entered in both Freestyle and Greco. At this level of competition I recall that he was too young and I was too old. However, it was a heck of an experience.

None of the returning Greco wrestlers

from the '72 US team finished on top of the ladder in the Trials. Dave Hazewinkel came the closest, placing 3rd behind Gary Alexander and Reid Lamphere.

Another veteran found more success. The 31-year old Olympian Gene Davis survived some see-saw matches in Cleveland. He downed Dwayne Keller 12-10 and then Jim Humphrey 5-4 on the way to the 136.5 pound Freestyle title. Davis would go on to make the US Freestyle team at the wrestle-offs in Brockport and was selected 1976 team captain.

Among the entrants were a couple of blind wrestlers. One of them, Jim Mastro of Minnesota Wrestling Club finished 3rd in Greco at 198 pounds and qualified for the Finals Camp in Brockport.

There were the usual disputes. At 125.5 pound Freestyle, Harold Wiley and many others thought Wiley had Jimmy Carr pinned early in their match, but it wasn't called. Wiley's corner cried 'politics' as he ended up losing to Carr, 15-7.

Injury struck one of the key Freestyle competitors at 163 pounds. In a third-round match, Carl Adams suffered a dislocated shoulder in a loss to Tom Keeley and had to withdraw from further competition. Just one year earlier, Adams had whipped both Dziedzic and Schalles to earn a spot on the US World team.

Despite a plethora of entrants from the northern Ohio area, not a lot of wrestling fans came to watch the matches. In fact, only 75 people bothered to attend the Greco finals on the last night of the competition, even though tickets were only $2 or $3 each.

Wrestling pundits couldn't agree about the potential for winning Olympic medals. The *Cleveland Plain-Dealer* carried the following quotes in its coverage of the Freestyle finals. Tournament director Gene Gibbons stated:

It was by far the greatest accumulation of wrestling talent ever under one roof.

That exuberance offset the grim remarks that same evening from National AAU Chairman Wes Brown:

Right now this figures to be a lean year for us in Freestyle and we don't have a thing in Greco-Roman.

Father and son – Coach Chuck Farina and 105.5 pound Greco champion, Mike Farina Photograph courtesy of Scholastic Wrestling News

105.5 pounds Freestyle — Mike Farina vs Bill Rosado vs Bobby Weaver

MANY considered high school senior Mike Farina of Elmhurst, Illinois the star of the Cleveland tournament. He beat out 31 entrants in the 105.5 Freestyle weight class and he was the sole wrestler to win in both Freestyle and Greco. Mike, the son of acclaimed Illinois high school wrestling coach Chuck Farina, talks about his experiences...

My father was a great motivator for me. I liked to wrestle and by my freshman year in high school he had me wrestling year round. I often worked out two or three times a day, increas-

ing it to four my senior year. I didn't wrestle for my father's team, though. I was at York High in Elmhurst, where we lived. During those years, dad coached in another district — at East Leyden High in Franklin Park.

In my sophomore year of high school I decided I wanted to be an Olympian. Freestyle and Greco were not really dad's area of expertise, though. From a technique standpoint, I credit Bobby Douglas's book, Takedown. Ironically, he was coach of my chief competitor, Bill Rosado. I really didn't have a Freestyle/Greco coach; I was pretty much self-taught.

Even with all this wrestling that I did, I only won the Illinois states once — as a senior in 1976.

[Author's note: That was the year that Yorkville won the Illinois Class A State Tournament under the tutelage of Coach Denny Hastert, better known as the Speaker of the House from 1999 to 2007.]

Farina continues:

Before the '76 Olympic Trials, I didn't wrestle in a National tournament other than the Juniors. I did win the Junior Greco title twice, in '74 and '75, but never the Junior Freestyle.

At Cleveland I had to wrestle five days in a row and make scratch weight every day. Making 105.5 was a big pull for me. I'd be up till 3am running to lose the weight, get just a little sleep, then weigh-in and re-hydrate six or seven pounds.

The Freestyle tournament was first up. For my opening match, I drew Rosado, who was the best wrestler in the weight class. I lost to him, 9-8. However, I made it to the final round as I pinned everyone else that I wrestled, while Bob Weaver pinned Rosado — in something like 20 seconds. Weaver was cradling everyone then. I wrestled Weaver in the final match and beat him 13-7 to take 1st place.

On the Greco side, I also lost an early-round match — to Karoly Kancsar, a Hungarian refugee who had been on the US World Greco team the previous three years. He scored ten points on me in the first period. From then on we wrestled evenly but I couldn't make up the difference. However, as the tournament went on, he ran out of gas and was eliminated. Meanwhile, I was winning all my matches, so I ended up 1st in Greco, too.

After the Trials I was due back in school to

> **From a technique standpoint, I credit Bobby Douglas's book, "Takedown". Ironically, he was coach of my chief competitor, Bill Rosado. I really didn't have a Freestyle/Greco coach; I was pretty much self-taught.**
>
> **— MIKE FARINA**

finish my senior year at York. Fortunately, the school was kind enough to let me out a month early so I could train at the Olympic Camp. I went to DeKalb and I showed up about 18-20 pounds overweight. I started working out with all the top guys at 105.5 and 114 in both Freestyle and Greco.

Truthfully, I really didn't like working out and getting beaten up by the bigger 114-pounders. I wasn't much of a practice room wrestler. I didn't like working out with Rosado and Weaver either. I never beat either of them at the Camp scrimmages. I give Rosado credit though. He gave me a lot of pointers that helped me at the Camp.

I spent more of my time practicing Freestyle. I really wanted to make the Freestyle team rather than the Greco team. It was more prestigious and I thought I'd have a better chance of placing higher in the Freestyle Olympics than the Greco Olympics.

When I went to the Brockport Finals Camp, I was doing much better getting my weight under control. I was recovering from some injuries I received at DeKalb — a broken toe and a sprained ankle. I had the opportunity to keep working with both the Freestyle and the Greco guys. That was helpful. It gave me some variety and a way to beat the grind.

At the Freestyle wrestle-offs, Rosado won the right to challenge me and he then beat me twice. He didn't take me lightly as he probably had done in Cleveland. Our scores were something like 7-4 in both matches. I just didn't have enough to beat him.

It was then time for the Greco wrestle-offs and the final challenger was a guy from California, Marty Lockwood. I remember feeling glad it was him and not Kancsar. I beat Lockwood twice to make the Olympic team. I was very happy to make the team as a high school senior but knew it would be tough facing the Eastern Europeans and Asians who were so talented in Greco.

I now concentrated solely in Greco and kept improving. A couple of my high school wrestling buddies from Illinois were at the Finals Camp - Khris and Keith Whelan and Jerry Kelly — and we had a good time wrestling and hanging out together.

Coach Jim Peckham was great. He had a lot of common sense and worked you very hard, yet gave you a chance to recover. He participated in all the workouts with us and he was tough. I respected that.

Farina's main competitor, Bill Rosado, was the National AAU champion at 105.5 and was wrestling for Bobby Douglas at Arizona State in '76. He relates a few stories of his own...

I was one of five children born into a Puerto Rican family originally from the Bronx. My dad was a staff sergeant in the Army, stationed in Puerto Rico. He was always telling me 'don't let anyone push you around', so he got me started in judo when I was 11. Judo taught me a lot about combat technique and how to take an opponent's motion and skillfully use it to my advantage.

The following year my dad was transferred to Offut AFB outside Omaha. That's when I started wrestling — in eighth grade.

The next year it was back to Puerto Rico where I was the island champion at 98 pounds. Then we moved to Arizona, where as a junior in 1972 I won the state AA high school tournament at 98 pounds. I also won the AAU Junior National Freestyle championship.

During that summer, the coach at the University of Arizona, Bill Nelson, asked me to come over to the University to workout with some other wrestlers. I did and received some excellent training, especially from Dale Brumit who became a good friend. However, Nelson made no mention of recruiting me for the Arizona wrestling team. When I asked him why, he told me, 'Billy, you are a fine kid and would be an asset anywhere, but you are too small to ever be a college wrestler.'

For my senior year at Tucson Santa-Rita I wrestled up at 112 pounds and made it all the way to the State Finals but lost in overtime. I was crushed.

I still hadn't received any college recruiting

> **My parents couldn't be at Brockport because they didn't have enough money to make the trip. Right after winning the final match I called them and my girlfriend. I was crying. I was really happy, but feeling very alone with no one there to share this exciting moment with me.**
>
> **– BILL ROSADO**

offers. I was feeling left out — a Puerto Rican nomad who wrestled all over the country but couldn't find a college interested in me. However, the coach at Phoenix Junior College talked to me after the State Tournament and said he'd take me at his school, so that's where I ended up.

Meanwhile, I was doing well in Freestyle back down at 105.5. I went to the World Team Trials and beat Wayne Holmes in two-out-of-three to make the 1974 US team. We went to Istanbul for the Games where I lost both my matches. We wrestled our matches outside in a soccer stadium. It was a pretty bad environment for everyone and the team didn't do well at all.

In 1975 Bobby Douglas was the Arizona State coach and he started talking to me about coming to Arizona State. He told me 'I am not at all sure you are Division I material, but if you come here and wrestle I will help you become a World and Olympic champion.' I believed him, except for the DI bit, and enrolled at ASU. A couple years later I proved Coaches Douglas and Nelson wrong when I finished 5th for ASU at 118 pounds in the 1977 NCAAs.

In April '76 I won the National AAUs, defeating Dave Range at 105.5. That qualified me for the Olympic Trials tournament in Cleveland. I was doing fine there until I came up against Bobby Weaver. That match ended quickly. I went in for the takedown, dropped my head and Weaver threw me right on my back with his patented cradle. It was all over. I finished 4th, but at least I qualified for the Camp at Brockport.

After the Cleveland tournament I chilled out for awhile at Dale Brumit's home in Akron. No workouts, just a little running and some meditation. I got my head together and headed out to the

Bill Rosado was pinned by Bobby Weaver at the Cleveland Trials but came back to win the two deciding wrestle-off bouts at Brockport *Photograph by Chris Poff, courtesy of* Scholastic Wrestling News

DeKalb camp.

By the time I got to Brockport, I was pretty focused and confident that I could win. I was in perfect shape and my weight was under control. Douglas was there as my personal coach and in my corner throughout. I beat both Weaver and Farina. Nothing spectacular, I just did it.

My parents couldn't be at Brockport because they didn't have enough money to make the trip. Right after winning the final match I called them and my girlfriend. I was crying. I was really happy, but feeling very alone with no one there to share this exciting moment with me.

Bobby Weaver, just a high school junior at the time, recalls his experiences:

Following in my older brothers' footsteps, I started wrestling as a grade-school kid at St. Anthony's Community Center in Easton, Pennsylvania.

I had a lot of family tragedy to deal with early in my life. My father and brothers were the ones that got me to take up wrestling. My father had a big influence on me in my early years. However, when I was eight years old he passed away and that was a huge loss. My mom was left to be the driving force in the family. One of my older brothers, Brad, was a good wrestler for Easton in the early '70s. He finished 2nd in the states his junior year, losing in the championship finals in the last second. He never got another chance to win states, though. That summer he was killed in an automobile accident. I had always looked up to Brad so much.

At Easton high school, I won the State Tournament three times — 1975, 1976 and in 1977. There was this guy at Easton, Henry Callie, who was my size and could beat me in grade school and my freshman year, too. My sophomore year he wrestled one weight above me and took 2nd in the states. He would push me every day in practice. At that time Freestyle was not big in eastern Pennsylvania, so I never wrestled that style until after the '76 season. That was the first year that I started wrestling year round.

My first Freestyle competition was the USWF state-wide tournament right after states in '76. I took 2nd and then entered the Olympic Qualifier tournament at Clarion. I weighed under 100 pounds while competing at 105.5 and I won the tournament which meant I got to go to the Final Olympic Trials.

The Final Trials in Cleveland were just my third Freestyle tournament ever. People had never heard of me and didn't know what I could do. I wrestled nine bouts there; I got eight pins, with seven of the eight with a cradle, including ones on the veterans Bill Rosado and Dave Range. I lost the final match to Mike Farina. He was bigger, stronger and more mature than I was. However, I finished 2nd and that was a big deal for me. I had earned my way to the next step — the DeKalb and Brockport camps.

That Trials tournament was a thrilling experience and for the first time put me on the national map. People called me 'the blonde bombshell'. It was an exciting ride that just kept getting better and better.

After the Cleveland experience, I went to DeKalb and started to learn more Freestyle technique. I remember DeKalb being just a small Midwest farm town. What I remember most though is the intense wrestling environment. I worked a lot with Rosado. Even though we were rivals, he was very generous in taking time to teach me new moves.

I went to the Final wrestle-offs knowing it would be tough for me to continue my success. I had 'caught' the guys in Cleveland with my cradle and they now knew what to avoid. I wrestled both Rosado and Farina at Brockport. Farina pretty much controlled the action in our match although at one point I had him on his back and nearly pinned him. But he won and then Rosado beat me soundly.

After the wrestle-offs, I stayed at Brockport working out with the lightweights and that experience meant so much to me. I worked out every day for close to a month with Rosado. He taught me a lot of offense, like the foot sweep and various throws. It was either sink or swim and I sunk more than I swam; he beat me up good but I didn't quit. He helped take me to the next level — really from the state to the national level. It was there at Brockport where I first felt that making the Olympic team could actually become a reality in another four years.

The Olympic Training Camp, DeKalb, Illinois, May 20 — June 17, 1976

WHILE most Americans in the early summer of '76 were merrily planning celebrations of our country's bi-centennial anniversary, over 200 wrestlers and coaches gathered at Northern Illinois University in DeKalb for a month of intense training prior to the Final wrestle-offs. Head coaches Baughman and Peckham directed the activities along with their assistants: Dan Gable, Bobby Douglas, J Robinson, Dave Auble, Bill Weick, Russ Houk, Vaughn Hitchcock, Lee Allen and Joe DeMeo.

Coach Baughman recalls his time at DeKalb:

At the Olympic Training Camp, I decided we were going to resume practicing upper body techniques. The only way to learn to defend upper body throws is to practice against people that could do it — so our guys had to learn the throws well enough to use them. I taught the wrestlers how to shoot takedowns off the underhook, over-hook and other upper body tie-ups. I was coaching the guys in close-in combat wrestling as opposed taking a step back and shooting from outside. Most importantly, we were learning how to better defend our opponents' upper body attacks.

During the practices I was keeping my eye on Schalles and Dziedzic. I didn't care which one of them represented the US. However, I had noticed that while Schalles did win the Tbilisi tournament, during the most recent trip by the Russians to the US they had him scouted pretty well. They had learned not to get into a scramble with him and that when they shot their takedown not to go for the back-points right away but instead sta-

> ❝ **I almost went to Northern Iowa, but I wanted to wrestle in the Big Ten. Iowa didn't recruit me – they said they were already happy with their lightweights. I liked the easy-going style of Coach Don Corrigan, so I went to Purdue. I loved it there. And I wanted the chance to kick Iowa's ass.**
>
> **– JOE CORSO**

• •

bilize him. They knew he wouldn't shoot first but would score off their move.

Anyway, one day during our usual 20 minute scrimmage, Schalles comes up to me saying he didn't have a partner. He wanted to wrestle me. Well, I took this as a challenge to my coaching. I weighed about 195; he was around 180, so I had some size and experience on him. I wrestled him the same way the Russian did. Take him down, stabilize him, and then turn him. Not one time did Schalles take me down. After our scrimmage, I warned him, 'Wade, you are waiting for your opponent to make a mistake. You can't afford to let the Russians just take your leg. You need more offense.'

The Final Camp, Brockport State College, New York, June 18 – July 12, 1976

FREESTYLE winners of the Cleveland tournament included Mike Farina, Jim Haines, Jimmy Carr, Gene Davis, Larry Morgan, Wade Schalles, John Peterson, Ben Peterson, Russ Hellickson and Mike McCready. At Brockport, they waited and watched the wrestle-offs between the other 70 wrestlers who were vying for a shot at them.

Feelings were mixed regarding the prolonged 90-day training sessions that were held at Iowa City, DeKalb and Brockport, as well as the selection of Brockport as the site of the Final Camp. In an *Amateur Wrestling News* interview in September of 1976, John Peterson's wife Nancy remarked:

We attended about two-thirds of the ninety-day camp that was conducted by the AAU and it was great to be with John and be able to encourage him while he was going through such grueling training. This was the first time the wives had an opportunity to live with their husbands during the Olympic camp and for us it was a great success. I enjoyed it. Don't get me wrong. There were a lot of problems in the camp administration. Some of the food was terrible and in Brockport the weather turned cold and we were all without blankets.

John Peterson is quoted as saying:

I can't say enough about [the camps]. Where else are you going to have four or five national champions to work out with? I was able to get individual help from a variety of great coaches. Sure there were a lot of problems. I didn't like moving from one place to another. But I know one thing. The camp made it possible for Nancy and I to be together. When you marry, your wife becomes part of you and in my case she's the better part.

Among the crowd of contenders at Brockport was Purdue's Joe Corso who finished a distant 6th in Cleveland at 125.5. He reminisces:

It wasn't until my junior year at Valley high school in West Des Moines that I started to become a successful wrestler. I finished 2nd in states and then won them at 112 pounds in my senior year, 1971. My coach, Larry Bock, was very instrumental keeping me involved in the sport. I learned a lot of discipline and intensity from him.

I did not have good grades – around a 2.0 average as senior. So, instead of a four-year school, I went to North Iowa Area Community College [NIACC] for two years. We won the JC Nationals my second year there.

After NIACC, I almost went to Northern Iowa, but I wanted to wrestle in the Big Ten. Iowa didn't recruit me – they said they were already happy with their lightweights. I liked the easy-going style of Coach Don Corrigan, so I went to Purdue. I loved it there. And I wanted the chance to kick Iowa's ass.

My first year I had a pretty good season, but come time for the Big Tens, I was worn down from cutting weight all year and ended up 4th. I just didn't have it. I told myself I wasn't going to cut that much weight ever again.

The next year I wrestled at 126 for Purdue and beat most all the 126-pounders around. I won the Big Tens and was named Outstanding Wrestler.

At the 1975 NCAAs I lost to John Fritz in the quarter-finals. I was very disappointed; I really thought I would beat him. I did come back to take 3rd place, beating Jimmy Carr in the consolations. That let me know not to be scared of him later.

I was wrestling Freestyle year-round now, placing but not winning the big tournaments. I trained hard for the Trials and thought I was ready for Cleveland. However, I finished 6th. The only good thing was that I beat Fritz, 6-1. Otherwise I didn't wrestle well at all. I remember being pinned by Northwestern's Mike Massery.

I felt very depressed. I wrestled crappy and went back home licking my wounds. I figured that I wouldn't even go to the Camp and that I'd wait till the 1980 Games to have a chance to make the Olympics. I was very down on myself and went out and partied and tried to have a good time. However my old coaches and my folks called me, talked to me and convinced me to keep going and to get myself to the Camp in DeKalb.

I did and I had a great experience. I felt a lot better and headed for the tournament at Brockport. There I faced Don Behm and Jack Reinwand and beat them both to win the mini-tournament. Massery didn't show up, so it was down to Jan Gitcho, Jimmy Carr and me. Gitcho had placed 2nd to Carr at Cleveland and was a stud from Southern Illinois. He also had wrestled on the US team at the Worlds in '74. In our first match he trounced me, 22-4. He just killed me. Everyone figured that I was done.

I got together with my coaches and we decided upon a new strategy. I had to tire Gitcho out and beat him with my conditioning. These were nine minute matches, so in our second match, I started to wear him down and I rallied at the end to win 8-5. I could see that I would win the third and deciding match if I could weather his early storm. I did and won the third match handily.

I thought, 'Wow, now I'm in the finals against Carr.'

Weigh-in was the next morning. I'm fine but Carr doesn't make weight the first go-round.

Finally, just before time is up, Carr makes weight. I am glad because I wanted to wrestle him. I knew I could beat him. And in the first match, I did... something like 9-7. It was an exciting, good match with lots of throws. I could see that Carr was dying, though, come the third period.

In the second match, it was all over — I pinned him. I caught him and stuck him and I had my ticket to Montreal.

Sandy Cageao was a referee at the Brockport Trials and offers his memories of the Carr — Corso competition:

Carr did not come to Brockport until the night before his finals match. Corso, meanwhile, had been wrestling his way up the ladder. Carr came in about eight pounds overweight. His brother Fletcher was furious. Jimmy spent much of the night losing the weight and just did make it. I think that took a lot out of him.

At one point during their first match, Carr takes Corso down right to his back. From where I am sitting — and where the Mat Chair, Steve Evanoff is sitting — it is a pin. It should have been considered a fall, but the referee didn't see it. The Mat Chair cannot initiate a score, he can only confirm one, so no pin was called. Anyway Corso ended up winning and I actually think he was the better wrestler to go to Montreal.

Wrestling official Rick Tucci recalls the Carr-Corso matches. He refereed the first one and has this to say:

Carr was the heavy favorite. The AAU officials wanted him in the US lineup. He was a past Olympian with lots of experience. Jimmy was cocky — the whole Carr family was — and they could back it up. No one gave Corso a shot.

I refereed one of their matches. There were lots of scrambles. Towards the very end of the match, Corso was ahead by two points when Jimmy went for a double-leg. He lifted Joe high in the air and took him down to the mat — on his belly. I gave Carr one point for the takedown and the match ended with Corso ahead by a point.

The AAU officials called me over to the sidelines. They wanted Jimmy to win and asked me if I couldn't give Carr more than one point for that move. I said that since Carr didn't put Corso in danger I could only award one point. They had a

Wisconsin native Russ Hellickson upended 1972 Olympian Henk Schenk on his way to winning the Trials at 220 pounds *Photograph by Pete Hausrath, courtesy of* Amateur Wrestling News

video replay, although I am not sure it was used. My ruling stood and Corso, nor Carr, got to go to the Olympics.

There was another former Big Ten wrestler who, unlike Corso, was pretty much head and shoulders above all the US competitors in his weight class. That would be 220-pounder Russ Hellickson. Russ tells his story:

In '74 I badly hurt my neck while practicing with Ben Peterson. I ruptured two discs and elected not to have surgery. That would have taken me out of action for too long. So I was cautious while wrestling and had to be selective as to how often I could wrestle in tournaments.

I qualified for the 1975 US World team. Ben went to the Worlds at 220 and I was at 198. I was having trouble keeping my weight down, so after

the Worlds I asked Ben if we could switch weight classes. He said, 'Yes', so I stayed up at 220 after that.

By the time the '76 Trials rolled around, I was still hurting with a lot of pain in my neck and arm. I had trouble sleeping. My toughest competitor was Larry Bielenberg who was good, but nothing like Ben. I beat him in the finals both in Cleveland and Brockport and was very happy to finally make the Olympic team.

A few words about Ben Peterson. We wrestled each other many, many times and worked out together many, many times. We made each other better. I saw him as a teammate, not as a rival. He could be brutal to wrestle but he had a lot of class. We shared the same concept that you didn't have to hate or hurt someone to beat them.

For me the sport of wrestling was a perfect fit. There were so many ways to be great – on your feet, on the mat, various pinning combinations. I was very glad to have the opportunity to be around so many good people.

Coaches and fans pretty much agree that the two most competitive weight classes at the Trials were 149.5 and 163. In 1972 Olympians Dan Gable and Wayne Wells won gold medals at these weights, but both immediately retired from international competition. Hence in the intervening years, several US Freestyle wrestlers were able to pick up invaluable international experience. Let's look at the competition.

149.5 Freestyle – Lloyd Keaser vs Larry Morgan vs Chuck Yagla

Larry Morgan beat 'Butch' Keaser four out of the seven times they wrestled in 1976, but Keaser won the deciding wrestle-off to make the Olympics
Photograph by Pete Hausrath, courtesy of Amateur Wrestling News

VETERANS Lloyd Keaser and Larry Morgan battled each other fairly evenly in most all the major Freestyle and Greco tournaments from 1973 to 1976. Meanwhile Chuck Yagla, the NCAA champion from Iowa, came out of the college ranks to mount his challenge.

Keaser tells his story from after the '72 Trials up through the '76 Final Camp:

After the '72 Trials I was stationed as a Marine Corps officer at Quantico, Virginia. I had a very successful '73 wrestling season. I competed at the Tbilisi tournament and finished 3rd. I beat Larry Morgan for the National AAU title though we actually tied in our match and I was declared the champion on fewer black marks. I won my World Cup matches at Toledo, and then I won the World Championship at Teheran, Iran in September.

It was unfortunate though that just one month before winning the gold medal, my dad passed away. He was the biggest believer in me and I wish he could have been alive to see it. I thought about him the whole time I was wrestling over there.

After winning a silver medal at Tbilisi in early '74 I cut back on my wrestling training and com-petition until six months before the '76 Trials.

In late '75 I put in for a transfer to Annapolis so that I could concentrate more on wrestling in preparation for the Trials. I was assigned to the staff at the Academy, where I helped coach the varsity team and started working out rigorously. I went to a 30-day Olympic Training Camp at the University of Iowa and then on to the Cleveland Trials.

I won my early round matches easily but then ran up against two good young guys. I had a very tough match with Chuck Yagla. I was way ahead of him early but he came storming back and put me on my back. I held on to win, 10-9. Then I wrestled Mark Churella who was a freshman at Michigan. I remember he took me down and got a back-point at the start, but I ended up beating him. The last match was with my long-time rival,

Larry Morgan. I believe we wrestled each other 13 times in our careers. We were always close. This time he whipped me, 9-6.

One of my best memories of the event was watching a high school junior from California — Dave Schultz — compete. He looked very good and had great technical skills even then. He came up to me after my first bout and asked if we could wrestle a simulated bout in the practice room. We did and I was impressed with the guy. He was always looking to wrestle — a 'gym rat' so to speak.

After the Trials, I went to the Camp in DeKalb and worked a lot on my counter techniques that I needed to improve to beat Morgan. The training camps at Iowa and Illinois really were excellent, although it was a bit odd practicing alongside the same people you were going to face in the final wrestle-offs.

I went to Brockport well prepared. I had to wrestle Yagla again and I beat him twice to set up my challenge matches with Morgan. In our first match I wrestled one of the best matches of my life. I beat him convincingly. That set up a second match, which I also won. The feeling after that match was hard to describe — I was floating on a cloud knowing that I had made the Olympic team.

The Camp environment after the challenge matches was very good. We had three workouts a day, six days a week. I wanted it to be physically challenging and it was. I am especially thankful to Coach Bill Weick. It seemed that he was the best man for me to be in my corner. I always seemed to wrestle my best with him there for me.

Larry Morgan, who grew up in Bakersfield, California and became a Division II national champion at Cal Poly, tells his story:

I was a good wrestler in high school in Bakersfield, winning the Junior Worlds in '69. Then I went to Cal Poly which is a great school academically. However, it was not a wrestling Mecca like Iowa or Oklahoma.

After graduating from Cal Poly in 1973 I made the US World Freestyle team that same year and placed 4th at 136.5. I realized California wasn't the right environment for me to get ready for the Olympics — not enough world class international wrestlers — so I moved to Iowa City to train. Iowa

> **I am especially thankful to Coach Bill Weick. It seemed that he was the best man for me to be in my corner. I always seemed to wrestle my best with him there for me.**
>
> — 'BUTCH' KEASER

was a great experience for me. The wrestling room at the University was a phenomenal place. There were so many excellent partners there — Gable, Joe Wells, Chris Campbell, J Robinson, plus college guys like Bruce Kinseth and Chuck Yagla. I was the only one there from California where you are by the beach, with lots of surfers and skateboarders playing there year-round. Iowa was totally different as you can imagine.

I went to Iowa thinking that I would be training and working out with Dan Gable on a daily basis. Wrong. Dan was known to all as 'the machine' and it was true. If I wrestled with Dan occasionally, say twice a week, I could keep up with him okay. He was a little bit bigger than me, but much stronger and had too much endurance. When I tried to wrestle him two or three days in a row, then he would start pummeling me. I soon changed my routine to work with him just on occasion.

In 1976 I beat Keaser four out of the five times that we wrestled prior to Brockport — at the Federation Nationals in Greco and Freestyle, at the National AAUs in Greco and at the Cleveland Trials in Freestyle. The one time he had defeated me was at the National AAUs in Freestyle.

After winning the Freestyle Trials in Cleveland, I also tried to qualify in Greco. I thought I could win both styles, although I really wanted to be in the Olympics in Freestyle. However, while I was beating a guy in our Greco match, I tore some cartilage in my rib and had to forfeit out of the tournament.

That injury hampered me in my subsequent training program for the Brockport Camp. My ribs hurt so much I couldn't twist and turn at all. Keaser was a great wrestler and competitor and he beat me twice. I can't put my finger on it exactly, why I didn't win. I felt very tired. I wanted to beat him so badly and felt like I could, but it just didn't happen.

Iowa's Chuck Yagla recalls his wrestling days and his Trials experience:

I grew up as the youngest of four boys in Waterloo, Iowa. As a youngster I played lots of sports — golf, tennis, football, baseball and wrestling. By the time I got to high school, I decided I liked wrestling the best. It was the only sport I went out for at Columbus, the Catholic high school in Waterloo.

I had an okay high school career. I made varsity as sophomore — but didn't make it past the sectionals. Ken Snyder was a teammate and my same size. I couldn't beat him, so I had to wrestle up a weight. In my junior year, I won the sectionals but lost in the district semis and didn't go to states. My senior year was better. My nemesis was Bruce Wilson from Waterloo West who beat me in the finals of the sectionals, districts and states.

I started wrestling Freestyle in high school. In my senior year I won the state Freestyle tournament and went to the USWF Junior Nationals in Iowa City where I won a couple of bouts but didn't place. I also went with a group of Waterloo West guys, including Dan Gable, to a national tournament in Oklahoma City. I won the tournament at 154, tying Gable's protégée Tony Cordes, but winning on fewer black marks. That was great exposure for me. I was not heavily recruited but I chose to go to the University of Iowa mainly because my brothers were there and I knew that my idol, Dan Gable, was an assistant there.

In college I made the varsity as a freshman, wrestling at 150 much of the year. In my sophomore year I started working out twice a day and set my goals to be in the top four in the country. The Gable influence started to take hold. I ended up 4th at the NCAAs. Good conditioning was making the difference.

My goal junior year was to be a National champ, Big Ten champ and Midlands champ. The season got off to a rocky start for me. The first tournament of the year was the Northern Open in Madison. I get to the finals and meet a freshman from the University of Wisconsin — Lee Kemp. He beats me in overtime. I'm

> ## "My best move was the 'seat-belt'. Over the years I pinned a lot of people with it but I don't think Keaser knew about it. Anyway, I worked it and put Keaser on his back. I thought I had him pinned but the ref didn't call it.
>
> **— CHUCK YAGLA**

crushed. Coach Gable comes up to me after the match and says, 'I don't know how you are ever going to figure out how to beat that kid.' That was his way of motivating me.

I made it to the finals of the Midlands where I promptly lost to Bob Holland of ISU. Then things started to get better. I came back and tied Holland in our dual. I beat Kemp three times that season — in our dual, the Big Tens and in the NCAA finals in overtime.

My senior year, I again faltered at the start. I won the '75 Northern Open. [Author's note: That's the tournament where Kemp spoiled Gable's comeback attempt, 7-6.] At the Midlands, I faced Michigan freshman Mark Churella and he beat me. I came back through the consolations and beat him to take 3rd. Later in the season, I beat Churella in our dual meet and in the Big Ten tourney. I went on to win the NCAAs without wrestling Churella.

Up until I won the NCAAs as a senior in '76 I had not thought much about entering the Olympic Trials. It was not one of my pre-season goals, but I decided, 'why not', so I entered the Cleveland tournament. I ended up 5th, losing to Lloyd Keaser and Larry Morgan in close matches. I think I wrestled Dave Schultz, who was a high school kid at the time, and beat him.

My match with Keaser was a good one. To me, he was the guy to beat. He was a World Champion. He had a great ankle-pick and used it effectively on me a lot. My best move was the 'seat-belt'. Over the years I pinned a lot of people with it but I don't think Keaser knew about it. Anyway, I worked it and put Keaser on his back. I thought I had him pinned but the ref didn't call it. Then we are back on our feet and Keaser goes in for his ankle-pick again. We are near the edge of the mat and Keaser not only gets a point

Kemp upset Dziedzic at the Cleveland Trials but fell to the more experienced Pennsylvanian at Brockport *Photograph by Chris Poff, courtesy of* Scholastic Wrestling News

for taking me down, but two more for my 'stalling' and for my 'running out of bounds'. I never did understand how he could get three points for that — maybe two at the most. Anyway, he ends up beating me, 10-9. The next day the ref comes up to me and tells me that he was sorry that he made a mistake giving Keaser three points, but it's too late to do anything about it.

I went back to Iowa City and worked out there getting ready for Brockport. Larry Morgan was training at Iowa City as well, but I don't think I ever worked out with him. I went to Brockport ready to go and won the mini-tournament. I then had to wrestle Churella and I did beat him in two-out-of-three. Next up was Keaser. He beat me twice in close matches. His darn ankle-pick still got me and he now knew to keep away from my 'seat-belt'. He went on to beat Morgan and in my opinion was the right guy to go to Montreal.

I stayed around for the rest of the Camp and was a team alternate. They took me to Montreal and that was a fantastic experience for me. It set my sights for what I wanted to accomplish in 1980.

163 Freestyle — Stan Dziedzic vs Lee Kemp vs Wade Schalles

DZIEDZIC and Schalles were two fierce middleweight rivals from Pennsylvania. Throughout their high school careers, save for Schalles' senior season, they were rather ordinary teenage wrestlers. There was little evidence that they would one day attain Hall of Fame stature. In the early '70s they attended small Pennsylvania state teachers colleges only 45 miles apart — Slippery Rock and Clarion — where they both became NCAA champions. Both later distinguished themselves as international Freestyle champion wrestlers. Prior to the '76 Trials their career record against each other was reported to be 7-7.

Meanwhile, Lee Kemp from Chardon, Ohio and just a sophomore at the University of Wisconsin, was the emerging star at 163. Several years the junior to the two Pennsylvania phenoms, Kemp proved his mettle in the college ranks by reaching the finals of the NCAAs as a freshman and winning them as a sophomore.

Kemp recalls his wrestling days leading up to and including the '76 Trials:

I was raised in inner-city Cleveland through sixth grade, at which time my family moved out to the country — Chardon, a small town of 4,000 people about 30 miles from Cleveland. I played junior high basketball with little success. My gym teacher told me that I should try wrestling since I had an athletic build. I watched a practice, thought it looked like a good sport for me and joined the freshman team.

For freshman and sophomore years, I had good physical ability but didn't know many moves. I was 11-8-3 as a sophomore on the varsity squad. That summer, 1972, I went to a wrestling camp in Ohio which changed my entire life. Dan Gable and the Peterson brothers were there and it was incredible watching them work out. When Dan was doing his teaching, I volunteered to be his demo partner. I picked up a number of his moves and his work ethic. From that summer on, I patterned my wrestling after Gable. He had a profound effect on me and was the person most responsible for me turning into the wrestler that I went on to become.

I won the Ohio state high school tournament the following year and again as a senior in 1974. During the college recruiting process, Iowa was not particularly interested in me because Gable said he already had Chuck Yagla filling the weight class. I was very interested in going to Michigan State but didn't hear too much from them, so I accepted a scholarship offer from the University of Wisconsin. The day after I accepted that offer, the Michigan State assistant coach, Stan Dziedzic, called me with an offer of a full scholarship to Michigan State. I had to tell Stan that I had already accepted the Wisconsin offer.

[Author's note: Within two years, Kemp wrestled and beat both Gable and Dziedzic.]

I wrestled a bit of Freestyle during high school in local tournaments. After my senior year I won the USWF Junior Nationals in Iowa City, beating both Mark Churella and Paul Martin at 154 pounds. I had a successful freshman year at Wisconsin, getting to the finals of the NCAAs where Yagla beat me in overtime at 150.

At the start of my sophomore year, the fall of 1975, I set my goals for the year — move up to 158, have an undefeated college season and win a NCAA championship. My coach, Duane Kleven, calls me in his office about two weeks before the start of the season and starts telling me that if I want to accomplish those goals, I better start getting back down to 150 pounds.

When I ask why, he says, 'We are going to the Northern Open for our opening matches and Dan Gable has entered at 158. I think you want to avoid him in order to go undefeated this year.'

I didn't understand where he was coming from. I was very excited about the prospect of wrestling Gable. No one took me seriously though and many people asked why I should even try. Well, I believed in myself and I did face Dan in the finals and I won. The interesting thing is that I was training in the same mindset as Gable and I had the physical capacity to be like him. From that point all the way back to the Ohio camp in '72, I tried to be as much of a Gable clone as I could. I viewed and wrestled the match as he would have instructed me. Yes, he wasn't at 100 percent since he did have a pinched nerve, but I had the physical ability and great conditioning and wasn't going to give up.

That match was a confirmation to me that I could beat anyone.

Come spring of 1976, I had just accomplished my sophomore year goals — an undefeated season and an NCAA championship. I didn't like to compete right after the season, so the Olympic Trials were not high on my agenda. I wasn't doing any training for them. However, as the time approached for the Trials back in my hometown of Cleveland, I figured I better go — even though I really didn't want to.

I easily won all my matches the first two days, and then had to wrestle Dziedzic. I think he overlooked me. I got an early lead and as the bout went on, the match started getting away from him. Stan was a very good counter-wrestler, but once I got ahead of him he couldn't pull-off a quick go-to takedown move on me. I ended up winning, 7-5.

Next I had to wrestle Schalles. I was terrible. I was intimidated by his reputation and so afraid. I froze up and just wanted to avoid getting pinned.

I ended up 2nd in the weight class, so I went to

> **Going into the match I was really motivated to beat him. We were both highly competitive and I told Wade at the start of the match that there was no way that he was going to win.**
>
> **— STAN DZIEDZIC**

• •

the DeKalb Camp for a month and trained with all the top wrestlers — Gable, Keaser, Dziedzic — but for some reason, not Schalles.

When we went to Brockport, Dziedzic earned the right to challenge me and he soundly beat me — twice. Stan was a great tactician and he totally beat me in this area. I had more physical ability, the strength and quickness, than Stan, but he totally outclassed me tactically.

I believe Stan was the right guy to go to the Olympics for the US that year. On a good day, Wade could beat him, but not two out of three times. Stan was just not going to lose to Wade to make that Olympic team.

Stan Dziedzic recalls his wrestling roots and the '76 Trials:

I was a 108-pound football player as a ninth grader at Allen High in Allentown. The wrestling coach came up to me and said he needed a 103-pounder on the team and asked me to try out. I did and I made the team. We had a good team with Geoff Baum and me both in the lineup. We were probably the only high school in the country with two future NCAA champions (not from the same family) on the team. I was never a state champion, never qualified for states, but I had enough success to enjoy the sport and wanted to continue to wrestle in college.

As a high school senior I competed at 133 pounds but had a big growth spurt after that and wrestled 152 as a college freshman at Indiana State. I then transferred to Slippery Rock when Fred Powell, who was an assistant at Indiana State, was named head coach there in 1969.

I remember wrestling Schalles just twice in college. I beat him in the finals of the Wilkes tournament once and then again in a dual meet at Clarion. In 1971, I wrestled at 150 and won the NCAAs while Wade was at 158 and didn't place.

The following year he dropped down to 150 and won the championship while I went up a weight and lost to Carl Adams, the defending champ at 158.

I tried out for the '72 Olympics and did well in my first taste of high level Freestyle wrestling. I finished 2nd — a distant 2nd, mind you — to Wayne Wells, and was an alternate on the team that went to Munich.

I knew that after college I wanted to stay active in the sport but didn't know where or how. By chance, I was sitting across the aisle from Grady Peninger on the airplane ride home from the Nationals and I told him that I'd like to get into coaching. Two months later an opening came up on his staff. Grady called me and offered me the job as his assistant. I took it.

That was a fortunate move for me. For the next several years, Jack Zindel was there and was an excellent workout partner. Don Behm and I became great friends and we would travel all over the country together wrestling in various tournaments.

In those days there was no such thing as a permanent Olympic training site. You had to go out and seek help and training partners. During that '72 to '76 period while stationed at Michigan State and wrestling for the NYAC, I received some good coaching from a variety of the best that were around — Dan Gable, Jim Peckham, Bill Farrell, Bobby Douglas and Sonny Greenhalgh. Each contributed in their own way to my success.

As I prepared for the '76 Olympic Trials, I had to be concentrating on two things — one, was the international guys that I'd have to eventually face like the Russians, Iranians, Mongolians, etc., and two, the US wrestlers like Adams and Schalles.

Schalles won the Tbilisi tournament early in '76 while I did not do well over there. But that didn't bother me; I knew I could beat him.

I thought that Adams would be my toughest competitor. He was very tough. Besides beating me in the NCAA finals, he beat me twice in the National AAU finals. Carl lost, though, early in the Cleveland Trials tournament and couldn't advance. However, Lee Kemp, as a college sophomore, came into play and that changed all the dynamics.

At Cleveland, I lost to Kemp, 7-5, and beat Schalles, 4-2. I never thought I would lose to

Kemp. I really underestimated his physical abilities. Schalles won the tournament when he defeated Kemp. They both had fewer black marks than me, hence I finished 3ʳᵈ.

The fact that I finished 3ʳᵈ was a benefit. I spent the next month working on those particular areas where I had to improve to beat both Kemp and Schalles.

I was ready for the Brockport Camp. As I expected, the winner of the mini-tournament at 163 was Jeff Callard, so I had to wrestle him first. I beat him twice to set up my challenge matches against Kemp. I had to win two matches against him, which I did. It was a little easier than I thought.

That result set up the Finals showdown with Schalles. In his defense, I believe he thought he'd probably be wrestling Kemp instead of me. Going into the match I was really motivated to beat him. We were both highly competitive and I told Wade at the start of the match that there was no way that he was going to win.

My biggest worry was the first two minutes of the match. I noticed that Wade had an extraordinarily long workout before facing me. I knew I was in better physical condition than he was and that the last seven minutes of the match would be mine.

True to form, Wade came out very aggressive and got me on a two-point move. Then he starts running. I could see he was tiring. We each got some points and I think the score was tied when the referee, Rick Tucci, cautioned him out. I think he could have been hurt, probably in the opening flurry where he scored.

That match was held in the morning and our second match was scheduled for the same evening. Sometime in the afternoon, the Wrestling Committee said that Wade had been injured and that the second match would be wrestled a week later. That was against the rules, but the officials said they were going to do it anyway. I said 'Okay' and went back to the dorm to take a nap.

Later that afternoon, the doctors re-examined Wade and declared him out of the competition with cracked vertebrae. The Committee declared me the winner. We never did wrestle that second match. While thrilled to make the Olympic team, I was disappointed at the time. I wanted the chance to prove I was the best, no

Schalles was sure that he wasn't going to be beaten by a collegian... not even NCAA champion Kemp *Photograph by Pete Hausrath, courtesy of Amateur Wrestling News*

questions asked, even though I knew I could beat Wade anyway.

Referee Rick Tucci talks about the Dziedzic—Schalles rivalry at the Final wrestle-offs:

There was lots of hype around the Schalles—Dziedzic match. Schalles was the 'golden boy' with his prominent story in Sports Illustrated. Stan was his toughest challenger.

Schalles was not a favorite of the old-timers — guys like Steve Garber, Dick Torio, Steve Evanoff. He was a bit too extreme for them. They preferred that the more orthodox Dziedzic represent the US. It was interesting to say the least.

Dziedzic had to come through the wrestle-backs and beat Kemp on his way. Wade was just waiting for him. Wade watched the matches — sitting in the stands, relaxed, with a nonchalant look on his face. He seemed to enjoy what was going on and gave the aura of 'here I am, fight it out to come get me.'

I knew them both from officiating previous matches of each, but never a match between them.

Come time for the match, it was really hot in the Brockport gym. There was no air conditioning. A large crowd was awaiting many big matches, but Schalles-Dziedzic was the biggest. I got the opportunity to referee it.

The two wrestlers went right after it and there was a big flurry. Schalles won opening points and had a two or three point lead. However, I could see at a particular point he started to wear down. Wade was getting tired. Both guys were sweating profusely and then Dziedzic scored as the two wrestlers went out of bounds. He goes back to the center circle but Schalles doesn't. The Mat Chair, Evanoff, yells at me to get 'em back in the middle. Schalles still doesn't move and I call an end to the match and award it to Stan.

For the second match, to be held in the evening, I again was selected as the referee. As they announced the wrestlers at the start of the evening, Schalles comes out with a brace on his neck. He had cracked the vertebrae in his neck in the first bout and had to forfeit.

Stan and Wade came together at the center of the mat, shook hands, and hugged each other. That was it.

The Mat Chairman for the Dziedzic–Schalles matches was the late Steve Evanoff. Wayne Baughman remembers Steve:

He was one of our country's greatest international officials and someone who never received the recognition he deserved for advancing the cause of American wrestling. Steve knew how to play the Russians' and Europeans' system of 'justice' and would fight fire with fire. That even extended to the Trials.

Finally, it's Schalles's time to tell his story:

My Olympic dream appeared at the end of my junior year in Hollidaysburg [Pennsylvania] high when I didn't qualify for states. I was moping around home and my mother said she knew why I didn't make it to states. She said, 'I never heard you say you wanted to go to states and if you don't dream it, and believe it, you'll never get there. You have to visualize it. That's your problem.' She then told me to dream not about states, but about going to the Olympic Games in 1976, pinning all my opponents, winning the most Outstanding Wrestler award and leading the whole US contingent of athletes in the closing ceremonies.

That became my dream for the next seven years.

The following year in high school, I went

> **I throw Stan and we both land on our backs. They give Dziedzic two points, none for me, and he was declared the winner of the match. That was maybe the first time I ever knew that I won the match but my hand didn't get raised at the end. I believe it came down to AAU-USWF politics. The head official was Steve Evanoff and he hated me.**
>
> **– WADE SCHALLES**

29-0 with 29 pins. High school wrestlers seem pretty meek when you are dreaming about being an Olympic hero.

Stan Mousetis took me to my first major Freestyle tournament after my senior year in high school. We developed a strong friendship and I asked him to be in my corner during the Trials. I wouldn't have done that if I knew what I now know. Your corner man is very important, particularly if he has a certain stature in the wrestling community. Stan was, and is, a good man, but he wasn't the equivalent of a Dan Gable or a Bill Farrell. Men like that can influence the referee in your favor.

I never really had a personal Freestyle coach on a consistent basis and that hindered me. Bob Bubb, my college coach, was too busy doing his job as head coach at Clarion. I needed to have someone train me and there wasn't really anyone. Not many coaches were around back then who could help me with my unique style. Today there would be, but not in the mid-70s.

Leading up to the Trials, I went to the Tbilisi tournament in January and got into final round-robin which consisted of three wrestlers in ten weight classes. Out of the 30 wrestlers in the finals, I was the only non-Russian. Usually Russians are very conservative wrestlers and don't mix it up like I do, but when I met them in Tbilisi they got into flurries with me. I was fortunate enough to pin them and win the gold medal.

After that I went to Iowa City to work out with the Iowa wrestlers to prepare for the Trials. Larry Morgan was my roommate and we hung out together. He was a very smooth wrestler — unlike

> "Dziedzic is so intense and competitive. I have him hoisted in the air and he is coming down – unceremoniously. I bow forward and he is wrapping himself around me. He is bear-hugging one of my arms and scissoring my other arm. He knew he was going down and was going to take me with him.
>
> — WADE SCHALLES

'Butch' Keaser who was a brawler and a cruncher. Iowa coaches tried to change Morgan but not successfully. Morgan could beat Keaser in the room, yet not that often in the tournaments. The intensity at Iowa was impressive — three to four sessions a day — but it was too much for me. I started dragging and had to take time off.

I went to Cleveland where I pinned my first six opponents. I figured it would come down to just me and my biggest rival, Stan Dziedzic, and I knew I could beat him. I was very surprised to see Lee Kemp beat Dziedzic. Lee was a good wrestler, but I didn't think any collegian could beat Stan or me. It was most likely a style match-up thing. When I wrestled Kemp, I didn't have much trouble with him.

My last match was against Dziedzic and it came down to one call at the end. We were even, although he was ahead on criteria. It was either 2-2 or 4-4 and I come close to taking him down but we go out-of-bounds. Back in the center of the mat with under 30 seconds left, in the area they call 'the zone', I get in behind Stan and initiate a throw. Now in those days if you initiated an offensive move from the zone, you couldn't have points scored against you. Anyway I throw Stan and we both land on our backs. They give Dziedzic two points, none for me, and he was declared the winner of the match.

That was maybe the first time I ever knew that I won the match but my hand didn't get raised at the end. I believe it came down to AAU-USWF politics. The head official was Steve Evanoff and he hated me. He was an AAU guy and I was one of the wrestlers that broke away from that organization and became a USWF guy. I had

been very outspoken about the way wrestlers were being dumped-on by the AAU. On top of that, I had no mentor telling me how to act and play the politics game. I bet if I had an influential person like Farrell in my corner, I would have received the points. Meanwhile, Dziedzic, who I've always said is a top-shelf quality individual, was more politically astute than me and remained friendly with the AAU and their officials.

Mousetis and I protested the call. Evanoff talked with the mat referee when we protested and I believe he intimidated the officials into giving the tilt points to Stan. That was a bad 'homer' call. The next week I got a letter (I still have it, by the way) from the referee of the match apologizing for the bad call. Nevertheless because of all my pins, I had fewer black marks than Lee or Stan, so I won the tournament anyway.

For the next month I went to the Camp at DeKalb to continue my training. I didn't work-out with the 163-pounders. Instead, I preferred wrestling the guys at 180. I wrestled a lot with John Peterson and could beat him pretty easily. I couldn't handle the bigger Peterson — Ben — though. In my estimation he was, by far, the better wrestler of the two brothers.

At Brockport, I was in the best shape of my life, both mentally and physically. I never felt stronger as an athlete. I had my weight under control; I came down from over 180. Physical test results from a sports camp I attended at Indiana State showed that I had more power in my legs than any of their college football linemen. I had great legs and thighs.

I really didn't care whether I met Kemp or Dziedzic in the finals. I knew I could beat both — at the same time if need be. If I was rational, I would have thought that I'd rather face Kemp, because I had his number, but I didn't give a shit who my opponent was.

Early in the match with Stan, we are on our feet and I am in on him below his under-hook, squatting in the fireman's carry position. I picked him up and due to our intense 'friendship' I had every intention of planting him on the mat like a daisy. Ha!

As an aside, when Stan and I would be entered in tournaments at different weight classes, we were very friendly and would work as a tandem — hang out together, have a beer or soda, look for girls, the things guys do — but when we were wrestling each other, it was a very different story.

Anyway, as I said, Dziedzic is so intense and competitive. I have him hoisted in the air and he is coming down — unceremoniously. I bow forward and he is wrapping himself around me. He is bear-hugging one of my arms and scissoring my other arm. He knew he was going down and was going to take me with him. I carried him with me as I dropped into a front bridge. I had no hands to break our momentum. My head was driven into the mat with the force of us both and I broke two vertebrae.

I got my two points but I knew something was not right. I was seeing double. The injury clock started and after 30 seconds, the mat judge, Steve Evanoff, barks at me, "Get up and wrestle." I got up and started, but I couldn't do anything. My chest was spasmatizing.

Stan was behind and was coming after me. He was pushing me and I was just trying to hang on. I got warned and then penalized two points in the second period for stalling. Was I stalling? You bet. I wasn't shooting. I felt like the boxer who, after taking a blow, clinches to buy time to shake the fog in his head. My fog never cleared.

At the end of the second period, my corner man, Mousetis, tells me 'Wade, you gotta suck it up.' I couldn't. My chest wasn't expanding and I was having trouble breathing. I went back out there but finally, with about 45 seconds to go, I collapse. The next thing I remember is waking up in the hospital later that day.

In a magnanimous but meaningless gesture, my buddy Evanoff announced that this first match with Dziedzic was null-and-void because of my injury and that we will have to wrestle two more matches. Well, the doctors said, 'no way, you cannot wrestle with a broken neck', so I was done. While I was very dejected, I was grateful that I didn't receive a life-threatening injury. I just had a compression fracture, the mildest form of a broken neck.

My thoughts went back to the day six years earlier when I was wrestling Ray Murphy from Oklahoma State in the semi-finals of a Freestyle tournament in Stillwater. I had Ray up in the air, brought him to the mat on his head and he broke his neck. Very badly; he was paralyzed and never walked again. After the Dziedzic match, I was still able to walk around and my mind told me it just wasn't meant to be for me to wrestle in the Olympics.

That evening, I join the rest of the wrestlers at the medal ceremonies. I am standing one rung down from Dziedzic. I reach up, shake his hand, congratulate him, and wish him good luck in Montreal. He replies, 'I deserved to go. I was the best wrestler.'

1976 OLYMPIC TEAM MEMBERS

	FREESTYLE	GRECO-ROMAN
105.5	Bill Rosado	Mike Farina
114.5	Jim Haines	Bruce Thompson
125.5	Joe Corso	Joe Sade
136.5	Gene Davis (3rd)	Gary Alexander
149.5	Lloyd Keaser (2nd)	Pat Marcy
163	Stan Dziedzic (3rd)	John Matthews
180.5	John Peterson (1st)	Dan Chandler
198	Ben Peterson (2nd)	James Evan Johnson
220	Russ Hellickson (2nd)	Brad Reinghans (4th)
UNL	Jimmy Jackson	Peter Lee (5th)

★ THE Soviet wrestlers dominated the Olympics, winning a total of 12 gold and 5 silver medals. In Freestyle, Communist block countries won 15 of the 30 possible medals. In Greco, Communist block countries won 27 of the 30 medals.

1976 PRESIDENTIAL ELECTION

★ WINNING a close race, Carter became the first president elected from the Deep South in more than 125 years. According to many, Ford's pardon of ex-President Nixon was his undoing, while Carter appealed to the masses as a Washington outsider.

THE SCORECARD

Jimmy Carter Walter F. Mondale	297 Electoral Votes 50.1% of Popular Vote
Gerald R. Ford Robert J. Dole	240 Electoral Votes 48.0% of Popular Vote

1980
THE BOYCOTT

> 66 At the Trials, the person that bothered me the most was Chris Campbell's wife. She was his corner person, believe it or not. Well, during Chris' matches, she'd not only stand up, walk around and holler, she'd get right down flat on the mat and yell. In our last Finals bout, Chris and I were wresting near the edge and Chris was on top of me. About a foot away from my nose there's her face. She's eyeballing me, and she's screaming, 'Common, Chris, he's beat, he's out of shape, turn him over.' I wanted to say – but didn't – 'I'm not out of shape, lady. Chris is just too slick for an old guy like me.'
>
> – **John Peterson, 1976 Olympic Champion**

VETERAN wrestlers across America remorsefully recall 1980 as the year of the boycotted Olympics. And they believe that President Jimmy Carter was truly the boogeyman.

The wrestlers' Trials stories just aren't as passionate; their experiences just don't seem as meaningful. Where were the Camps where the guys grinded each other into the mat, ran the unforgiving stadium steps and hung out together in the dorms? Some wrestlers said, 'What's the point?' and decided to bag it. Others, including many who believed the boycott would never really happen, still trained excruciatingly hard, cut weight and busted a gut so that they could be forever called 'An Olympian'. But it wasn't quite the same.

What were the reasons behind this US – and more than 60 other nations – boycott anyway?

Historians tell us that in 1979 Afghanistan was in the midst of an internal revolution between the government and the insurgent anti-communist Mujahideen forces. Sometime in '79 it is believed that US President Carter signed a directive authorizing CIA aid to the Mujahideen. The US was backing the revolution. The Russians were supporting the existing communist government – to a certain extent.

After a palace revolt in September of '79, Deputy Prime Minister Hafizullah Amin took over as President in the capital city of Kabul. Within weeks of Amin's ascent, relations between Afghanistan and the Soviet Union soured. The KBG reported that Amin was purging his opponents, including Soviet sympathizers, and was ignoring advice from Moscow. Citing earlier requests for military assistance from the central government of Afghanistan, the USSR deployed the 40th Soviet Army to Afghanistan on Christmas Eve, 1979 for the purpose of destroying the revolutionary CIA-backed Mujahideen forces.

Russia also intended to get rid of Amin. The Soviets accomplished that mission three days after Christmas when Amin was killed by KGB Special Forces in a bloody attack on the Tajbeg Presidential Palace in Kabul.

Some people, including Carter advisor Zbigniew Brzezinski, believe that the administration was rather Machiavellian in its approach and was baiting the trap to encour-

Previous spread: Joe Corso and Gene Mills were beset by injuries. Mills recovered to win the 114.5 spot on the Freestyle team. Corso's broken leg kept him out of the final wrestle-offs. *Photograph by Roy Hobson, courtesy of* Amateur Wrestling

age a Soviet offensive into Afghanistan, thus providing Russia with its own Vietnam War.

Meanwhile, over in Iran, just a month earlier, a group of 300 radical Muslim students stormed the US Embassy in Tehran and took 66 Americans as hostages. President Carter was now facing dual crises in the Middle-East. Did Carter feel compelled to demonstrate his country's disdain for the actions of the Soviets and the Iranians because he was facing reelection in less than a year?

Carter's decisive but shallow answer came on January 20, 1980 when he announced that unless the Soviets withdrew their troops from Afghanistan by February 20, the United States would boycott the Olympic Games slated to be held that summer in the Soviet Union.

The Russians did not retreat, thus the President followed through on his promise. On March 21, Carter made his official announcement confirming the boycott. In April, the United States Olympic Committee and their many delegates met at the Antlers Hotel in Colorado Springs. The Olympic Assembly voted overwhelmingly to keep the US athletes home; the US athletes were not going to Moscow.

Stan Dziedzic, National AAU Coach at the time, recalls:

I found out about President Carter's announcement of the boycott as our US team disembarked from a plane in Moscow at the start of an annual AAU wrestling exchange. We were headed for Tbilisi and a couple other tournaments in Russia. We were pretty much speechless and didn't really believe that the boycott would actually happen. It didn't seem to make any sense. We thought, well, maybe the country won't go, but individuals could go on their own. In the US, that wasn't the case.

As mentioned, Carter was up for reelection as President and was facing a strong challenge from within his own party. Senator Edward Kennedy campaigned vigorously in the Democratic primary elections. Carter gained the nomination at the Democrat National Convention but looked a bit foolish when, in his acceptance speech, he referred to the late Hubert Humphrey, whose middle name was Horatio, as 'Hubert Horatio Hornblower.'

The Republicans were feeling optimistic about regaining the White House; popular Californian Ronald Reagan was pulling comfortably ahead of George Bush in the party primaries.

Muhammad Ali proposed a personal solution for the Iran hostage crisis. He offered to fight his comeback heavyweight title match against Larry Holmes in Tehran if the Iranians would free the US hostages. Ali was quoted in an Associated Press release, "I'm serious, I have many, many fans in Iran. If they let the hostages go, me and Holmes will fight for the title in Iran." That never happened.

On the economic front, the stock market continued to stagnate. The Dow-Jones Industrial average bounced around in the mid-800s in the summer of 1980, about 100 points lower than it was during the 1972 and 1976 Trials.

And, a revealing sign-of-the-times anecdote about the 1980 NCAA wrestling championships hosted by Oregon State. According to wrestling historian Jay Hammond:

The 1980 NCAA tournament had a record total of 128 schools (some non-DI) qualify their wrestlers. Over 40% of those schools no longer (as of 2007) have a wrestling program.

The Outlook for the US Wrestlers

IN THE intervening years since the '76 Olympics, the US wrestlers broke through with some record-setting performances in international competition. We came up with our sixth-ever gold medal winner in the '77 Worlds when Stan Dziedzic won the Freestyle championship at 163 pounds. Jim Humphrey won a silver medal as the US finished 4th overall. In 1978, Lee Kemp continued the US dominance of the 163-pound class when he won his first World Freestyle championship. The following year Kemp defended his crown and enjoyed the honor of being the first US wrestler to win a second World championship. The US was the runner-up in team scoring to the Soviets. We won ten medals overall, with Bobby Weaver, Jim Haines, John Peterson and Russ Hellickson winning silver medals in Freestyle. The Greco team had its best finish ever, placing 4th, led by Abdurrahim Kuzu's 2nd place finish at 136.5 pounds.

Perhaps our most impressive performance was winning the World Cup in March of 1980. Except for the '60 Olympics, in the previous 21 years of international competition between the US and the Soviet Union, the US had never beaten their bitter rival. However, before a crowd of 6,000 fans at the University of Toledo's Centennial Hall, the Dan Gable and Stan Dziedzic coached US Freestyle team finally beat the Russians, 7-3. Bobby Weaver, Gene Mills, Dave Schultz, Lee Kemp, John Peterson, Ben Peterson and Jimmy Jackson won their matches to lead the US to victory. Weaver and Jackson pinned former Olympic champions.

Based on these results, observers felt that the US had the makings of a Freestyle and Greco team that would have been favored to win a dozen Olympic medals, including three or four gold ones. In some cases, it would have been harder to make the US team than to come home with an Olympic medal.

Wrestlers and fans listening to officials within the USWF and the AAU may have had reason to be confused about sentiments surrounding the boycott.

USWF Executive Director Steve Combs announced in February:

As an organization, we totally and completely support the President, the Congress, and the vast majority of the American people in repudiating any competition in Moscow while the Soviet Union continues its invasion of Afghanistan.

Meanwhile, the AAU proceeded forward.

The Trials Process

T HE AAU organized 21 Regional Qualifier tournaments in March and April. They announced that the Final Team Trials would be held as planned in Madison in May and the Final wrestle-offs and training Camp at Brockport in June. The top six place-winners from Madison would be eligible to advance to Brockport.

The Wrestling Division of the AAU nominated Gable as head Olympic Freestyle team coach and Dziedzic, who retired from competition and became the National AAU wrestling coach, as Freestyle team manager. On the Greco side, Californian Lee Allen was selected as the Greco team coach and Wayne Baughman as Greco team manager.

Before hearing the stories of the wrestlers who did compete in the Trials, here is one from a highly ranked US wrestler at the time who decided not to participate – once he learned of the boycott.

Boycott Victim

M ARK Lieberman was a three-time National prep champion at Blair Academy and two-time NCAA champion at Lehigh University. Lieberman talks about his experience at the '76 Trials and his decision not to enter the 1980 competition:

In 1976, while I was red-shirting at Lehigh, my brother Mike and I entered the Olympic Trials. We decided to go to the Regional in Glassboro, New Jersey at different weights so we wouldn't have to meet each other. However, Mike missed making weight at 180.5, so we both ended up at 198. Sure enough, we ended up facing each other. I beat him 5-3. That was somewhat shattering – beating my older brother, and idol, for the first time.

We both advanced to the '76 Final Trials in Cleveland at 180.5. That was a tough weight class. Wouldn't you know, Mike and I meet each other once again and I pinned him – not pleasant. I ended up 5th and qualified for the Final Camp.

I didn't make the '76 team, but had some great collegiate and Freestyle competition over the next few years. I went to the Tbilisi tournament, which was an unbelievable experience. It was an awakening to see the true competitive nature of the international sport. I never won a bout there.

In the years and months of training leading up to the '80 Trials, I faced top Freestyle competition, particularly John Peterson and Chris Campbell.

Russ Hellickson, top, had little trouble winning his second Olympic team spot at 220 pounds
Photograph courtesy of Amateur Wrestling News

The first time I ever wrestled Peterson, sometime in the mid-'70s, he beat me by 20 points. The next time it was 8-3. Then in the Midland finals I lost to him, 3-2. I was getting closer. However, the next time out he got me, 17-6. Finally, in the '78 USWF Nationals held on Long Island, I pinned him. That was great, but bittersweet. Like my older brother, for many years he was my hero.

I wrestled Campbell a number of times. He usually beat me, although I did pin him at the '77 National AAUs on my way to winning the 180.5 title.

During those years from '76 through '80 I wrestled for the NYAC but elected to stay at Lehigh to do my training and continue my education. Thad Turner was a phenomenal coach, yet I realized that I was missing out. I had no world-class competition in my regular workouts. The reality was that I needed a more intense environment to reach my goal of becoming an Olympic champion.

Beginning in January of 1980, I went out to the Midwest for some training. I remember spending a week at Iowa, and another week or so at Nebraska and Minnesota. My body was in pretty fair shape but I knew I had a tough task ahead of me with Campbell and Peterson still in my weight class. They were among the best in the world. I thought that if I could win the Trials, I would win an Olympic medal.

I went to the National AAUs in April and met Campbell in the finals. He beat me decisively. I was aware of the pending boycott of the Moscow games. I added it up and decided to forgo the Trials. The odds were against me actually wrestling in the Olympics, which was my goal. I made the decision to stay at Lehigh and continue working on my MBA. It was a difficult decision but I convinced myself to look for new challenges.

The Final Olympic Team Trials, Madison, Wisconsin, May 8-13, 1980

THE announcement of the boycott severely affected the number of wrestlers competing at the Trials. Only 150 or so turned out, less than half the total in '76. Besides Mark Lieberman, other highly ranked wrestlers such as Lee Kemp, Bruce Kinseth and Brad Reinghans decided to skip the Madison tournament altogether.

Quite a few wrestlers got knocked by the wayside due to injuries received either right before the Trials or during the Trials themselves. Don Shuler, always in the mix with the best US 180-pounders, broke his leg prior to the Trials and couldn't compete.

The Oklahoma wrestlers seemed particularly snake-bitten. Lee Roy Smith, who was voted the Outstanding Wrestler at the USWF National Open Freestyle championship in April, injured his leg in the Trials and finished 7th at 149.5. He withdrew from further competition. Andre Metzger, a finalist in the '79 and '80 National AAUs, broke his leg and was done while battling NCAA champion Steve Barrett in a late-round 149.5 match. Eric Wais, 1979 NCAA Champion at 190, injured his knee and withdrew. Heavyweight favorite Jimmy Jackson injured his shoulder, finished 3rd and did not make it to the final round-robin at Brockport.

Bobby Weaver sprained his shoulder and dropped to 6th place, just making the Brockport wrestle-offs. Gene Mills was injured in his match with Joe Corso and didn't place, but earned a medical hardship waiver to wrestle-off at 114.5 at Brockport.

Twenty-year-old Dave Schultz pulled off a surprise move. In late March, Schultz's dramatic victory over his Russian opponent at 149.5 was key to helping the US team beat the Russians in the World Cup. Six weeks later at the Trials, Schultz moves up to 163 — the weight class that Lee Kemp had dominated internationally for several years. Was Schultz expecting Kemp to compete or not?

Finally, after six days of bouts at the

Andre Metzger, right, was a favorite at 149.5 but had to drop out of the Trials after breaking his leg
Photograph by Roy Hobson, courtesy of Amateur Wrestling News

University of Wisconsin Field House, 20 wrestlers emerged victorious. Seven former Olympians won their weight division — Bill Rosado, Jim Haines, Joe Corso and Russ Hellickson in Freestyle and Bruce Thompson, John Matthews and Dan Chandler in Greco. The Peterson brothers were runners-ups to Chris Campbell and Laurent Soucie, respectively. The other Freestyle winners were Randy Lewis, Steve Barrett, Dave Schultz, and Greg Wojciechowski. Other Greco winners included T.J. Jones, Brian Gust, John Hughes, Tom Minkel, Mark Johnson, Greg Gibson and Wojciechowski.

It was on to Brockport six weeks later for the Final Camp and the wrestle-offs.

The Final Camp, Brockport, New York, June 18 – June 22, 1980

A DIFFERENT, almost indifferent, atmosphere pervaded the 1980 Final Camp. It really wasn't a Camp per se, not as the wrestlers and coaches knew it from their experiences at prior Olympic Trials. Wrestlers kind of just showed up, wrestled and went home.

Some wrestlers who did not compete at Madison, like John Azevedo, Lee Kemp and Brad Reinghans, decided to come and wrestle at Brockport. A couple of Trials champions, Jim Haines and Steve Barrett, decided it wasn't worth it and didn't appear at all. The 1976 Olympian Joe Corso broke his leg while playing soccer shortly after winning the Trials and was unable to enter the wrestle-offs.

Nevertheless, there were some awesome performances and heightened competition between some very, very good wrestlers. Bobby Weaver fought his way up from 6th to take the 105.5 spot. Chuck Yagla turned into a pinning machine. Lee Kemp and Dave Schultz had two of their most intense matches ever. And at 180.5, Ed Banach, Chris Campbell and John Peterson threw each other around in a wild three-way wrestle-off.

Freestyle team manager Dzeidzic explains why Brockport was selected as the site for such an important event:

Brockport was chosen, both in '76 and '80, because of Don Murray, the head coach at Brockport State University. Don was well known as a worker in the international wrestling community. He wanted to host the Trials at Brockport and was willing to do the work to bring them there.

Bobby Weaver talks about the time between the '76 Trials and '80 Trials and his personal experiences:

It took me two or three years to catch up with Bill Rosado and take command of our rivalry at 105.5. He set the bar and I gradually started climbing it. Finally, I beat him to win the National AAUs in '78 and again to make the US World team in '79. We'd work out a lot together and by the '80 Trials we knew each other's offense and defense thoroughly and what to avoid.

In the meantime, I graduated from Easton High in '77 and went to Blair Academy for a post-grad year. That helped me both academically and athletically. I got my grades and SATs up high enough to qualify for admission to Lehigh, which is where I wanted to go to college. Tom Hutchinson was a great coach for me at Blair especially teaching me how to get out from

underneath. I won the National Preps in '78. My freshman year at Lehigh I was on the wrestling squad, but my record was only 1-2-1. I was competing at 118 even though I only weighed around 110. I sat out the '79-'80 college season, working on my studies and preparing myself for the Olympic Trials.

By the time the Trials came around I had been wrestling well in Freestyle. I won my weight class in the '80 World Cup, won the USWF Nationals at 114.5 and the AAU Nationals at 105.5. However, when I went to the Trials at Madison, I ran into a problem. While wrestling Richard Salamone, a teammate from the NYAC, I sprained my shoulder. I didn't forfeit, but I couldn't wrestle well at all and lost to Salamone and then to Rosado.

In the one month interim, my shoulder recovered and I headed up to Brockport. I had to beat three guys to get into the final two-out-of-three round-robin. I did so and it was down to Rosado, Salamone and me.

I can't remember for sure who I wrestled first in the round-robin. I think it was Rosado. I decisioned him once and then pinned him. Then I had to wrestle Salamone, whom I pinned to win the tournament.

Chuck Yagla was probably the most dominant wrestler at Brockport. He recalls his campaign to make the US Olympic team and some thoughts about the Soviets:

After using up my college eligibility in '76, I needed a fifth year at the University of Iowa to get my degree. I was an Education major, married and working part-time in construction. On the mats, I turned all my attention to Freestyle.

In November of '76, I went to the Great Plains tournament, hoping to win and to qualify to wrestle in Tbilisi. I got to the finals where my opponent was a high school senior from California. This young guy had been following me around all weekend asking if he could have his picture taken with me, asking for tips on wrestling, and so on. I was a two-time NCAA champion now and didn't worry much about high school wrestlers. However, this 16 year-old kid, Dave Schultz, pinned me and he got to go to Tbilisi — the first of many trips he made to Russia. Oh, yea, I forgot, they gave me the Sportsmanship award.

After getting my degree from Iowa, I went looking for work. The University of Oklahoma called and offered me the job as their second assistant. I talked to Coach Gable to see if Iowa had anything similar for me. He said he wasn't allowed to hire another assistant coach. The next day, I got a call from the Iowa athletic office. They said they would match the Oklahoma offer, so I eagerly joined Gable's staff and also became the Executive Director of the Hawkeye Club.

By 1979 I was basically on target to meet my goal of making the US Olympic team. I won the National AAUs in '77, ' 78, and '79 and made the US World team in '77 and '79. I lost to Kemp while wrestling up at 163 in trying to make the '78 team — which is the year that he went on to win the Worlds.

In November of '79 while training, I tore something in my right knee. I had surgery but it wasn't successful. They had to cut me two more times to get it right. I couldn't wrestle at the Midlands, though I started practicing again in January. My first live competition was the National AAUs. I lost to Andre Metzger and someone else and placed 6th. From there I went to USWF Nationals, lost to Doug Parise and finished 3rd.

I had lost my aggressiveness; I didn't feel comfortable going down to my knees.

At the Madison Trials, I went up against Steve Barrett. I had worked out with Steve many times and never had much trouble with him. However, he beat me in a wild-scoring match. I never thought I could lose to him, but I did. It really hit me bad. I remember after the match I went outside the gym and cried. I was so frustrated that it wasn't the same 'me' out there on the mats as it had been for the past four years. I ended up 4th behind Barrett, Jim Humphrey and Andy Rein.

However, I was not about to give up. I went back to Iowa City and worked extremely hard for the next month in preparation for the wrestle-offs in Brockport. My knee kept getting better.

For some reason, Barrett didn't come to the wrestle-offs. I think he knew we weren't going to be competing in the Olympics, so why bother to make the team. Anyway, that boosted me up to 3rd place and I didn't have to enter the mini-

tournament. Phil Anglim ended up winning that competition.

So now it was the four of us, Humphrey, Rein, Anglim and me, in the round-robin, having to wrestle three days straight. I was feeling good and had my weight pretty much under control. My first round-robin opponent was Rein. He was the one I feared the most. I wrestled well and beat him in the first match 12-7 and then pinned him in the second match. The next day Humphrey and I wrestled each other and I pinned him twice. Then, on day three it was Anglim and me, and again I got two pins. I felt great, especially with all those pins.

Making the US Olympic team was huge for me. It had been my goal for years. Obviously I was disheartened; I was disappointed that I couldn't compete in Moscow, but I also saw another side of it. I had already been to Russia twice and I knew how bad it was over there. I also knew that they were going to sensationalize the USSR during the Games and the world wouldn't be seeing how truly bad it was there. I figured that we might as well not give the Russians their chance to sensationalize their country and way of life.

Lee Kemp, World Champion in 1978 and 1979, had a change of heart after skipping the Madison Trials and received permission to try to make the team through the wrestle-offs at Brockport. In an article years later in the *Boston Globe*, Kemp called his wrestle-off match with Schultz "probably one of the hardest battles we ever had and it was just to get a uniform."

Kemp recalls:

I had been training hard all year and won my match in the World Cup, helping our US team beat Russia for the first time. However, by the time of the Trials in Madison, the word was out that we weren't going to Moscow. Like a number of other wrestlers I said 'heck with it'. I didn't go to the Madison Trials. I wasn't interested in just making the Olympic team; I was interested in winning the gold medal.

Shortly after the Trials, my former college coach, Duane Kleven, talked to me and challenged me to make the team. He told me, 'Go do it. Some day it will be important to you'.

So, I went back into training and the AAU

> **The University of Oklahoma called and offered me the job as their second assistant. I talked to Coach Gable to see if Iowa had anything similar for me. He said he wasn't allowed to hire another assistant coach. The next day, I got a call from the Iowa athletic office. They said they would match the Oklahoma offer.**
>
> **– CHUCK YAGLA**

● ●

allowed me to go to Brockport to compete. Only three guys showed up at 163 — Grant Smith from the University of Wisconsin, Dave Schultz and me. I beat Smith and was then supposed to wrestle Schultz two-out-of-three. Dave came up to me a few hours before the scheduled matches and said that he wouldn't be able to wrestle. He had a boil on his neck. The officials agreed and decided the matches would be postponed one week. I went back to Wisconsin for some more training.

I knew Dave would be tough, although at that point I had beaten him every time we had met, going back to my senior year in college.

About a week later Dave and I finally wrestled our Trials bouts. It was just the two of us, the officials and a small handful of wrestlers in the gym. Those were very hard-fought matches. I won the first one real close. The second one I remember the most. Dave was the young, upstart underdog, a favorite of the fans and the officials. In that second match, the officials started getting on me for stalling and that bothered me. I took offense, literally, and started to get more physical. I beat Dave worse than I ever had before. There is a picture of me having my hand raised by the official at the end of the match and I had a terrifically intense look in my eyes.

I felt empty, yet I was relieved to win. My coach was right; making the '80 Olympic team did become important to me, especially since I never actually did get to wrestle in the Games themselves.

The decision to boycott hurt a lot of people. It was frustrating because we had such a great

team. We had just beaten the Russians in the World Cup and we felt we were ready to show the world that the American wrestlers could beat the Soviet wrestlers in the Olympics.

Mitch Hull, who was in the mix with Mark Johnson, Laurent Soucie and Mike Houck to make the Greco team at 198, notes this about his Wisconsin Wrestling Club teammate:

Lee Kemp was the athlete most affected by the boycott. He lost more than any other wrestler in our country's decision not to participate in Moscow. Being the World Champion in '78 and '79, Kemp would have won the Olympic Gold and then retired. Instead he had to hold on for four more years to try and win the Olympics, which, as we now know, didn't happen.

125.5 pounds Freestyle — Nick Gallo vs John Azevedo

EAST Coast against West Coast. It was a bit of a surprise to see Nick Gallo and John Azevedo wrestling-off in the final round-robin for the Olympic berth at 125.5. Not that they weren't accomplished wrestlers — both were NCAA champions. However, Joe Corso had more or less dominated that US Freestyle weight class since the '76 Olympics, with his main competition coming from Jack Reinwand and Mark Mangianti. With Corso now on the sidelines, the field opened up.

Nick Gallo tells his story:

I was small as a youngster and other kids would constantly pick on me. Being Italian, I'd mouth off back to them and usually get into a fight. So, I learned some wrestling moves early on and then I could beat up the bullies and no one picked on me. The other reason I started to wrestle was because the high school wrestlers were the 'coolest' guys in school. When I made the Deer Park [New York] varsity team as a ninth-grader the older guys took me under their wing and I felt great.

I was a naturally good wrestler, but the best I ever did in the New York states was 4th place as a senior. I wasn't a very mature teenager — I didn't start shaving until I got to college.

I was only mildly recruited; no one was ter-

John Azvedo and Nick Gallo went down to the wire in their quest for an Olympic team berth. Azvedo won out at the end. *Photograph by Mike Miller, courtesy of* Amateur Wrestling News

ribly interested in me as a potential college wrestler. I remember writing Dan Gable a letter to see if Iowa was interested in me. He wrote me back saying that they only looked at the top two or three wrestlers in any state and wished me well. I still have the letter and I kid Dan about it to this day.

After looking at a couple of out-of-state schools, I decided to stay nearby and go to Hofstra. I finally matured physically after my senior high school season and I picked up an incredible amount of strength. I did well my freshman year, going 13-0 at 126. I wasn't cutting any weight. I got the basic moves working better and was stronger than anyone I wrestled, even though I didn't look it. My body was very flexible and I had a 'gumby' style that worked for me.

In my sophomore year, 1975, I made it to the NCAAs in an incredibly tough weight class, 118 pounds. I lost to Jim Brown of Michigan by something like 15-13 in the semi-finals and finished 4th.

[Author's note: Ten wrestlers competing in that weight class would be Division I NCAA finalists at one time or another, including six who were crowned NCAA champions.]

In my junior year I had some problems with my weight, injuries and the coach. I didn't wrestle particularly well. After the season I entered the '76 Olympic Trials in Cleveland. Bill Farrell and the NYAC wanted me to compete at 125.5 but I didn't want to cut all the way down there. So, I went at 136.5, not as a NYAC team member, and did okay, placing 6th. That qualified me for the Brockport Camp. While I didn't make the team, I got to stay on at the Camp as a workout partner and that experience helped me immensely. I remember wrestling a lot with Gene Davis. He would really beat up on me but I learned a lot in the month that I worked out with those great wrestlers.

My senior year at Hofstra, I wrestled most of the season at 134 and really wrestled well. I went into the NCAAs with a great attitude and ended up cruising through them. I never had the goal of being named the Outstanding Wrestler, but they did award it to me and that was like icing on a great cake.

After graduation in '77, I had a nice offer to go out to Colorado as the second assistant coach with their University wrestling team. However, I think Bill Farrell went into a panic when he heard about it and made me an offer to stay home and work at his company — TW Promotions — where I have been employed ever since.

I wrestled competitively in Freestyle for several years, always placing but never winning the big one. I think I was caught between weight classes. 125.5 was very difficult for me to make and at 136.5 I was often wrestling guys bigger than me, such as Randy Lewis and Andre Metzger.

In the spring of 1980, I made the US World Cup team and competed in Toledo at 125.5 against Japan, Canada and Russia. I won my matches against Japan and Canada easily. I then wrestled Sergei Beloglazov and stayed even with him for a while. I ripped his shoulder hard midway through the match. He got mad and came back to trounce me. He was so technically sound; I could never catch him leaving an arm, leg or elbow behind.

I tried to prepare myself for the Olympic Trials but I had an awful lot going on in my life, particularly my job — supplying equipment for wrestling camps, running our shoe sales program, and so on. I was also the head wrestling coach over at Hofstra. There were a lot of distractions that kept me from clearly focusing on my wrestling. In May I went to the Trials tournament at 136.5 pounds and finished 3rd behind Randy Lewis and Tim Cysewski.

Gable asked me to take a leave of absence from all the work stuff and come out to Iowa and train for the Final Trials. That was my plan until I heard about the boycott and then I decided to stay back East. I was no longer that interested in making the team.

After the Madison Trials, Gene Mills called me and said that he was going to go to Brockport at 125.5 and that as his NYAC teammate I should go at 136.5 and both try to make the team. The NYAC coaches, Sonny Greenhalgh

> **I was preparing myself to wrestle-off at 136.5 until I showed up at Brockport. That's when Gene tells me that he's decided to drop down to 114.5. Now the coaches want me to be at 125.5. Meanwhile, I am weighing around 145.**
>
> — NICK GALLO

and Bill Farrell, wanted to see both of us on the team. So I was preparing myself to wrestle-off at 136.5 until I showed up at Brockport. That's when Gene tells me that he's decided to drop down to 114.5. Now the coaches want me to be at 125.5. Meanwhile, I am weighing around 145.

I kill myself getting those 20 pounds off, but I do make weight. I find out that Joe Corso, the top seed, injured himself and is not wrestling. I have to wrestle Jack Reinwand twice and I beat him by seven or eight points each time. Meanwhile, in the other round-robin, Mark Mangianti beats John Azevedo in their first bout, but is injured in the second match and cannot continue. The tournament coordinator, Stan Dziedzic, pulls me aside and tells me that even though I have won my two bouts and Azevedo lost one before the injury, the Wrestling Committee wants a best-of-three wrestle-off between the two of us. This is a Thursday and he tells me that the wrestle-off will be on Sunday.

I say 'okay, but I need a weight allowance.' He tells me, 'no, you gotta go at flat weight,' so I have to sit around for a couple of days dehydrated and keep my weight in check. Come Sunday, I am feeling like garbage — like I had some sort of electrolyte shock from pulling weight. I couldn't run or do much of anything. I don't know how I made it through the matches. Azevedo and I split our first two bouts but by then I am feeling really numb. Before our third and deciding match, my coach and trainer, Chick Murano, gives me a rubdown but I can't feel anything. I go back out for the last match hoping to score early and hang on. I couldn't do it. I had nothing left and John won.

I don't use these as excuses for losing to John. I underestimated him and he was a good, smart wrestler. He was very flexible and wrestled a lot like me. He did everything right and I have a lot of respect for him.

I have no regrets about my career even though I never became an Olympian. I knew I didn't have to prove anything to anyone, so there was no real disappointment. My career was as good as I ever envisioned.

California native John Azevedo recalls his wrestling days:

I started wrestling in sixth grade after seeing my older brother wrestle. I trained and competed in AAU Freestyle tournaments exclusively my first three years until I entered high school. That would be Grace Davis High School in Modesto where I became a two-time California state champion.

During my high school days I was already wrestling year-round. In my junior year, I finished 2nd in the Junior Nationals and won them my senior year, 1975. I was undefeated in Folkstyle and Freestyle as a senior and was recruited to wrestle at Oklahoma State. I went there because I wanted to be with the best.

I wrestled at OSU as a true freshman, splitting time with another wrestler at 118. I went to Midlands, finishing 2nd. However, I lost the team wrestle-off at the end of the season and didn't go to the Big 8s or NCAAs. I was pretty bummed out. I thought I was a better wrestler than the starter in competition, but lost out in the practice room.

I returned to Oklahoma State my sophomore year, but left before the wrestling season started and transferred to Cal State Bakersfield. I did much better there; my record at Bakersfield was 122-2. I red-shirted during the transfer year, but made it to the NCAA finals both my sophomore and junior years. I lost both times, the only two losses during my three years at Bakersfield.

My senior year, 1980, was a very good year for me. I had two goals — win the NCAAs and make the US Olympic team. I trained year round, working with Dan Gable and Stan Dziedzic at the summer Freestyle camps and with Joe Seay as my personal coach and college coach. The NCAAs were my first priority and I finally did win them in March at 126 pounds.

From there I went to the National AAUs in Madison and finished 5th. I don't remember much about that tournament or why I didn't return to Madison in May for the Trials tournament. I think that perhaps I didn't have to qualify at Madison in order to get to Brockport.

I do remember Brockport though. In my first match I wrestled Mark Mangianti, who was runner-up to Joe Corso at the Trials tournament. He beat me in our first bout. I remember going back to my dorm room after the bout and contemplating how quickly it could all be over if I didn't win the next two bouts. I remember telling myself to relax and I asked the Lord for His help.

During my next match with Mangianti, he gets hurt, has to injury-default to me and drops out of the tournament. I don't remember how or when he was injured. On the other side of the round-robin, Nick Gallo and Jack Reinwand are fighting it out. Gallo beat Reinwand, so now it was between the two of us for the Olympic team.

In our first match, Gallo is ahead of me until the last few seconds when I pick up a couple of points to win by one. Then he beats me in our next bout. These are fierce battles. In the third bout, I don't recall the details but I was ahead most of the time and end up winning in a closely contested match. What a relief for me. I was very happy to make the Olympic team, but it could have gone either way. All those matches at Brockport were tough, grueling matches for me.

I credit my faith in God — He was in control. I was thankful that I had made the Olympic team and that I fulfilled my goal. Actually, for a good while after making the team I really thought we'd go to Moscow. I thought they would never really follow through with their threat to boycott. When they did, it was disappointing, but I wasn't ever angry like some others were. I was relatively young, 23, and I said, 'Well, I'll make it next time.' Actually, I was more disappointed with losing out in 1984 than I was in 1980.

The Brockport Trials wrestle-offs were really a great event. They were certainly not as glamorous an event as they are today, but it was tough, high caliber wrestling with family, coaches and close friends supporting each wrestler. It was fun and very, very competitive.

> "I remember the scene at Brockport when we understood that we were definitely not going to participate in the Games. Gene Mills took the news particularly hard – as did Campbell and Chuck Yagla. These guys were on top of their game, were cutting a lot of weight and knew that this was probably their last chance to wrestle in the Olympics. It was very sad to see.
>
> **– ED BANACH**

● ●

180.5 pounds Freestyle – Ed Banach vs Chris Campbell vs John Peterson

SEVERAL former and future Olympic and World champions competed in the 180.5 weight class. Teenager Mark Schultz didn't make it into the top six in Madison. In the final round-robin, the three left standing were the young gun (Banach), the chiseled veteran (Campbell) and the aging warrior (Peterson). Their stories follow.

Ed Banach, a freshman NCAA Champion in '80 from the University of Iowa, recalls:

While watching the 1972 games on TV where the US won three gold medals, I decided then and there that my goal was to be an Olympic wrestling champion.

I was born in Newton, NJ a few minutes ahead of my twin brother Lou. I was one of 15 kids in my family. At the age of two our house burned down. I remember standing outside holding Lou's hand and watching everything our family owned go up in flames. Our family disbursed. Lou and I and our older brother Steve ended up being adopted by a family in Port Jervis, New York.

I wrestled a bit in junior high and then wrestled for Mark Faller at Port Jervis high school. In the summer of '76, even though I was just a sophomore, Faller urged me to try out for the

Olympics. I went to the District Trials and went 2-2. I was not good enough to qualify for the Final Trials tournament but it exposed me to the type of training I would need to get in order to reach my Olympic goal. I saw then that my dream of being an Olympic champion could be a reality. As I watched the '76 Olympic Games on TV I would daydream in my mind that I was there and that I would pin John Peterson to make the team.

In 1977 I finished 2ⁿᵈ in the NY states and I won the title as a senior in '78. I competed in the Junior Nationals out in Iowa City and was impressed with the field house and overall wrestling atmosphere. My brother and I were exposed to Gable and we decided that Iowa would be the best place for us — both for a college wrestling experience and also as a way to fulfill my Olympic dreams.

I won the NCAAs as a red-shirt freshman and then set my sights on the Trials. I entered the Trials tournament in Madison and took a 5ᵗʰ place, which was good enough to get me to the wrestle-offs in Brockport. I was a good upper-body wrestler and could pin guys off my throws.

At Brockport I was in the final round-robin with Chris Campbell and John Peterson. I first had to wrestle Campbell. I was really in awe of Chris since we had worked out together some in the Iowa practice room. I came out very aggressive, caught him several times with my throws and beat him, 15-7.

However, Chris came back to beat me twice in succession, 7-4 and 15-8. He was really a lot better than me technically.

When I wrestled Peterson, it was the first time we ever met. I pinned him in our first match — just like I had dreamed while watching the '76 Games. I basically caught him with a high-crotch move. But he was too good for me and never let me get that move on him again. He beat me with his double-leg drops in the next two matches.

I had come so close, but I knew that I needed to work on things so that I could beat the top competition consistently. After my matches with Peterson and Campbell, Gable came up to me and asked, 'How come you beat Peterson? How come you then lost to him? How come you beat Campbell? How come you then lost to him?'

Gable was very canny in his way of getting me to ask myself why they beat me, what they did to win, and what I didn't do. I recognized that in wrestling both Peterson and Campbell, that I was fortunate the first time around with each of them. The next times, they caught-on to me and beat me because they were more disciplined and had sounder technical skills.

I remember the scene at Brockport when we understood that we were definitely not going to participate in the Games. Gene Mills took the news particularly hard — as did Campbell and Chuck Yagla. These guys were on top of their game, were cutting a lot of weight and knew that this was probably their last chance to wrestle in the Olympics. It was very sad to see that they had set their sights on a goal, they worked so hard for it and made it — and then that goal was taken away from them. The whole atmosphere after the final round-robin was a true sense of loss.

Chris Campbell remembers his experiences:

I started wrestling at the YMCA while in grade school. In seventh grade I played basketball, but wasn't particularly good at it, so I went out for wrestling. In ninth and tenth grade I was on the JV team at Westfield [New Jersey] high school, but didn't wrestle the next year since my mother wouldn't let me compete. I did, however, workout with some junior college wrestlers. I was always quick and that year my strength really developed. When my mom did finally sign the waiver allowing me to wrestle for Westfield my senior year, I went undefeated and won the states, pinning all 26 of my opponents.

I went to the Junior Nationals in my senior year, 1973, and finished 2nd to Mark Johnson.

I accepted a 'walk-on' invitation from Dan Gable to wrestle at the University of Iowa. Richie Sofman, then the coach at Montclair State, tried to recruit me but once I told him that I didn't want to go to Montclair State, he told me to go wrestle for Gable.

When I got to Iowa in the fall of '73 it was a huge culture shock. It was really different from New Jersey in several aspects. There was the college party life which I never saw before; also, I was a black kid in a very white Midwest envi-

ronment. The University of Iowa didn't have black wrestlers. However, the coaches, Gable and J Robinson, were so good it made up for all the other distractions. They were both geniuses in their own rights.

I wrestled as a freshman on the Iowa team in '74 at 177. I had a good year, winning the Big Ten tournament and being voted the Outstanding Wrestler. However, at the NCAAs, I lost in the first round to a guy from Rutgers — my home state — and was eliminated. That was terrible. The following year, I made it to the NCAA finals which were held at Princeton University, not far from my hometown. I lost to Mike Lieberman by a point. That really upset me, but I came back to win the NCAAs my junior and senior year.

After graduation, I got my first taste of international wrestling when I made the US team for the '77 Worlds in Switzerland. I really didn't understand the significance of the Worlds and finished a disappointing 5th. I didn't wrestle smart; I didn't think; I just wasn't focused.

During the next two years, I wrestled in Freestyle tournaments off-and-on but the big turning point for me was when Harold Nichols offered me the job as an assistant wrestling coach for the '79-'80 season. Iowa State was a more favorable environment for a black guy like me. They were accustomed to recruiting good black wrestlers and I felt comfortable there. I had some great training partners, particularly Willie Gadson. I changed my habits, became a vegetarian and really focused on the upcoming Trials.

I felt that by 1980, I had pulled far ahead of anyone in my weight class. What spurred me on was the feeling that in the past few years, I had been losing some close matches due to stalling calls. I thought that maybe those stalling calls were racially biased. I decided that I needed to train myself to beat the other guys so badly that I couldn't get screwed by a racist call. I knew that I couldn't afford to keep the score close and I needed to beat everyone by at least ten points.

I won the National AAU freestyle tournament at Madison, beating Mark Lieberman, 23-6 in the finals. I then went back to Madison for the Trials and defeated John Peterson to win the tournament. At Brockport, again Peterson was my toughest competition. In our first bout

Chris Campbell and John Peterson fought it out for the 180.5 Olympic slot
Photograph by Scott Conroe, courtesy of Amateur Wrestling News

it was close as John hit me with a crotch lift and when he took me to the mat I thought he almost broke my neck. I squeaked by him in that match and then beat him convincingly in our second match to make the Olympic team.

I was incredibly angry at President Carter for sacrificing the ambitions of many American athletes for what was an empty justice. Carter was a coward, which is a polite way to state how I felt.

John Peterson has his say:
After the '76 Olympics, Ben and I set one more goal. We wanted to win a gold medal in the World championships. Well, we didn't achieve that; the closest we got was my silver in '79. So we decided to give the Olympics one last shot. We were both over 30 years-old and knew going in that this would be our last competition.

Before the Trials started I knew that we were going to boycott the Olympics and that made it tough to get motivated. Plus my wife was very pregnant and that was on my mind. See, I got my excuses.

I had been out in California working with the Athletes-In-Action team and in the spring of '80 I came back to the Midwest to start some intense training. I really don't recall much of the Trials tournament in Madison other than it was held at the old Field House on the University campus which was very familiar to me. That's where I had wrestled in the high school state tournament about 15 years earlier. Anyway, I finished 2nd to Chris Campbell.

I remember our Brockport matches much more vividly. In our first match, we ended up tied, but Chris was victorious because I had received more points on penalties that were called for his stalling. Doesn't that seem weird? I guess in this case stalling paid off. Think about it.

In our second and final match, I went out ahead and took him down a couple of times. My double-leg was still my best move. At one point I took Chris down and thought I had him turned for back points. I was putting a lot of pressure on his neck but the officials stopped the match fearful of a neck injury. Chris always accuses me of trying to hurt his neck, but I tell him, 'Chris, if you would have just turned over on your back, your neck wouldn't have been hurting so much.'

Anyway, he took me down with his slick high-crotch move more than I took him down with my double-leg and he beat me in my final match of my career. I didn't like going out losing my last bout, but I was not ashamed of who I lost to. There were some great matches and I had no animosity at all towards any of my competitors.

You know, 180.5 was a tough weight class with Lieberman, Campbell, Shuler, Banach, Mark Schultz and me. I'll share a couple of thoughts about some of these guys.

In '78 Mark Lieberman beat me in the Federation Nationals. I hadn't lost to him before but this time he pinned me. However, a month or so later we wrestled in the National AAU championships and I got back at him and beat him. For awhile, whenever I wanted to get motivated, I'd put on a Lehigh wrestling shirt.

Don Shuler was very tough. Unfortunately, he broke his leg before the Trials started. Otherwise I think he would have made the final round-robin along with Campbell and me.

And Ed Banach was coming on strong. He was a real whirlwind out there. After our final match at Brockport, I remember shaking his hand and saying to him, 'It's all yours from here on in, Banach. I'm not going to try to wrestle you again. This is my last competition.'

Several other wrestlers who won berths on the Olympic team talk about their experiences and their feelings about the US boycott.

Greco competitor and three-time Olympian Dan Chandler speaks out:

We were in a tournament in Budapest in early 1980 when I heard that President Carter said America was going to boycott the Olympics. I didn't actually believe that would happen. I held out hope that the USOC would allow our athletes to compete. Finally the IOC said they needed the final list of entrants and when the US didn't submit one, only then did I understand that we weren't going.

I grew up in Anoka, Minnesota, which was a hotbed of Greco-Roman wrestling. I wrestled for Coach Ron Malcolm in high school and got involved with Greco through the Minnesota Wrestling Club and their great people like Alan Rice and Larry Lyden. I wrestled for the University of Minnesota, but found better success in Greco. I was six foot one, almost all legs. When I saw that in Greco my opponents couldn't get to my legs like they could easily do in Folkstyle and Freestyle, I took to it and learned how to use my height to my advantage.

The event that elevated our wrestling club to new heights was an extended visit by the Polish national Greco team to Minnesota in 1974. They brought over their Olympic stars like Kazimierz Lipien and Czeslaw Kwiecinski and showed us techniques we had never seen before. That put us at the top of the US Greco world; in fact, in 1979 seven of the Greco wrestlers in the Pan-Am games were from our club.

Through the '80 Trials, I really didn't have any competitors that I couldn't beat rather handily. My toughest opponents from prior years changed weight classes. Mark Johnson went up to 198 and Abdul Raheem-Ali went down. I ended up in the finals, twice beating teenager Phil Lanzatella to win my second Olympic berth.

We did go as a team to the White House that summer. That was fun with lots of parties and state dinners. Each Olympic team went through a reception line and shook hands with the President, his wife and daughter. The President was very smooth. The activists on the women's rowing team wore wrist bands that said, 'I'm here to make sure this never happens again.' I remember Chris Campbell somehow got one and when he went to shake the President's hand Chris gave it to him. The President smiled, said something like, 'Oh, you are giving this to me. How very kind of you.' He then put the bracelet in his pocket and introduced himself to the next person in line.

I was extremely pissed off about the whole

> " I went and told Coach Dziedzic that I wasn't going [to Tbilisi]. He threw a fit. I still wasn't going... until he said, 'Gene, I'm going to get you a whole bunch of Commies to wrestle and I'm sure you'd like nothing better than to get out on the mat and work them over.' That did it for me. I went on the trip and went 9-0.
>
> **– GENE MILLS**

thing myself. A lot of us put our careers on hold for a number of years. I had been in the top six in the world the prior three years and thought I had a great chance of winning a medal. I was sick, not only because I was being prohibited from competing, but also not being able to see my friends compete.

Gene Mills, the Freestyle 114.5-pound Olympian, tells a story or two:

I was an 88-pound butterball as a high school freshman when I began wrestling in Wayne, New Jersey. Wrestling was the sport for me and I went on to win the states as a senior and two NCAA championships at Syracuse University in '79 and '81.

My father taught me my favorite move — the half-nelson. I had a lot of trouble breaking guys down conventionally, so I learned how to put in the half and run it up over the top. It worked great for me.

In January of 1980 I made the US team that was traveling to the Tbilisi tournament. However, while training out in Nebraska, I heard that the President warned that no Americans should go to Russia or Iran because it was too dangerous for us over there. I believed him and was frightened that I might be held hostage. My parents told me, 'Don't go, Gene.' I made the decision not to make that trip.

I went and told Coach Dziedzic that I wasn't going. He threw a fit. He said I had to go, and that in the last 22 years we only had four Americans win there and he was sure I could do it. I still wasn't going... until he said, 'Gene, I'm going to get you a whole bunch of Commies to

wrestle and I'm sure you'd like nothing better than to get out on the mat and work them over.' That did it for me. I went on the trip and went 9-0.

After that trip I focused on getting ready for the Olympics. My buddy Ron Jones from New Jersey quit his job and stayed with me for three months to help me train.

I went to the wrestle-offs in Brockport still thinking we were going to compete in the Olympics. I wanted to pin my way through the Olympic Games and knew I needed to drop down to 114.5 to reach my goal. That was a tough pull for me but I made it. It was only after I won the wrestle-offs that I finally realized that we wouldn't be wrestling in the Games.

I was so mad. I wasn't pulling all that weight to have a good time. I was devastated, furious, angry, you name it. I would have liked to have been locked in a room with the president and make him pay. I had worked my ass off, earned the right to go and I wanted him to feel my pain.

Obviously, I didn't do that but I did get to see him on our team visit to Washington. One of his advisors had told him a little about me so as I approached him in the reception line, he says, 'Hello. I've heard about your half-Wilson, Mills'. I chuckled. I wanted to pin him right there. But, I kept my cool and just kept on walking through the line.

Heavyweight Greg Wojciechowski, coached and managed by the infamous Toledo trio of Dick Wilson, Joe Scalzo and Dick Torio, made good in his fourth try after finishing as the runner-up in the three previous Olympic Trials. He tells how happy he was to make the 1980 Olympic team:

In 1968 as a high school senior I qualified for the Trials and lost early in Freestyle. However, I made it to the finals in Greco before losing to Bob Roop. In '72, I finished 2nd to Chris Taylor in both styles.

In '76, I competed in the Trials at 220. Russ Hellickson was considerably better than me in Freestyle and Brad Reinghans came out of nowhere to beat me in the Greco finals. I had worked my way up the ladder, wrestling something like 21 matches, but to no avail.

Wojo finally made the Olympic team after finishing runner-up at the Trials in '68, '72 and '76
Photograph courtesy of Mark Osgood

a hell of a team. Gable was a great coach — the best one I ever had for international wrestling. He was my coach on the '78 World Team, too. He was sensible and realized that not everyone was a Dan Gable.

My goal was to make the team and after three near-misses, I finally did it. I knew when I won the final matches at Brockport that even though I wasn't going to compete in the Olympics, I had made the US Olympic wrestling team.

Now I could at least die happy.

I wrestled at heavyweight from '77 to '80 and won the AAUs three times. I was the best US heavyweight around at that time. I weighed around 250, had a wife and three kids, and was 30 years-old when 1980 rolled around. I was trying to raise a family on my teacher's salary and working on the loading docks part-time. I had to be selective in how much I could wrestle. For instance, I couldn't afford to tryout for the Pan-Am games.

In '80, I didn't go to the AAUs, but I entered the Trials and I peaked at the right time. I had no close matches in Freestyle or Greco. I beat Bruce Baumgartner in the District Qualifier pretty easily and again at Madison. He gave me some closer matches up at Brockport; you could see he was getting better all the time. I beat Jimmy Jackson pretty handily and he dropped out.

At the Brockport Camp, it was a bummer, knowing that we were not going to have a chance to wrestle in the Olympics. We could have had

1980 OLYMPIC TEAM MEMBERS

	FREESTYLE	GRECO-ROMAN
105.5	Bob Weaver	Mark Fuller
114.5	Gene Mills	Bruce Thompson
125.5	John Azevedo	Brian Gust
136.5	Randy Lewis	Dan Mello
149.5	Chuck Yagla	Tom Minkel
163	Lee Kemp	John Matthews
180.5	Chris Campbell	Dan Chandler
198	Ben Peterson	Mark Johnson
220	Russ Hellickson	Brad Reinghans
UNL	Greg Wojciechowski	Jeff Blatnick

★ TEAM members, along with two guests, were invited to Washington for two weeks. They had pictures taken with President Carter, had tours of the White House and were given two Olympic medals - one from Congress and one from the USOC. It is doubtful if everyone kept theirs.

1980 PRESIDENTIAL ELECTION

★ AS THE incumbent, Carter was acknowledged to have a slim lead in the polls until the final weekend of the campaign, where Reagan outshined him in the TV debate. Carter's reference to his consultation with 12-year-old daughter Amy on nuclear weapons policy didn't help him either.

THE SCORECARD

Jimmy Carter Walter F. Mondale	49 Electoral Votes 41.1% of Popular Vote
Ronald Reagan George H. W. Bush	489 Electoral Votes 50.7% of Popular Vote

PASSING THE TORCH

SINCE it was still recognized by FILA as the national governing body in the US, the wrestling division of the AAU maintained its control of the 1980 Olympic Trials. The ongoing fight between the AAU and the USWF for recognition as the official body involved many leaders in our sport and reached the international borders of Switzerland and the court rooms of America. No one knew it for sure at the time, but after eight decades of AAU control, 1980 would be the last time that the Olympic Wrestling Trials were organized and run by the AAU.

The Trials were about to be transfigured.

THEY DOTH
PROTEST
TOO MUCH

1984

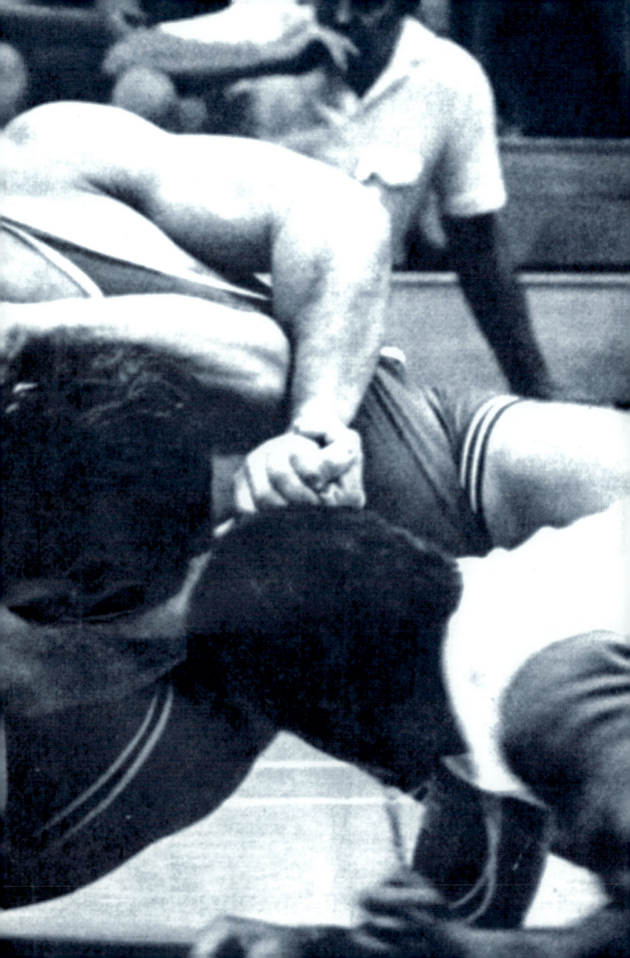

Nineteen Eighty-Four has, at times, been seen as revolutionary and politically dangerous...

– Wikipedia, the online encyclopedia, describing George Orwell's dystopian novel

AND IT'S not a bad way of describing the 1984 US Olympic Wrestling Trials. Talk about revolutionary... we no longer had the AAU; we had USA Wrestling running the show.

We also had the Freestyle and Greco 'Final Qualifier' (in previous Olympic years called the 'Final Trials') tournaments taking place in separate cities on separate weekends. We had six-minute matches, down from twelve minutes in the '60s and then nine minutes up through 1980. We had video replays, and official protests galore.....and protests of protests.

And as for 'politically dangerous', see the next chapter, '1984 Addendum', to learn first-hand stories of the Randy Lewis – Lee Roy Smith – Dan Gable saga which was intertwined with messy politics and finally settled by an Arbitrator in a Chicago courtroom. That was just one of three individual competitions which ended up being decided in court.

US wrestlers faired well in international Freestyle competition in the 1981 to 1983 period. As a team the US finished 3rd, 2nd, and 3rd in the Worlds. Chris Campbell won a World title in 1981 and Lee Kemp won his third World championship in 1982. Dave Schultz brought home a gold medal from the '83 Worlds, while Lee Roy Smith and Greg Gibson (who also won a silver medal in '81) won silver medals.

The Greco wrestlers were far less fortunate. They did not finish among the top ten countries in any of the three years and had no medal winners.

On the national political front, President Reagan was enjoying a swelling tide of popularity as he ran for re-election with his vice-president, George Bush - the elder. The Democrats considered Walter Mondale and Gary Hart as potential candidates who could derail the Reagan candidacy. Mondale's foreign affairs experience won out in the minds of the delegates, who eventually nominated him at their National convention at the Moscone Center in San Francisco. Mondale then went on to appeal to female voters by naming Geraldine Ferraro from New York as his vice-presidential running mate.

In other political news while the Trials were taking place, former Princeton grappler and 1956 Trials contestant Donald Rumsfeld resigned as President Reagan's Middle East envoy, citing his demanding responsibilities as President and CEO of the G.O. Searle pharmaceutical company.

Football coaches from Oklahoma made headlines. Oklahoma State's Jimmy Johnson left the Cowboys after five successful seasons and accepted the job as head coach at the University of Miami. The University of Oklahoma's Barry Switzer failed a sobriety test.

In business news, the Dow Jones Industrials dipped down to the 1100s in May, off from a high of 1300 in January of '84. Interest rates in the US were soaring. People could open a money-market checking account with a $1,000 minimum and receive better than 10% interest; or, they could invest $1,000 in a one year money-market certificate at rates above 13%.

The IBM PC, introduced in 1981, faced new, aggressive competition. In June '84 AT&T moved into the PC market, unveiling their version of the personal computer with

Previous spread: Steve Fraser scored with a big move to defeat Mike Houck and secure a spot on the 1984 Greco team for the LA Games *Photograph by Dan Lucas, courtesy of* Amateur Wrestling News

user memory of 256kb. Earlier in the year an upstart California company, Apple, launched the innovative McIntosh machine. Both home computers were priced in the $2,500 - $3,000 range.

On the foreign front, the bomb (figuratively speaking, of course) dropped on May 8, when Russia announced its boycott of the '84 Los Angeles Olympic Games. They were obviously retaliating for the US boycott of the '80 Games held in Moscow. Russia also convinced 13 other countries to join them, including Bulgaria, East Germany, Cuba and Poland. This action meant that the majority of the world's Freestyle and Greco wrestlers who won medals in the 1983 World Championships (seven Russians had won gold in Freestyle, five in Greco) would not be competing in the upcoming Games.

The Trials Process

FOLLOWING much deliberation, USA Wrestling chose Dan Gable as the 1984 head Freestyle coach and Stan Dziedzic as team manager. For Greco-Roman, Ron Finley was selected as the head man, assisted by Pavel Katsen, an Oregon resident and a former coach of the Russian national teams.

USA Wrestling announced the Trials schedule in December of '83. Wrestlers would compete in a series of Freestyle Regional tournaments culminating with the National Freestyle Open in March. From these tournaments, the top Freestyle wrestlers would advance to the Final Qualifier held in May in Iowa City.

For the Greco wrestlers, there was a separate schedule. The National Greco-Roman Open tournament would not take place until May. The Greco Final Qualifier was scheduled for Minneapolis in early June.

Six wrestlers per weight class in both styles would vie in the last wrestle-offs — the Final Trials. These matches were scheduled to take place at Grand Valley State College in Allendale, Michigan from June 17-23.

According to USA Wrestling President

Warner Holzer, 1,892 wrestlers from across the country tried out for the '84 Olympic wrestling team. Only 20 made it to the Olympics.

The Final Qualifier Tournaments
Freestyle — Iowa City, Iowa, May 18-20
Greco — Minneapolis, Minnesota, June 8-9

THE Final Qualifier format was a giant pool of approximately 20 wrestlers per weight class. It was double-elimination, held over two days with the winner usually wrestling six or seven bouts.

One of the 400 or so wrestlers who qualified in the Regionals did not make it to the Final Qualifier. Rocco Liace, a 198-pound Freestyler from LSU, was delivering pizza for a Baton Rouge take-out the weekend before the tournament. Unfortunately, he was robbed and stabbed in the chest with a 14-inch kitchen knife. Liace was hospitalized but lived through the ordeal. His coach, Larry Sciacchetano, was quoted as saying:

Rocco can't go. He's got a hole in his chest.

One of the surprises at the Freestyle Final Qualifier in the Carver-Hawkeye Arena was Paul Widerman. While in college and competing for Harvard University, Paul never qualified for the NCAA tournament. Nevertheless, after graduation he turned his attention to making the '84 Olympic team at 105.5 pounds. Paul incorporated numerous sports psychology techniques in his training routine while he honed his on-the-mat skills in the University of Iowa wrestling room.

Paul relates his story:

I started wrestling in seventh grade in Huntington, New York. I had to beg my parents to allow me to wrestle. They thought a little Jewish boy should be playing tennis, not wrestling. In ninth grade the Huntington coach, Lou Giani, brought me up to the varsity to wrestle at 98 even though I only weighed 88. I ended up a two-time New York state champion. I also was the class valedictorian and had a straight A average all through my school years.

Coach Giani was fabulous. He could really

get into my head. I remember right before the State Championships my junior year, having gone 28-3 during the season, he told me, 'I don't expect much from you, Paul, just a gold medal.' He also ran very demanding practices. After going through Giani's program, when I went to the Iowa practice room to train for the '84 Trials, I felt comfortable.

I was recruited by several good schools and it came down to Lehigh and Harvard. Lehigh coach Thad Turner came to my home and I knew I'd probably get a better wrestling experience there. But two things happened. I knew they had Bobby Weaver coming in and if I couldn't beat him I might not make the team. And I was blown away by the Harvard environment and their diversity of students. I chose Harvard.

When I first walked into the Harvard wrestling room I saw that I knew more wrestling than anybody there, including their coach. Fortunately, I hooked up with Rod Buttry who was living with Jim Peckham in Boston at the time. I'd go with them to work out at the Boston YMCA. Buttry could beat me, so at least I found someone I could learn from.

In my sophomore year two good wrestlers, Jim Phills and Andy McNerney, came to Harvard. Jim Bennett, the former NCAA champion from Yale, was attending the Harvard Business School and would work out with us. Jim had two great moves — a single-leg takedown and a crab-ride. He taught the crab-ride to McNerney that year and more than a few years later McNerney taught the crab-ride to his neighbor friend on Long Island, Jessie Jantzen.

The highest I ever placed in the Easterns was 6th my senior year, 1983, at 118. Bobby Weaver pounded me in the semi-finals, 10-0. I was strong enough — I could bench-press over 225 pounds — but still too small. I was doing much better at Freestyle, though, finishing 3rd at the '81 National AAUs.

After graduating from Harvard, I tried out for the 1983 World team. At those Trials, I had to wrestle Weaver twice. The first time he beat me, 13-1. After that match, Chris Campbell came over to me and showed me in ten minutes how to defend against Weaver's best move, the Russian 'two-on-one'. Weaver beat me in the second match by only 3-2 and couldn't take me

> ## I came to realize that Gable was a genius in his handling of different wrestlers. He was always outsmarting you.
> — PAUL WIDERMAN

down any more after that.

Campbell suggested that if I wanted to make a run at the '84 Olympics that I ought to come out to Iowa City with him and train with the Hawkeye Wrestling Club. I talked my Boston-based buddies, Buttry and Phills, into joining me.

So, in the fall of '83, the three of us went to Iowa — by way of California. I had been a yoga devotee for several years and I wanted to learn more about training the mind from a noted sports psychologist in Mill Valley, Dr. Joel Kirsch. Buttry, Phills and I drove in two cars to Iowa City, left one there, added Campbell to our group, and drove to California. We spent three exceptional weeks there learning the benefits of meditation and visual training from Dr. Kirsch.

Back in Iowa, I rented an apartment just 100 yards from the Hawkeye arena and joined an unbelievable wrestling environment. I came to realize that Gable was a genius in his handling of different wrestlers. He was always outsmarting you. I have fond memories of eating Thanksgiving dinner at his home.

I flourished in the Iowa environment, training twice a day, plus meditating for 20 minutes each morning and each evening. Campbell took me under his wing and I became great friends with Chris and his wife, Laura. I told Chris that I was in Iowa to get my Ph.D. in wrestling. In return I'd help him write his essays for his Law school applications.

I only competed once during the '83-'84 season — at the Cerro Pelado tournament in Cuba. I went at 105.5 and ended up in the finals against the reigning Pan-Am champion. I was scared, but I beat the guy 13-1 and realized then that I could beat world-class guys. I was also now 'one of the boys' back at the Hawkeye Club.

I was well prepared for the Trials starting with the Qualifier right in Iowa City. I beat Tim Vanni in a close bout and then faced Weaver in

Paul Widerman upset Bobby Weaver at the Final Qualifier to earn the top seed for the final wrestle-offs in Allendale, Michigan *Photograph by Jim Phills, courtesy of Paul Widerman*

the last match. We had both won all our matches up to that point. Though I was nervous at first, I built an early lead, throwing him to his back. I think it was 5-1 in my favor after the opening period. In the second period I started to freeze-up and stall. I'm thinking to myself 'I'm beating him and I just hope this match ends soon'. Weaver comes back to tie it 6-6 and he's on top with under ten seconds to go; we are near the edge of the mat. He's ready to put me on my back with a gut-wrench.

My mind flashes back to the rule book that I had memorized during my training — 'If your head is on the mat and over the boundary line, you are out of bounds'. Just as I'm about to get rolled, I stretch my head out and plop it down outside the line. Weaver completes his gut-wrench and the referee signals two points as the match ends. However, I yell out to my corner man, Jim Peckham, that my head was out-of-bounds. He goes over to the head table, tells them about my situation and they take Weaver's last two points away. I win on criteria and earn

the number one seed at the Final Trials.

Winning that match culminated five years of training for me.

Morris Johnson participated in the Greco Qualifier in Minneapolis. He grew up in inner city Sacramento and wrestled at Cal State-Stanislaus for two years. In 1981, he placed 3rd at the FILA World Juniors in Greco at 220 pounds. Johnson moved on to San Francisco State, winning the Division II Nationals at heavyweight in '84 while training for his run at an Olympic berth in Greco. He recalls his Qualifier experiences:

In '84 I was competing in Greco for the Peninsula Grapplers, coached by Lee Allen and Bill Martell. In tournaments, Dennis Koslowski and Greg Gibson would beat me regularly, but I was improving. I pinned Koslowski in the finals of the University Games Trials and came close to beating Gibson a few times. I was feeling pretty good about my chances with these guys going into the Olympic Trials. I was a good thrower and thought if I could catch them early with one of my throws, I'd have a chance.

I entered the West Regional Trials and won them in both Greco and Freestyle. I knew all along my best shot was in Greco, so I went to their Qualifier in Minneapolis. I pinned four guys the first day and was actually in 1st place because Gibson lost to Jeff Simon. However, my first match the second day was against Koslowski and he not only thrashed me, he cracked one of my ribs. I also lost to Gibson that day, although I caught him with an arm throw. He couldn't take me down, but he had such a powerful gut-wrench that once we got on the mat, he would get his points on turns. I ended up 3rd behind Koslowski and Gibson.

In the week between the Qualifier and the Final Trials in Michigan, I stayed in Minneapolis and lived in this huge house with many of the Greco wrestlers from Minnesota. I slept on the floor. There was a lot of camaraderie amongst the Greco wrestlers and I remember guys such as Jim Martinez, Dan Chandler and Evan Johnson being particularly nice to me.

The Final Trials – Allendale, Minnesota, June 16-23, 1984

THESE wrestle-offs were set up ladder style, best two-out-of-three, with certain exceptions. The top three place winners from the Final Qualifier were top seeded, while the 4th, 5th and 6th place winners would wrestle-off in a mini-tournament to determine the true 4th seed. Then, #4 would wrestle #3, that winner wrestle #2, that winner wrestle #1. That was fine, unless there was no clear-cut winner in the Qualifier final round-robin (say, a beats b, b beats c, c beats a); then the top four wrestlers would compete in a Final Trials round-robin. One Freestyle weight class and three Greco weight classes were wrestled round-robin format.

USA Wrestling established a formal video replay protest procedure for the Trials. For a fee of $20, a wrestler could petition a six-person Protest Committee to review the

The 33-year-old Peter Lee, left, couldn't use his weight advantage over Jeff Blatnick, who won the Trials match in overtime *Photograph by Dan Lucas, courtesy of* Amateur Wrestling News

tapes of the match in question. If the protest was upheld, the match would be re-wrestled. At the Final Trials more than 25 protests were lodged. Most were denied, but several bouts were re-wrestled or the outcome of the bout was reversed.

USA Wrestling National Teams Director Greg Strobel recalls:

I didn't get to see many live matches at the Trials. It seemed like I was in the video room the whole time. There were quite a few protests.

Morris Johnson picks up his story at the Final Trials, adding in a couple of other anecdotes:

I wasn't so confident at the Final Trials in Michigan. My ribs were really hurting. However, I had nothing to lose and gave it my best shot. My first matches were against Lester Ware from the Adirondack Club in New York. Joe DeMeo was Ware's coach and he was always trying to intimidate the referees. Ware beat me in the

> **Paul Widerman lost in the Final Trials to Bobby Weaver at 105.5 on an illegal move. Several people, including J Robinson and Jim Peckham, told me it was the biggest screwjob that they had ever seen, that Paul should have wrestled in the Olympics. Talk to Paul about it.**
>
> **– MORRIS JOHNSON**

first match. I remember being so tired, but I came back to win a close second match and then won easily in the third and deciding bout.

There was a scary scene in Michigan. I was warming up for my second match against Ware and nonchalantly watching Tony Thomas wrestling-off with John Guira. Thomas went for a headlock, Guira stepped aside, and Thomas fell to the mat square on his head. His heart actually stopped. The CPR people were trying like mad to revive him and his coach was yelling, 'Tony come back'. Somehow the medics did bring him back to life. The officials shut down all the mats for a few hours, which fortunately gave me a needed break.

After defeating Ware I then wrestled Koslowski and Dennis easily beat me. Dennis was getting really good by the time 1984 rolled around. He had learned how to wrestle defensively on his feet and became extremely tough. Again I ended up 3*rd*, but I was happy that I placed and qualified for the pre-Olympic camp at Big Bear, not far from my home. I got in a month of great training there with the best guys and realized that I still had a chance to make the Olympic team in four more years.

One more thing – Paul Widerman lost in the Final Trials to Bobby Weaver at 105.5 on an illegal move. Several people including J Robinson and Jim Peckham told me it was the biggest screwjob that they had ever seen; that Paul should have wrestled in the Olympics. Talk to Paul about it.

By virtue of his victory in the Iowa City Qualifier, Paul Widerman earned the top seed

at 105.5 and had to wait to see who emerged from the pack to wrestle him for the opportunity to compete in the Olympics. Widerman picks up his story as he enters the last round in Allendale:

I go to the Final Trials in Michigan and sure enough Weaver wins his ladder matches and the right to wrestle-off against me.

In our first match once again I go out to an early lead, taking Weaver down several times. I'm ahead 5-4 until the last few seconds when Weaver puts a full-nelson on me with the legs in – an obvious illegal move – tilts me for two points and is declared the victor, 6-5. He should not have received the two points – actually he should have lost a point for the illegal hold.

In the process of using the full-nelson, Weaver hurt my neck and I was unable to wrestle effectively in our second match. He crushed me and made the team. Afterwards, I realized that I made several off-the-mat mistakes. I didn't have an authoritative figure as my corner man. I should have had either Jim Peckham or J Robinson and they would have seen Weaver's illegal move and immediately protested the match.

Secondly, a short while after the match, Robinson comes up to me and tells me that I should file a protest. I didn't have the protest fee of $20 on me, so he pulls $20 out of his own pocket. I go to the protest room, pay my money and ask to file the protest. They tell me that 36 minutes have gone by since the match ended and the time limit for filing was 30 minutes. They do not accept my protest.

I should have refused to wrestle the second match until the protest was remedied. However, I was just 22 and didn't have any saying power, nor understand the politics of the sport at that point. I am convinced the powers-that-be wanted Bobby Weaver on that Olympic team.

Mark Schultz was a three-time NCAA champion at the University of Oklahoma. He talks about his wrestling days, his relationship with his older brother, Dave, and their quest to make the '84 Olympic team together:

I didn't start wrestling until the second half of my junior year in high school. I originally was a gymnast, the Northern California champion,

Mark Schultz, left, defeated his main rival Don Shuler to win the 180.5 spot on the Olympic team
Photograph by Dan Lucas, courtesy of Amateur Wrestling News

but the sport wasn't giving me the confidence I needed at the time. My brother Dave would constantly beat me up, so I quit gymnastics to get into the Chuck Norris style of martial arts. After several months of that training, I took up wrestling so that I could become a better fighter.

As a junior I made the Palo Alto high school varsity team, but with no experience I had a losing record. That summer, 1977, I wrestled quite a bit and won a small Freestyle tournament. I came back my senior year wrestling at 154 for Coach Ed Hart. I had a 16-2 dual meet record

and went on to win the league and region title and qualified for states. At states, I was behind in every one of my matches, but ended up winning them all.

I was only recruited by two schools — UCLA and Oklahoma State, where my brother Dave was finishing up his freshman year. Dave told me not to go there. He had some problems with the coaching staff — he wanted to wrestle at 158 but Ricky Stewart was already there so they made Dave drop to 150 and he didn't like that. He called it 'a bad scene'. Meanwhile, I got to know the UCLA coach, Dave Auble, pretty well and liked him a lot. He was a fun guy, my type of person and was putting together a power-house team. I wanted to be part of that, so I went there, as did Dave, who transferred from Oklahoma State.

My freshman year I went something like 18-8 and finished 3rd in the PAC-10 at 158. Dave had to sit out the year. I enjoyed the wrestling there and we had a NCAA champion in Fred Bohna. But a problem arose. Our assistant coach tried to undermine Coach Auble and it divided the team. It turned into a messy situation and brought the whole program down. Dave and I sided with Auble but we were sick of the UCLA conflict. We had to leave.

Dave and I both made the Junior World team that year and Jim Humphrey was our coach. He recruited us to the University of Oklahoma where he was the assistant. Dave and I had to sit out the '79–'80 season because of the trans-fer, but we had a good year of training with the Oklahoma wrestlers. We'd beat each other up but always saved enough to pick on Isreal Shep-pard to take out what other frustrations we had left.

Dave and I had an intense sibling rivalry. We were best friends and no one was more instru-mental to whatever success I achieved than Dave. But when we were on the mat scrimmag-ing together, it was all out. He'd continually beat on me. Interestingly, Dave never taught me any moves himself; I would just watch and copy him.

People always thought we had such different styles – Dave the technician and me the 'mauler', but our wrestling styles were actually very simi-lar. We both wanted to kill our opponents. Off the mat though, I was a lot quieter, while he was friendlier to more people. Basically, Dave was the leader and I was the follower.

Dave and I were back on the Oklahoma team for the '80-'81 season. I had grown to fill the 167-pound class, which was Oklahoma's weakest weight, while Dave went at 158. At the NCAAs we both made the finals, but Dave was upset by Ricky Stewart, getting pinned off of a fireman's carry. I wrestled Iowa's Mike DeAnna, doing all the offensive scoring even though the referee kept calling me for stalling. I won, 10-4.

The following year I went up another weight

class, to 177, where Ed Banach of Iowa was the defending two-time NCAA champion. He had beaten me four times prior to '82, but I finally beat him in the Iowa-Oklahoma dual match when I took him down with two seconds left to win, 10-9. I beat him again in the NCAA finals, 16-8, and won the Outstanding Wrestler award. Meanwhile, my brother won his NCAA title at 167, defeating his nemesis, Mike Sheets, in overtime.

The next year, 1983, was a nightmare for me. I was all alone at Oklahoma. Dave had gradu-ated. Coach Stan Able was going through a divorce and really wasn't there for me. Assis-tant coach Humphrey left to coach the Cana-dian team. It was a tough emotional year men-tally and I wasn't up to par physically – I hurt my back and missed some dual meets. I won the NCAAs, but barely. I was happy to get out alive and felt the whole world was lifted off my shoulders.

I was ready to quit wrestling, but my brother wouldn't let that happen. He said, 'Let's go make the US World team together' – and we did. We went to Kiev where Dave wins the gold medal and I finish 7th. I was disappointed and pissed off at Dave's wife, Nancy. She decided to join us on the trip and went over there to have fun. Dave and I, meanwhile, were cutting a lot of weight and trying to focus on the wrestling. The three of us were living together and I let her distract me and it screwed up my mental state. I told Dave after the tournament that she was a problem for me. After that Dave and I started to separate a bit.

Our next goal was to make the Olympic team together. We both won the US National Open in Stillwater and the Qualifier in Iowa City. I felt very confident that we'd both make it.

Don Shuler was my main competition. We had met several times in college and I remem-ber that he was the only guy I never defeated at Lloyd Noble Arena in Norman. We tied in that dual between Arizona State and Oklahoma. In '84 I beat him in the finals of the National Open and then again at the Iowa City Qualifier. I was mentally and physically ready for my final wres-tle-off matches against him. I wanted to win so bad I was willing to do anything.

In our first match, I won but got frustrated.

At one point I was on top of Shuler trying to turn him with a gut-wrench. My hand was under his stomach, but I couldn't turn him. Finally, I just grabbed a hunk of his skin and stomach and yanked. He let out a terrible scream but still wouldn't budge. I went on to win that match, but lost the next one to him, 7-2.

That set up a third and deciding bout. It was close and I won on a move that I never had done before. I was on top and while I was trying for a leg-lace I grabbed Shuler around the body and rolled up on my side. The ref gave me two points for exposure and that's what I won by.

163 pounds Freestyle — Dave Schultz vs Lee Kemp

LEE Kemp was part of the 1980 US Olympic team that boycotted the Moscow Games. In order to compete in the 1984 Olympics, he stuck around for another four years, winning his third World Championship along the way. However, by 1984, Kemp had a formidable foe to contend with — the 1983 World Champion from California, Dave Schultz.

Kemp tells his story:

When I won the Worlds in '82 in Edmonton, I received a bad gash above my eyebrow that needed constant attention. There really were a lot of close, hard-fought matches for me in that tournament. It was anything but easy.

In '83 I started thinking about my future. I beat Dave Schultz in a close match right before the World tryouts, but the night before I was to drive to Iowa City for the World Trials, I decided to skip the tournament.

I had just two classes to go to get my graduate degree and I decided to go to school during the fall semester and skip the Worlds which were being held in October. I figured taking classes in the fall was better than going to school second semester, which would have interfered with my training for the Olympics.

Up until then I had the mental edge over Schultz. I had wrestled him at least ten times and he had beaten me only once — to make the World Cup team in the spring of '83.

Well, Schultz got to go to the Worlds in

> **My strategy was wrong, actually. I could take Dave [Schultz] down, but late in my career he had the ability to turn me when we were down on the mat. I should have focused on taking him down more and build an early three or four point lead. Instead, I'd get my takedown and keep it close. Then when we'd go down on the mat, I'd be susceptible to his turns.**
>
> **— LEE KEMP**

Kiev and won them. He beat the next best 163-pounder in the world, Martin Knosp, the West German who was a former World Champion. I defeated Knosp in the '82 Worlds but lost to him in '81.

Dave was starting to peak then and become a really great wrestler. At the same time, I was having some problems.

At the start of the '84 year, I was questioning whether I wanted to do this anymore. I had a difficult time training. There was no coach for me at Wisconsin and not the tough workout partners I needed. I finally called Dan Gable and asked him if I could come to Iowa City to train. He was kind enough to say 'Okay', which was very generous of him since he had one of his own Iowa wrestlers, Mike DeAnna, trying to make the team at 163.

My match with Schultz at the Iowa City Trials and our first match at Grand Valley were very close — and very similar. Both ended even and he won on criteria. My strategy was wrong, actually. I could take Dave down, but late in my career he had the ability to turn me when we were down on the mat. I should have focused on taking him down more and build an early three or four-point lead. Instead, I'd get my takedown and keep it close. Then when we'd go down on the mat, I'd be susceptible to his turns. He'd get ahead of me, and in the final minutes he'd give up a takedown to me, but it was meaningless as he'd already have the criteria advantage.

When I lost my second match at Michigan, I was done. I was pretty frustrated and did not

After years of narrow defeats to Lee Kemp, Dave Schultz finally got the advantage over his long-time foe in the 1984 Trials *Photograph by Dan Lucas, courtesy of Amateur Wrestling News*

wrestle anymore. I didn't go to the Olympic Camp. I moved forward with the rest of my life, immediately taking a job in St. Louis and leaving wrestling behind.

I am glad that I tried to make the '84 team. I never would have known whether I could have done it or not. But in reality, I should not have wrestled. Actually, I believe 1981, 1982 and 1983 were declining years for me even though I won the World Championship in '82. I really peaked in 1980 and just never felt the same after that. I have no doubt that I would have won that Olympic gold medal in 1980. I very much wanted to be an Olympic champion.

From an *Associated Press* story describing Dave Schultz's first match with Kemp at the Final Trials in Michigan:

Schultz won by 2-2 on criteria. First period — Kemp TD, 1-0; second period — Schultz 2 point tilt, 1-2, Kemp TD, 2-2. Schultz two-point tilt wins on criteria.

The media reported Dave Schultz's comments: "...used an ankle cross move that I learned in the Soviet Union to make the two-pointer... It was a tough match. I wanted to beat him bad, but I didn't. I couldn't. That guy's tough. I'm going to try to beat him bad next time."

Mark Schultz, on his brother's chances against Lee Kemp:

I couldn't imagine anyone beating Dave, including Lee Kemp. I had gotten to know Lee a bit and I liked him. He seemed very friendly and we played some racquetball together. However, I remember thinking this 'friendly' quality might be a detriment to him. Dave was much meaner. Now, Dave was a great guy, but on the mat he showed you no mercy or sympathy.

I wasn't surprised when Dave beat Lee two in a row at the Final Trials.

Stan Dziedzic was the Freestyle team Manager for the US 1984 Olympics. He offers his insights on the Kemp–Schultz rivalry:

From '78 to '84 Lee Kemp controlled Dave Schultz. The turning point was Lee studying for his MBA at the University of Wisconsin in the fall of 1983. Up until then I don't believe Kemp had ever lost to Schultz, although all their matches were close. Heck, all of Kemp's matches were close, no matter who he wrestled. Anyway, that September the World Championships were held in Kiev.

Lee had just won the Pan-Am Games in August, but he decided not to try out for the US World team because he wanted to start the final semester of his MBA program.

I was disappointed because Lee had a great chance of winning the Worlds, but I, along with the other coaches, respected his decision. Besides, we had a pretty darn good replacement at 163 pounds — Dave Schultz.

As we all know, Dave went over there, beat the Russian and four others to win his first World title. He was our only gold medalist. Kemp created his own monster by opening the door for Schultz.

That decision I believe changed the whole dynamics of their rivalry. By winning the gold in the Russians' own backyard, Dave gained too much confidence for Lee to overcome in '84.

149.5 pounds Freestyle — Nate Carr vs Andy Rein

THE 149.5 pound class had its share of past, present and future NCAA champions in the competition — Steve Barrett, Jim Heffernan, Ken Mallory, Andre Metzger, Kenny Monday, Pete Yazzo. Under-rated Oregon standout Bill Nugent managed to place above all those champions, garnering a 3rd at the Final Trials.

The top two wrestlers left to vie for the right to wrestle at 149.5 on the Olympic team were both multiple-time National champions, Nate Carr and Andy Rein. Carr was a three-time NCAA champion at Iowa State and would go on to become a three-time US National Open Freestyle champion. Rein was a two-time National AAU champion, the Pan-Am champion, a Tbilisi champion and a

> " In the third match the score was close when Rein slipped behind me while on our feet and I had his leg hooked. Suddenly, the referee taps me on the shoulder and says to us to break the hold. As I unhook my foot Andy throws me and the judges award him the points and I lose the match.
>
> — NATE CARR

• •

NCAA champion at Wisconsin.

Nate Carr's story:

I followed the same pattern as my older brothers. I was the sixth of nine boys — I also had seven sisters. Dad was a church pastor and we were brought up in a strong Christian family environment.

Like the others, I practiced in Coach Canvan's garage. If I didn't do a move right, some older brother was there to hit me until I did. Early on people said 'this guy is going to be good'. I was quick and strong.

At Erie Tech I wrestled 126, 132, 138 and 145 my four years there. I really wanted to be a state champion but it eluded me for a while. My junior year, I lost at the State Tournament due to being disqualified for a slam. In my senior year the best advice my coach gave me was, 'Don't slam anyone.' So, I just smashed everyone to win the state title.

The first school to recruit me was the University of Iowa. I was flown out there with other top recruits and Gable told us that if we all came to Iowa, we'd build a dynasty. They had Chris Campbell look after me and he put some pressure on me to attend Iowa. However mom had this dream that I shouldn't go there. She liked the idea of an older guy as my coach, like Harold Nichols, so I went to Iowa State instead.

I remember J Robinson, Iowa assistant coach at the time, telling me that if I went to Iowa State I'd never be a NCAA champion, never an Olympian and Iowa would always beat Iowa State. That was a lot of motivation for me over the next four years. By the way, J

Kenny Monday and Nate Carr had a heated rivalry that went back to their college days in the Big Eight Conference *Photograph courtesy of Bobby Douglas*

and I are now good friends.

I was very excited to be at Iowa State. I wasn't the greatest student, but I was determined to study hard and earn my degree. Getting that degree was a championship for me, too.

I won the NCAAs as a sophomore, with Scott Trizzino from Iowa being my main competition. I had beaten him twice during the season and then we each made it to the finals. On the day of the finals, I went into the steam room to lose a few pounds before weigh-in. Who is in there but Trizzino. I was a little slow to shut the sauna door and Trizzino yells, 'hurry up and shut the door, Carr.' I didn't care much for that, so we start wrestling right there in the sauna. After 30 seconds of beating on each other he says, 'Okay,

let's stop now and finish this off tonight on the mats.' We did. We went right after each other and he head-butts me in the opening period. I go to my corner, tell the coaches to quickly slap a butterfly on my brow and then run over to Trizzino's corner where he's talking to Gable. I drag him by the arm to the center of the mat and say, 'Let's go, Trizzino.' I was so fired up. I ended up beating him 10-5 to win my first NCAA title.

I won the NCAAs again the next two years as I developed a close, tough rivalry with Kenny Monday. Both in '82 and '83 Kenny beat me in the Big Eight finals. Both times I tell Kenny after our match, 'Good job, Kenny. But the next time we meet is the one that counts.' We'd always have a little bit of smack talk between us — we were both so competitive. In both the '82 and '83 NCAA finals, I beat him in overtime.

Those summers between 1980 and 1983 I was really concentrating on Folkstyle, wanting to increase my chances to be a three-time NCAA champion. I really didn't do much Freestyle. After graduation, I did tryout for the World team, and surprisingly, I made it, beating Lenny Zalesky, one of the Kistlers and Andy Rein. After those wrestle-offs, however, I immediately went into the hospital to have surgery that would dissolve a disc that I had injured. They gave me an injection that was potentially very dangerous, but I elected to have it done in order to cure my bad spine. It worked but it took me away from wrestling for a month right before the World Championships in Kiev. Coach Gable wanted to replace me with his wrestler from Iowa, Lenny Zalesky, but I told him that while I understood his desires, no way am I going to give up my rightly earned position on the US World team.

I didn't place in Kiev. I was really just starting out in the international world of Freestyle wrestling. I thought I could wrestle with these world-class guys and while I had great ability, in '84 I had no personal coach or trainer. No one was personally looking out for me. It was a struggle. I really wasn't all that focused on the Olympic Trials.

I remember that in Iowa City I won all my matches easily, but dropped a close match with Rein.

[Author's note: Carr's victories included two pins and dominant decisions by scores of 9-0, 13-0 — over Monday — 11-3, 6-0.]

Then I went to the Final Trials in Michigan and again end up meeting Rein in the last round. I knew that I was close to winning it all and all I had to do was to wrestle smart and I would make it to the Olympics.

I had two tournaments, of sorts, to win in Michigan — making weight and wrestling the matches. I had a whole lot of weight to pull to make 149.5. That was very tough on me, but I did it. Then, in my first match with Rein I wrestled very conservatively and won by a point. Then came my downfall. I was so pumped that I didn't have to weigh-in again, I decided to 'go for it' in

Tbilisi champion Andy Rein survived some harrowing matches against Nate Carr to make the 1984 Freestyle team *Photograph courtesy of Amateur Wrestling News*

my second match. I went out there trying to kill him, all full of vim and vigor. Well, he threw me a couple of times and soundly beat me.

No one told me just go out there and wrestle a solid match.

In the third match the score was close when Rein slipped behind me while on our feet and I had his leg hooked. Suddenly, the referee taps me on the shoulder and says to us to break the hold. As I unhook my foot Andy throws me and the judges award him the points and I lose the match.

I didn't complain. It just didn't mean enough to me at the time. But, coming so close in those Trials gave me a burning desire to really go for it four years later.

Andy Rein relates his story about his active wrestling days:

I grew up on a farm, only three miles from Russ Hellickson's place. I went to the same high school as Russ and had the same coach, Mr. Pieper, who was a pioneer in developing youth wrestling programs.

Our wrestling team won three Wisconsin state championships. I didn't place as a sophomore and that propelled me to win the next two years. At graduation, Nancy Steckbauer, the wife of my high school guidance teacher, gave me a note that said, 'I enjoyed watching you wrestle here the last four years, and I look forward to watching you in the 1984 Olympics'. That was a very motivating item that I never forgot.

Since I was not heavily recruited out of high school it was an easy choice to go to the University of Wisconsin. While there as a sophomore I finished 2nd in NCAAs; my junior year was not so good as I had a separated shoulder; then I won the Nationals as a senior in 1980. Hellickson was my driving force. In 1976 I saw Russ, our local hero, achieve success when he won a silver medal in the Olympics. I always looked up and listened to him.

Russ always got his wrestlers involved in Freestyle. After my junior year I made the Pan-American team and won a gold medal. I was too young and stupid to realize how good the opponents were. After graduation I competed for the Wisconsin Wrestling Club. Lee Kemp was great workout partner for me there. Occasionally, very occasionally, I would do something good against him.

In 1982 I went to Tbilisi where I lost six matches in a row to different Russians. I almost hung it up after that, doubting my ability.

In 1983 I again went to Tbilisi and this time I won the tournament, beating the defending Olympic champion. I remember afterwards Dave Schultz coming up to me, congratulating me and saying, 'You are just like them. You don't do anything and you win. I'm going to try that'. Winning Tbilisi was the biggest achievement of my wrestling career. J Robinson was my coach and I give him a lot of credit.

The first time I lost to Nate Carr was in '83 at the World Trials. He totally beat me and it was a shock to my system. I was devastated. Driving back from Iowa City to Madison I didn't say a word the whole time, but I put myself on a mission to beat him to make the '84 Olympic team.

I would not only work out every day but I would do 100 sit-ups and 100 push-ups every night before I went to bed.

I told myself that if I did this, without fail, I would make that '84 team.

As for the Trials in '84, I knew many of my competitors would be tough, but I knew at the end it would be between Carr and me.

The biggest win was my victory over Carr at the Final Qualifier in Iowa City. I don't remember much of the bout other than it was close and I picked him up and turned him with a gut-wrench. I won that and now had the top seed and only had to focus on beating Carr, because I knew he would beat all the others.

At Grand Valley, Carr did advance to the Finals and we went two-out-of-three. I had been dreaming of him every night for several months and I knew he was a quality wrestler and athlete. It was a huge battle.

In the first bout, it was 1-1 towards the end of the second period and I was ahead on criteria. I kept telling myself to keep my elbows in, stay cool. However, with about ten seconds left we go out of bounds; Carr gets a point and wins the match.

Now, we go to the second match and we are on our feet and I get this throw that I had never done before — basically he came in with his duck-under and I got my feet planted, slipped in a double under-hook and threw him over my head for a four-point move. Later in the match I do the same thing for another four-point move and I win by a big margin.

In the third and deciding match, I again throw Carr for four points, that's all I can remember and I win. I am feeling very beat up, but relieved. Coach Hellickson was in my corner and we rejoice. I had reached my goal of being an Olympian.

198 pounds Greco Roman — Steve Fraser vs Mike Houck

MICHIGAN native Steve Fraser was comfortable and successful in both Freestyle and Greco-Roman wrestling. He won the US Nationals titles in Greco-Roman in 1981 and 1983 and was a US Nationals Freestyle champion in 1984. Mike Houck was a Greco-Roman fanatic from Minnesota. Unable to even win a match at his state high school tournament, two years later he was the US Junior Greco champion. The two arch rivals, yet friends, wrestled each other countless times. The last one was for the 1984 Olympic berth.

Fraser tells his story:

I started wrestling in eighth grade in Hazel Park, Michigan. My gym teacher, Frank Stagg, wanted me to go out for wrestling. One day in the hall, he put the 'sleeper' hold on me and told me I better show up that afternoon in the wrestling room for practice. I went and never turned back.

Though I liked the sport, I was terrible my first year, but started to develop some muscular strength as a ninth-grader and got a little better. The big change came in the summer after my sophomore year when I attended Masaaki Hatta's wrestling camp. The following season I lost only three matches and my senior year I was undefeated, won the State Championship and earned a scholarship to the best school in the country — the University of Michigan.

At Michigan I was a two-time All-American, but never a Big Ten or NCAA champion, so when I graduated I felt unfulfilled about my college wrestling career. I needed to decide if I was going to continue in the sport. Right after graduation, I went up to a cabin on Lake Huron with some buddies, contemplated my career and considered how far I had come. I could quit now or continue on giving it all I had. I chose to re-commit myself to wrestling and see where it could take me. I accepted Coach Dale Bahr's offer to be his graduate assistant and continued training with the Michigan Wrestling Club, while also working at the local sheriff department.

One day during the winter of '83-'84, Dean Rockwell, the head of the Michigan Wrestling Club, pulled me aside to give me some advice. He told me that I needed to give up wrestling both Freestyle and Greco, and that I should focus on one or the other. And he told me that I was too small to wrestle 198. He said I should drop down to 180.5.

Actually, though I loved Dean, I was somewhat offended by his remarks. I enjoyed both Freestyle and Greco and wanted to make the Olympic team in both styles. I thought the double competition

> **The thought of wrestling [Mark] Johnson really inspired me. While out on my early morning runs in the dead-cold Michigan winter, I'd visualize wrestling Johnson and how I would set him up for my headlock and pin him. I thought about him every day for a good two months.**
>
> **— STEVE FRASER**

helped me. Plus, I hated cutting weight and hadn't done it since Hatta advised me against it at his camp years ago. Not cutting a lot of weight was one of the biggest reasons for my success. I normally weighed about 205 and I saw it as crucial to wrestle at 198. I rejected Rockwell's advice.

Going into the Trials I knew my biggest competition would be Mike Houck. We wrestled each other probably 30 times and I think we went 15-15 against each other. However, rumor had it that 1980 Olympian Mark Johnson, who would beat up on me badly in the Michigan room during my freshman year, was making a comeback and would be there at 198 as well. In fact, I think Rockwell was trying to tell me to drop down a weight class to avoid him.

The thought of wrestling Johnson really inspired me. While out on my early morning runs in the dead-cold Michigan winter, I'd visualize wrestling Johnson and how I would set him up for my headlock and pin him. I thought about him every day for a good two months.

I ended up wrestling Johnson four times in '84 at the Nationals and the Trials. I beat him each time and head-locked him in almost every match.

In the spring of '84 I competed in both the National Freestyle Open and National Greco Open. I won in Freestyle, beating Bill Scherr, but did not successfully defend my Greco title, losing to Houck. Then I entered both the Freestyle and Greco Qualifiers. Freestyle was first and I ended up 3rd behind Ed Banach and Mitch Hull. In the Minneapolis Greco qualifier I again placed 2nd to Houck.

I was very frustrated and took a couple of days off between the Greco Qualifier and the Final

Dan Severn, left, gave Lou Banach a good tussle but Banach survived to make the Olympic Freestyle team at 220 pounds *Photograph by Dan Lucas, courtesy of* Amateur Wrestling News

Trials. I went back up to that cabin in Northern Michigan to get away from it all. The recuperation made me feel good.

I made the decision not to pursue the Olympic spot in Freestyle but to put all my effort into making the Greco team. I knew I had a tougher road ahead in Freestyle. I would have had to defeat Banach, Hull and Scherr. Plus, dropping out of Freestyle gave my buddy Willie Gadson a chance to make the Freestyle team.

In the Greco finals, I beat Johnson twice to set up the best two-out-of-three showdown with Houck. In our first match, I got him with my favorite slam-headlock and won, 3-2. Mike then came back to beat me by a shutout in the second match. I was really down.

I remember sitting behind the bleachers about 45 minutes before the deciding match. I was depressed, feeling lousy about everything. Joe Wells, a former assistant coach of mine at Michigan, walked by and said the usual, 'Let that match go, this next one is the one that counts'. Then he told me a joke and made me laugh. That changed my whole mood. I started to feel better. I got out of my funk and started focusing on what I had to do in the last match.

I got a good warm-up in but started out slowly. Houck gut-wrenched me in the opening minute, so I fell behind, 2-0. Traditionally, whoever scored first in our matches won the bout. However, I told myself I had nothing to lose, to go for it, now. Near the end of the first period I got a double-under-

hook on Houck and threw him to his back for three points to go ahead 3-2. In the second period I just focused on keeping it scoreless and there was no further scoring.

I won the match. It was a dream come true but I could only relish the victory for a couple of minutes. Out of the corner of my eye I saw Houck's coach walking to the protest area. I was immediately deflated and depressed. Who knows what was going on in there? I understood that if the Committee overturned my victory I would have to wrestle the match all over again. The next 45 minutes were miserable. Finally, Gable came out of the room and just gave me a nod of the head — meaning things worked out okay for me.

Mike Houck tells his story leading up to and including the '84 Trials:

When I was in fifth grade, my father took my younger brother to the local sporting goods store and bought him a jock-strap and a pair of shorts. 'He's going out for wrestling,' my dad told me. I looked at that jock-strap with wide eyes and thought it was so cool. I wanted one, so I told dad, 'I want to go out for wrestling, too.' That got me started.

I wasn't a talented athlete and just a so-so high school wrestler. I made it to states my last two years in high school but never won a match there. My real enjoyment in the sport came from Greco-Roman wrestling. I remember watching the Polish national team wrestle the Minnesota

Wrestling Club guys at Augsburg College when I was in ninth grade. It looked great and I fell in love with that style. I started wrestling in as many Greco tournaments as I could.

I was a terrible student but wanted to both wrestle and play football in college, so I went to junior college after graduating from high school in 1977. I played football the first semester, but then flunked out of school. I was not ready for college. I decided then to give Greco a dedicated effort and in January I walked into the Minnesota Wrestling Club. I saw Olympians like Dan Chandler and Brad Reinghans there — America's best Greco guys — and they welcomed me with open arms. They encouraged me and taught me so much.

In the summer of '78 I met Ben Peterson at a summer camp. He was the wrestling coach at Maranatha College in Brooklyn Park, Minnesota and talked me into going to school there. I entered the college in the fall of '78, wrestled for Ben and ended up earning my degree from Maranatha in 1989.

He was very helpful to me all during my career.

Meanwhile I was wrestling year round in Greco for the Minnesota club. In 1979, I made the US Junior World team. I entered the Olympic Trials in 1980, finishing 3rd at 198 pounds. In 1981 I wrestled for the US in the Greco World Championships and went 0-2. In 1983, I wrestled in them again and won a match to tie for 8th. I could feel myself getting a lot better.

Going into the 1984 Trials, I was the top guy and I knew my main competition was Steve Fraser. There was no one close to him and we were very even in our career bouts against each other. I beat Steve to win the '84 National Open, and then it got down to the two of us at the Minneapolis Qualifier. I had my strongest showing there, pretty much dominating Steve. I came out of there thinking 'I own this weight class.' I was preparing myself to wrestle in the Olympics.

At the Final Trials in Michigan, I was the number one guy on the ladder. I saw this as a disadvantage. I would be going in cold in the finals while Fraser had been wrestling and gaining momentum. Anyway, in our first match, Steve headlocks me in the first minute of the bout and nearly pins me. It was a really tight headlock and my immediate thought was to give up and save my energy for the next bout.

> " I was sorry that I had to go out like that. I felt the system was against me and that the influence of Olympic team coach, Dan Gable, was to favor his own Iowa wrestlers. The system was just terrible.
> — CHARLIE GADSON

However, I knew wrestling is a lot about mental toughness, so I dug in and fought him while on my back until the period ran out. I thought that was a moral victory and I got my momentum back. I took him down in the second period but it was not enough, so I lost that one.

In the second match I felt good and beat him 2-0. I felt like I was dominating again. I went ahead 2-0 in the deciding third match. I was feeling in control. Suddenly, late in the match Steve slipped in a double-underhook on me, did a change of direction and threw me on my back for a three-point move. That was what he needed for the victory.

I was literally shocked and devastated. I stayed up all night thinking about the match. However, the next day I adjusted and told myself that I had laid it all on the line, but Steve wrestled better yesterday than I did. He was a great competitor. We were two guys who were just average athletes but had the heart and commitment which set us apart. I have a lot of respect for Steve. He made me the wrestler that I was.

Most hardcore fans of Freestyle wrestling readily recall the 1984 tussle between Randy Lewis and Lee Roy Smith that ended up in arbitration, yet interestingly enough two other protests from the 1984 Trials also ended up in the hands of an Arbitrator. Dan Severn lost an arbitration hearing, enabling Lou Banach to keep his Olympic berth at 220 pounds. Charlie Gadson won in arbitration against Bill Scherr, but Scherr won the rematch. Thus, Scherr remained the first alternate to Ed Banach at 198.

Charlie Gadson recalls his unhappy Trials experiences:

Prior to the Iowa City tournament I was among the top four guys in my weight class — 198. I didn't perform well in Iowa City and didn't place in the top six. I petitioned to the Committee to let me advance to the Michigan Final Trials and was accepted.

I got myself well prepared for Michigan and won my early matches to advance to the last four wrestlers. I then had to wrestle Bill Scherr two-out-of-three. He won the first match fair and square and I won the second match. In the third match there were problems.

I got an early takedown and a clear tilt but was awarded just one point. I was in control most of the time and built up a lead. Near the end Bill tilted me to tie the score but I thought I was ahead on criteria. He then dove in on me and drove me out of bounds, earning one point. There were just a few seconds left when I took Bill down, but in the process I grabbed his kneepads.

While I was awarded the takedown points and won the match, Scherr's people protested. His protest was upheld, my takedown points were erased and he was awarded the victory and advanced to the next round.

The Protest Committee did not follow their own procedures. They did not have us re-wrestle the match. They only had one video to review rather than the required two videos.

I wanted them to review the early takedown where I did not receive the back-points. However, they would not entertain watching another video that Thad Turner had taken in the stands which clearly showed me getting a tilt.

I was frustrated and upset. I wasn't going to let it die. I hired an attorney and sued USA Wrestling and went to arbitration. The day of the hearing I drove early in the morning from Ames to the arbitration site, Chicago, arriving there around noon. The Arbitrator heard my story and USA Wrestling's.

Around 11pm he comes back with his verdict that I was in the right and asked me how fast I could be in California. I had to be there the next day to re-wrestle Scherr.

I flew to California that next morning, drove to Big Bear where the training camp was being held and weighed in at 2pm. At 4pm I was wrestling Scherr, who had been training there as the Olympic alternate.

[Author's note: Ed Banach was the Freestyle Trials winner at 198.]

Bill was a serious competitor and a great wrestler. I hold nothing against him. We fought it out and he beat me in an empty gym, 5-5 on criteria. If I had won that match I would have had to wrestle Ed Banach for the Olympic team spot. They made it almost impossible for me to win. It was very frustrating. Making the Olympics had been a goal of mine since I was in high school.

I was sorry that I had to go out like that. I felt the system was against me and that the influence of Olympic team coach, Dan Gable, was to favor his own Iowa wrestlers. The system was terrible.

1984 OLYMPIC TEAM MEMBERS

	FREESTYLE	GRECO-ROMAN
105.5	Bob Weaver (1st)	Mark Fuller
114.5	Joe Gonzales	Bert Govig
125.5	Barry Davis (2nd)	Frank Famiano (5th)
136.5	Randy Lewis (1st)	Abdurrahim Kuzu (4th)
149.5	Andy Rein (2nd)	James Martinez (3rd)
163	Dave Schultz (1st)	Chris Catalfo
180.5	Mark Schultz (1st)	Dan Chandler
198	Ed Banach (1st)	Steve Fraser (1st)
220	Lou Banach (1st)	Greg Gibson (2nd)
UNL	Bruce Baumgartner (1st)	Jeff Blatnick (1st)

★ WITH the Soviet Bloc boycott, and having the advantage of wrestling on their home mats, medals flowed more freely than ever to the US. Observers say Andy Rein was robbed of a gold on the final day, when the officials decided on their own that the US already had enough gold medals.

1984 PRESIDENTIAL ELECTION

★ ANOTHER landslide, with Mondale only winning his home state of Minnesota and the District of Columbia. The Reagan campaign briefly used "Born in the USA" as a campaign song, without permission, until Bruce Springsteen, a lifelong Democrat, requested that they stop.

THE SCORECARD

Ronald Reagan George H. W. Bush	525 Electoral Votes 58.8% of Popular Vote
Walter Mondale Geraldine Ferraro	13 Electoral Votes 40.6% of Popular Vote

In the Matter of the Arbitration concerning)
)
RANDY LEWIS)   Case Number
and)   51 199 0159 84L
USA WRESTLING and)
U.S. OLYMPIC COMMITTEE)

AWARD OF ARBITRATOR

The arbitration hearing on this matter commenced the morning of Thursday, 5 July, 1984, when evidence was submitted over a period of almost eleven hours (without breaks for lunch or din and finally closed the morning of Sunday, 8 July, 1984, when additional evidence was submitted on behalf of the responde

Almost all of the evidence was submitted in the for sworn testimony, which was extensive, from the followi individuals:

On behalf of the claimant-petitioner:

DAN GABLE   Age 35.   Selected by USA Wrestling ("USAW") States Olympic Wrestling Team coach for t Former United States, World, and Olympic wrestling champion. Head coach of wrest Not a FILA certified official but quali

CHAD CROW   Age 33.   Former amateur wrestler wh a FILA "category-one" certified of some matters in Iowa City. Appea official to view tapes." Is a St living in Jackson, Minnesota.

J. ROBINSON   Coach of Randy Lewis for Oly matches. Selected as the U assistant coach for the 19 at Iowa University for el from Oklahoma (State?) U

TRIALS AND TRIBULATIONS

1984

ADDENDUM

s.
alist)
niversity.
fication.

74.   Now is
officiated
terested
ance agent

the disputed
stling Team
restling coach
years.   Graduated
en years ago.

Summary of Key Events and Timelines

August 20, 1982: Federal District Judge Aldrich orders the AAU removed from FILA and the USOC. Subsequently, USA Wrestling gains recognition by FILA and the USOC as the governing body for amateur wrestling in the US. USA Wrestling assumes responsibility for organizing and setting procedures for the 1984 Trials.

March, 1983: USA Wrestling names Dan Gable head Olympic team Freestyle coach.

January 23, 1984: The Executive Committee of USA Wrestling approves and issues the 1984 Olympic Trials procedures.

March/April, 1984: Randy Lewis wins Central Qualifying tournament to become eligible for the Olympic Trials. Lee Roy Smith wins the World Cup Trials to become eligible.

March 22-24, 1984: Ricky Dellagatta defeats Darrell Burley 13-4 in 136.5 pound finals of the National Open Freestyle championships. Dellagatta and Burley qualify for the Trials. Randy Lewis and Lee Roy Smith do not compete in the tournament.

May 18-20, 1984: US Freestyle Olympic Trials (Final Qualifier) at Iowa City. Results at 136.5 pounds:
  1st place, Dellagatta (loses to Smith 6-2; pins Burley; defeats Lewis 20-10).
  2nd place, Smith (defeats Dellagatta 6-2; loses to Lewis 11-9; defeats Burley 16-4).
  3rd place, Lewis (loses to Dellagatta 20-10; defeats Smith 11-9).

June, 1984: For the Final Trials wrestle-offs, USA Wrestling decides that the 136.5 pounds Freestyle weight class (and several Greco-Roman weight classes) will be a four-man round-robin series rather than a ladder challenge. This adheres to the January 23 Trials procedure document.

June 21, 1984: Final Trials, Allendale, MI. Results at 136.5 pounds Freestyle, day one:
Dellagatta vs Burley - Dellagatta wins two-out-of-three matches: 4-6, 6-4, 15-6.
Lewis vs Smith - Lewis wins the first bout on criteria, 7-7. Smith protests; protest is denied. Second bout - Lewis defeats Smith 7-6. Smith protests, protest is upheld by the Protest Committee, bout ordered re-wrestled in its entirety. Third (re-wrestled) bout - Smith defeats Lewis 13-0. Fourth bout - Smith defeats Lewis by injury default at 1:19, with Smith ahead at the time.
The Protest Committee includes three officials - Chuck Almeida, Vince Zuaro and Ron Ogelsbury and two USA Wrestling staff members, Greg Strobel and Bernadette Norris. Head coach Dan Gable participates as an ex-officio member with no voting rights.
Lewis, through his attorney, presents an appeal letter to USA Wrestling protesting the decision that the second match be re-wrestled.

June 22, 1984: Results at 136.5 Freestyle, day two:
 Smith vs Burley - Smith wins 14-2, 11-4.
Dellagatta vs Lewis - No matches wrestled. Dellagatta weighs in but Lewis defaults to him and withdraws from the tournament due to a knee injury.

June 23, 1984: Results at 136.5 Freestyle, day three:
Smith vs Dellagatta - Smith wins 8-3, 13-8.
Smith is announced as the Freestyle 136.5 Trials winner, Dellagatta as the alternate.

Late June, 1984: USA Wrestling denies Lewis appeal; US Olympic Committee denies Lewis appeal.

July 5, 1984: Lewis, under provisions of the Amateur Sports Act, brings his case (Randy Lewis vs USA Wrestling and the US Olympic Committee) to arbitration in Chicago. Individuals testifying at the hearings: on behalf of Lewis - Dan Gable, Chad Crow, J Robinson, Scott Fulton, Stan Dziedzic; on behalf of USA Wrestling - Steve Combs, Werner Holzer, Greg Strobel.

July 12, 1984: Arbitrator Ken Denzel announces his verdict. It states that the actions and decisions of the Protest Committee are reversed and vacated; the results of the third' and fourth Lewis-Smith matches are vacated, over-turned and of no effect; and, that Lewis and Smith are directed to re-wrestle the disputed match from the point of the controversy, with Lewis leading 5-4 with 84 seconds remaining. Lewis and Smith are directed to wrestle the next day; Dellagatta and Lewis are directed to wrestle the day after that.

July 13, 1984: Lewis and Smith wrestle the 84-second match in Big Bear, CA behind closed doors. Lewis wins 7-4. Smith is eliminated.
Smith files a state court injunction in Oklahoma. USA Wrestling files an application in US District Court in Illinois in attempts to vacate the Arbitrator's decision. Both are denied.

July 14, 1984: Smith's family files a restraining order on the arbitration ruling in Federal Court in Los Angeles. The judge turns down the request.
Lewis defeats Dellagatta, 5-2 and 16-4 at Big Bear behind closed doors.
Lewis's name is submitted to Los Angeles Olympic Organization Committee (LAOOC) as the US representative in the 136.5 freestyle division. July 14 was the final day for the US to submit the names of US Olympic contestants, per LAOOC mandate.

July 19, 1984: Letter from Don Sondgeroth, President of US Wrestling Officials Association, on Association letterhead, to Warner Holzer, President of USA Wrestling, asking that freestyle team coaches Gable, Dziedzic and Robinson be severely reprimanded and their resignations tendered as coaches after the Olympics.

July 26, 1984 - Date of a letter from Rick Dellagatta's parents to USA Wrestling protesting the Trials results at 136.5 due to lack of conformance with the Trials procedures. Greg Strobel writes back to the Dellagattas on August 8 addressing the questions posed in the protest letter.

July 30, 1984: Personal letter written by USA Wrestling Executive Director Steve Combs to Dan Gable stating Combs' strong disapproval of Gable's appearance in the Arbitrator's court and before the Federal judge in Los Angeles in support of Lewis. Despite media reports to the contrary, Combs does not actually ask Gable for his resignation as Olympic coach, though he ends the letter, "with total disrespect for your title and actions, I am challenged to rectify the situation."

August 7 - 11, 1984: Wrestlers compete in the Olympic Games.

September 11, 1984: The Board of Directors of USA Wrestling officially censure Dan Gable for taking the side of an individual athlete (Lewis) in the dispute and for challenging the integrity of several USA Wrestling representatives. Gable accepts the censure, stating that "my actions were motivated solely by my interest in a fair outcome, rather than any personal interest in one of the competitors" and that he was not in any way attacking the integrity of the Protest Committee members.

May, 1985: Steve Combs resigns as Executive Director of USA Wrestling.

> **I was the mat official for the disputed Lewis – Smith match. I knew it was going to be a 'hot match'. It was Iowa vs Oklahoma; two great, great wrestlers both going for a probable Olympic gold medal.**
>
> **– Referee Rick Tucci**

ARGUABLY, the most highly contested and most controversial Freestyle weight class in the history of the US Olympic Trials was 136.5 in 1984. There are more plots and sub-plots than your favorite Hitchcock thriller.

Twenty-three years later many of the wrestlers, coaches and officials (Randy Lewis, Ricky Dellagatta, Lee Roy Smith, Stan Dziedzic, Rick Tucci, Steve Combs, Greg Strobel and Dan Gable) who were involved in the melee present their views of the controversy.

Randy Lewis

LEWIS had a remarkable record at Rapid City, South Dakota high school, winning three state titles. As a high school junior he made it to the '76 Final Trials in Cleveland, losing 20-9 to the eventual runner-up at 114.5. In 1977 Lewis won the Junior World Championship, pinning the Japanese wrestler who became a Senior World champion the following year. Lewis enrolled at the University of Iowa, making the NCAA finals as a true freshman. He won the NCAAs as a sophomore and a junior, but a severe elbow injury kept him from winning his third straight championship. Lewis made the 1980 US Olympic team at 136.5 and was the 1983 Pan-Am champion:

He talks about his early wrestling days and the '84 Trials:

My father was the catalyst of my wrestling career. He let me chase my dream and told me what I had to do to reach my goals.

I started wrestling in sixth grade and hardly ever lost. Here is an original story that hardly anyone knows. In 1971, the AAU had its initial age-group National tournament. I entered the 11-and-under youth group at 65 pounds and won. I was the first National AAU age-group champion.

Jumping ahead to the '80s, I had a lot of injury problems starting in 1981. From '81-'83, I never won any tournament anywhere. I had lost my 'mojo', but I started getting it back in '84. I picked up a great trap-arm gut wrench from watching one of the Russians and that became my best weapon. I could work it on anyone in the world.

I didn't enter the National Open in '84 because I had already qualified for the Trials. At the Iowa City Final Qualifier I wrestled both Smith and Dellagatta.

Up to our Iowa City match, I had wrestled Smith five times with only one victory over him. It always seemed that I was hurt when I wrestled him, but not this time. I was injury-free and in good condition. I turned Lee Roy four times with my gut-wrench and beat him, 11-9.

Then I wrestled Dellagatta. I was 5-4 against him lifetime, always high-scoring matches. This was no exception. He beat me, 20-10. I knew he was injured and not wrestling up to his usual high level. I think I overlooked him. He came out and put it to me, throwing me a couple of times and running up a big early advantage. I started chasing him trying to catch-up. If I had wrestled conservatively and only lost by eight points or less, I would have won that Iowa City Qualifier. As it was, because of the score differential, Dellagatta finished 1st, Smith 2nd [because he beat Dellagatta] and I was 3rd because of losing by that major decision.

I knew that winning that tournament was meaningless, since USA Wrestling had pre-

Randy Lewis and Ricky Dellagatta *Photograph by Scott Conroe, courtesy of* Amateur Wrestling News

determined that the Final Trials matches in Michigan at 136.5 would be round-robin format rather than the usual ladder format. The top four wrestlers [Dellagatta, Smith, Darryl Burley and Lewis] were too even to give anyone the distinct advantage of being the top person on the ladder. The Committee also did this for three Greco weight classes.

I worked out at Iowa City right up till the time of the Final Trials in Michigan. My first opponent was Lee Roy, while Dellagatta and Burley squared off. I went ahead early with a takedown and two gut-wrenches to lead 5-2. He came back and took me down a couple of times towards the end of the bout and it ended with my winning by criteria. Smith's people protested that match, but the protest was denied.

I won the second match. I was ahead 8-5 and then gave up two easy takedowns at the end to make the final score 8-7. I thought I had won and was getting focused on wrestling my next

opponent, Dellagatta.

However, again the Smith team protested the match. The Protest Committee went into a closed room, watched a tape replay and made up points for Lee Roy. They wanted Lee Roy on the team. They said that with 1:24 left and me ahead, 5-4, that Smith should have received three points (a one and a two) for a move that put me on my back. They decided that we should re-wrestle the entire match right away.

I was working out in my sweats back in the practice area with no idea I'd have to wrestle Smith again. When I heard my name announced over the loud speaker to report to the mat to wrestle Smith, I was in shock. I remember nothing about that match except that I lost by 13-0. So, now it was tied at one apiece in matches, and we had to wrestle our fourth match. In that one I hurt my knee early-on and couldn't continue. I defaulted to Smith. I also defaulted my matches against Dellagatta the next day.

Luckily for me, USA Wrestling screwed a lot of things up. First, the protests were not allowed on 'judgment calls', only for procedure mistakes like awarding points to the wrong wrestler. Second, there were suppose to be five officials on the Protest Committee but they only had three; and, third, two of the people on the Committee were from Stillwater, Smith's hometown. In fact, Greg Strobel was a Committee member and he was Smith's roommate for a year.

We took our case against USA Wrestling to binding arbitration in Chicago. Both sides agreed that the Arbitrator's ruling would be final. Our lawyers brought six witnesses to the hearing. They all testified that after watching the tapes of the match that there was no possible way that Smith could have been awarded a 'one and a two' for the move in question. Meanwhile USA Wrestling could not explain how they ever got to the score they did.

The judge listened to and believed our witnesses. However, I think he felt bad in taking something away from Smith, so he compromised and told us to re-wrestle the last 84 seconds of the bout with me leading, 5-4.

I got a call at 6pm that evening telling me to get on a plane for California and that I had to wrestle Smith and Dellagatta. Because of my injured knee, I hadn't worked out at all in the intervening three weeks. All I had been able to do was lift some weights and ride the stationary bike. I never saw a doctor so I never knew exactly what the knee problem was, but I didn't want to take any chance on hurting it more in drills. When I went to California I was just betting on the knee holding up in my matches and it did.

I fly out to California and Smith, Dellagatta and I get together to determine the weigh-in situation. We are all weighing around 150 so we decide there will be a three kilo weight allowance.

We all make weight and then Smith and I wrestle-off the last 84 seconds starting with the score 5-4 in my favor and I beat him, 7-4. I have to then wrestle Dellagatta the following day. Because of the protest, he has the door re-opened for him to make the team. If he beats me twice and scores at least 22 points, he gets to go to the Olympics. That was not an impossible task as we had wrestled each other a dozen

times before and in nine of those matches he scored at least ten or more points. However, I am up for the matches with him and beat him twice to make the team.

Meanwhile, USA Wrestling goes back on its word and tries to get an Oklahoma state court to overturn the Arbitrator's decision. That's not allowed in binding arbitration, but they were so determined to get Smith on the team they did it anyway. What USA Wrestling put me through was criminal. It haunts me to this day. They lied and cheated and then tried to blame it on Gable. He did nothing wrong, he just wanted this to be over.

Let me make this clear, I can guarantee you this — not one person, not even Lee Roy Smith, can watch that film and tell me that Lee Roy won that match.

Ricky Dellagatta

AN OUTSTANDING wrestler at Buena, New Jersey high school, Dellagatta compiled a 73-3 record. He subsequently wrestled at the University of Kentucky where he became a three-time All-American. In 1981 he was named the Athlete-of-the-Year at the University which is best known for its basketball and football prowess. Dellagatta won the National AAUs at 136.5 in 1980, 1983 and 1984 and twice defeated the great Russian champion, Sergei Beloglazov, in international competition.

Dellagatta's motor was always racing when out on the mat. High-scoring matches and Outstanding Wrestler awards (such as at the 1983 National Freestyle AAUs and the 1982 Canadian Cup) were the norm.

Dellagatta tells his side of the '84 Trials controversy:

I believe that I was a victim of a system that did not allow the purest sport in the world to be pure.

At the age of 12, while watching the '72 Olympics on television, I decided I wanted to be an Olympic wrestler. The wrestlers became my heroes and my biggest hero was Dan Gable. He turned out to be my nemesis, which is too bad.

I was taught never to make excuses and I accept that wholeheartedly. However, in my college and Freestyle career, I faced a lot of prejudice, controversy and politics. That's not what our sport is all about, but it was there. I just didn't feel it; I knew it.

It was at the University of Kentucky where I first felt the politics and prejudices in wrestling. I was a little Italian-American and our team captain for two years. I was the only white guy on the team. We received a lot of taunting on our road trips because of the racial makeup of our team, especially when we wrestled down in Alabama and Louisiana.

In the 1982 National AAUs, I went 7-0-1, but still finished 3rd. I wrestled this match against Lee Roy Smith and it ended up 10-10, with me winning on criteria. The referee raised my hand and I walked off the mat victorious. However, the officials got together afterwards and changed the score and gave the victory — and 1st place — to Lee Roy. Why? I think it was because I wasn't a Midwesterner and wasn't supported by honchos at the AAU and USA Wrestling.

In 1983 and 1984 I won the US Open Nationals beating Smith 15-3 and Darrell Burley 13-4 in the two finals. I wasn't losing any more, but I wasn't allowed to compete in the World Cup wrestle-offs because some people thought I wasn't good enough. I was told by the NYAC head coach, Sonny Greenhalgh, that the committee felt Smith was 'heads and shoulders' better than me, even though I just beat him badly in the US Nationals and was named Outstanding Wrestler.

It was getting time for the '84 Olympic Trials and I entered a pre-Trials tournament in Chicago where I hurt my knee pretty severely. I questioned whether I should even enter the Trials, but I told myself I had to give it a shot. My gift was speed — I was quicker than any of the guys I wrestled — and I hoped my knee injury would not hurt my speed.

In the Iowa City Trials, I won all my matches except the one against Smith. In our bout, I did what I call a sit-duck from a front headlock and had him pinned. The refs never called it and he ended up beating me. I pinned Darryl Burley in 1:34 and beat Randy Lewis, 20-10. Meanwhile, Lewis beat Smith so I finished in 1st place going

into the Final Trials in Michigan.

I thought I had the luxury of waiting for the ladder wrestlers to wrestle-off for the chance to challenge me, like all the other Freestyle winners at Iowa City. I was back home in New Jersey — training, priming myself to weigh-in and wrestle on Saturday. I figured on flying out to Michigan on Thursday.

However, on Tuesday I get a call from Greenhalgh telling me I have to be in Michigan the next day to weigh-in or else I forfeit. Now, I am coming down from 149 pounds to 136.5. For some reason they changed the format from the ladder system to a four-man round-robin just for my weight class.

Well, I fly out there immediately and proceed to shed all the weight overnight. But, I did get sick doing so. On Thursday I have to wrestle Burley. For whatever reasons my NYAC coaches don't arrive in Michigan until Friday evening. Burley beats me in our opening match but I beat him in the next two to advance. I am not feeling good and I have to make scratch weight the next day, too. Lewis forfeits to me so I don't have to wrestle, but I still have to make scratch weight the third day. I face Smith on Saturday. I am still sick and he beats me.

The tournament ends. It is not at all what I expected. Why did they change the process to a four-man round-robin format for 136.5? Why did I have such a short notice? Did the other wrestlers know of this round-robin in my weight class? Why didn't someone tell me early on the change in format and that I'd have to make weight three days in a row and wrestle starting on Thursday rather than Saturday? Why didn't anyone standup for me?

Anyway, I tell myself, 'They got me', and I wish Lee Roy the best. I grudgingly accept that he's the one going to the Olympics. I think that my emotional roller-coaster is finally over. I'm not going to wrestle any more — ever. My dream as a young man was shattered!

A couple weeks later I get a phone call from Sonny. He tells me that they are going to wrestle the 136.5 Trials over again out in the Olympic Training Camp at Big Bear Lake. I couldn't believe it.

Without any training, I hop on a plane to California. Lewis and Smith have already wrestled their 84-second rematch with Lewis winning, which I can not believe. I then had to wrestle Lewis. We were given a couple kilo weight allowance and early on the morning of the weigh-in — and it was a beautiful California blue-sky morning — Randy and I show up at the scales with no one else around. He jumps on and is on weight; I'm about a half-pound over. I say, 'Okay, Randy, I'll weigh you in; you're good' and he takes off, drinking his Gatorade. A few minutes later, Gable and a couple others walk in. Now Gable is the US team head coach, supposedly impartial. He sees me and proclaims, 'I want it to be on the record that Dellagatta missed weight.' I am on the scales and by now the bar is even. I am on weight. I tell Gable, 'Well then you better weigh in Lewis because if I didn't make it, neither did he.'

I knew then that the playing field wasn't level. That was an indicator to me that this was an orchestrated wrestle-off by Lewis's coach who doubled as the US coach.

I lost the two bouts to Lewis, even though in the first bout I thought I had him pinned, but once again it wasn't called.

I have no disrespect for either Randy Lewis or Lee Roy Smith. They were both great wrestlers. It is no disgrace to lose to either one. But, the system betrayed the purest sport.

I have a great deal of respect for what Dan Gable has done for wrestling in America; however I do feel his love for competition interfered with his ability to select the best men for the 1984 team. While he's called a legend, he is also a legend-breaker because of the number of great wrestlers that saw they couldn't compete on his terms. I believe the USA Wrestling censorship of Gable was the start of making wrestling a better sport in this country.

Lee Roy Smith

SMITH was a two-time Oklahoma state champion at Del City high school and a two-time Junior National champion. He was recruited to Oklahoma State where he placed 5th and 4th in the '77 and '79 NCAAs before becoming an NCAA champion in 1980 at 142 pounds.

A wrestling icon in the Sooner state, Smith was voted the Outstanding Wrestler at the USA Senior Freestyle Championships in 1980 and won the National AAUs in 1981 and 1982. He placed 2nd at the World Championships in Kiev at 136.5 in 1983.

He recalls the 1984 Trials.

In preparation for the Trials I worked out in Stillwater with anyone I could get in here. I didn't have the backing of a big-time club so I was personally involved in raising funds for myself and others in the Cowboy Freestyle Club effort. I didn't have a strong club coaching affiliation either. Joe Seay was making the transition to Oklahoma State that summer so he really wasn't involved that much in my training process prior to the Trials in 1984.

In my weight class there was a talented pool of wrestlers — Burley, Dellagatta, Lewis, [Mike] Land. I trained with those guys in mind, but I couldn't concentrate on any single one. Lewis and Dellagatta had unorthodox styles with different strengths and techniques. My strategy was to stay away from their strengths and dictate my own strategy against them.

I don't remember much detail from the '84 Trials in Iowa City. I do recall that the only loss I had was to Lewis. I figured his only chance to beat me was at the University of Iowa. I remember coming away feeling I didn't have one of my better tournaments and felt I gave little hope to my competitors and would need to make sure I peaked for the Final Trials.

I also don't recall much detail on my matches with Burley and Dellagatta in Michigan, or my matches with Lewis. I remember that he came out aggressive with a leg attack, which caught me by surprise in the first match which I protested.

I do recall the situation that led to the protest in our second match. It was a scramble while I was finishing on a high crotch crack-down finish. Lewis attempted to counter and exposed himself as we rolled around. We were each awarded points. Coach Seay said that we should protest the scramble because Lewis should not have been awarded any points, that those points should be awarded to me since I initiated the action and exposed his back to the mat.

Seay filed the protest according to the procedures. Once the Protest Committee reviewed the

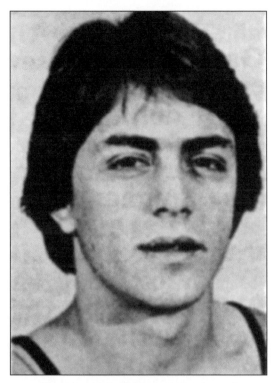

Lee Roy Smith *Photograph courtesy of Amateur Wrestling News*

tape of the match, they voted unanimously that I won the protest and said that the match must be re-wrestled from the start.

Randy was obviously discouraged when he came out to wrestle the rematch. I scored first and built a big lead. I sensed he was giving up. I'm not sure if it was from an injury, as he appeared to be limping, or his spirit was broken. I won the match and my hand was raised. He showed up for the final tie-breaker match limping. I was ahead 5-3 when he injury defaulted the match. The next day I had to wrestle Ricky Dellagatta and won two straight matches to earn the spot on the Olympic team. I received the plaque, and I still have it, and they took my picture along with all the other team members for winning the Trials in 1984.

I left the Trials in Michigan believing I was going to wrestle in Los Angeles, only to quickly find out that Lewis had filed for an arbitration hearing that was going to take place in Chicago. Although I was being told I had nothing to worry about, I could not just focus on training

and winning a gold medal. Over the next several weeks, I entered an unfamiliar legal world. With my fate and dreams being in the hands of others, it just all seemed so surreal to me.

Lewis's arbitration defense was well supported. Mine was not. They had better technical and tactical expertise on their side — and the Olympic coaching staff. I suffered a major blow in my defense at this hearing. USA Wrestling underestimated the tactics of Lewis' appeal which had the head Olympic coach testify on his behalf. In USA Wrestling's communications with my father, they told us there was no need to come out to Chicago for the arbitration and that I didn't need to hire a lawyer.

I was told the arbitration judge ruled that the match should be re-wrestled from the point of the protested call with me behind by one point with 84 seconds to go. All the top competitors knew going through the Trials process that we were wrestling-off to win a gold medal in LA, whether the Russians were there or not. There was a lot at stake. My family responded to the arbitration results by filing a restraining order on the ruling in Federal Court in Los Angeles to no avail. Rarely will a Federal Court over-rule an arbitration court. So, I thought, 'What I have to lose? Go to Big Bear and go for it.'

I do recall that no one other than Lewis, myself, the officials and coaches were allowed at the match. Lewis took a defensive strategy and kept me at a distance. I couldn't crack it to set up my moves. As time ran down I started to have to force things and time ran out. I lost.

I chose not to stay in California and watch the Olympics. Actually, I left the country during the Olympics to get away from it all.

I regretted keeping the match as close as it was with Lewis. I should have created situations that were more clear cut — but that's hard to do especially against a good wrestler and scrambler.

Looking back on it all, I believe no one had any other motive than just being competitive. I think it hurt my parents more than me. In retrospect my father thought that Gable overstepped his boundaries at the arbitration hearing.

As one person told me, and I agree, 'If that's the worse thing that happens to me in my life, then I am a lucky person.'

Stan Dziedzic

DZIEDZIC was the manager of the 1984 US Olympic Freestyle wrestling team. He was finishing up his tenure as National team coach at the time of the Trials and was an on-the-scene observer.

Dziedzic discusses the controversy from his point-of-view:

At the time of the Trials, I was still on the payroll of USA Wrestling. Though I was deemed to be at the arbitration hearing on behalf of Lewis, it correctly could be considered that I was also there on behalf of USA Wrestling and, thus, Smith.

The arbitration was thought by most as a 'we versus they' deal; the people even sat on separate sides of the table — Gable, Robinson and myself on one side; Combs, Holzer, Strobel on the other.

I didn't see it that way so much. I did not initiate, seek or request to be part of the arbitration but, once called, was required by the Amateur Sports Act.

I suspect I could have requested to be deposed in lieu of appearing at the hearing but as the USA National coach I felt that would have been a dereliction of my duties. And given their positions, it would have been equally derelict for Werner, Steve, Greg, Dan or J not to attend.

Regarding the arbitration hearing, a key point to consider is this — the judge didn't rule on the merits of the match or the officiating, He was arbitrating the 1978 Amateur Sports Act. In effect he was deciding if Lewis was given full and fair treatment under the Amateur Sports Act.

The judge admitted that he knew little about amateur wrestling and was not interested in watching the video tapes.

Some background is important. This was the first year that US Wrestling ran the Trials. They wanted to take away any notion that coaches would decide who made the Olympic team. They wanted to eliminate any sense or perception of bias. Their Trials procedures basically said that the Olympic coaches could only be spectators. I believe this is a good thing.

Now, I believe Bob Dellinger [deceased Hall Of Fame wrestling writer and Director of the National Wrestling Hall Of Fame in Stillwater from 1976 to 1993] was the Tournament Director in Michigan.

He had a relationship with the Smith family and may even have been the godfather to Lee Roy or one of his brothers. Anyway, as Tournament Director, Dellinger could exert his powers. This plays an important part in the whole arbitration scenario.

The night before the Lewis-Smith matches, Jim Scherr and Melvin Douglas were wrestling the last of several matches against each other and the match went into several overtimes. Now, the USA Wrestling rules said that certain rounds had to be completed by certain days, and the Scherr-Douglas matches had to be completed that night.

However, I remember Dellinger saying that if the score of the Scherr-Douglas match was still tied at the end of the next overtime, he was going to make the executive decision to over-ride the rules and continue the match on the following day. That was probably a good, fair decision. However, it set a precedent.

The next day, Lewis and Smith wrestle. Lewis wins the first match, then there is the protested match. At the end of the match, Lewis is ahead, but Smith's coach [Joe Seay] files a protest with the Protest Committee. After viewing the tapes of the match, the Committee overturns the bout score and announces that the bout must be re-wrestled according to the rules.

Lewis and his father, obviously upset with the ruling by the Protest Committee, ask to have the rematch moved to the next day in order to give Randy time to recover. Dellinger denied the request. Smith went on to beat Lewis that day and was subsequently declared the winner of the Trials at 136.5.

As I mentioned before, the arbitration hearing was about the Amateur Sports Act and potential bias against Lewis. I believe the arbitrator, in making his decision, looked at two key factors:

1) Should Dellinger, because of his relation-

ship with the Smith family, have recused himself before making the decision to deny Lewis' request to move the make-up match until the following day?

2) The make-up of the Protest Committee. I do not think that the make-up of the Protest Committee necessarily followed the guidelines set out by USA Wrestling. I believe that there were suppose to be at least four officials on the Committee and the presence of Strobel, who lived in Stillwater, Smith's home town, led the judge to believe that Lewis was not given fair treatment.

Lewis could still have gone to arbitration even without those points in his favor, but his case would not have been nearly as strong. Remember Rick Tucci and Chuck Almeida were two of the most capable officials in the world.

I certainly did not agree with the Arbitrator's decision to re-wrestle the bout from the time of the dispute. He should have said, 'Wrestle the full bout over or the best two-out-of-three bouts.'

I think people argued over the wrong issue, like did Gable's presence influence the Arbitrator. That didn't happen. Or if Gable should even have been there. The Arbitrator later sent a letter to Gable saying that he had the right, and even the obligation, to be there at the hearing. He said the organization [USA Wrestling] can't rebuke you.

During the arbitration process, Lee Roy was with the team members out in California, but my sense was he felt like he was an outsider. It was a trying period for him. I believe he was psychologically so affected by the whole thing that he could not perform up to par in his 84-second rematch.

For me it wouldn't have mattered but I sensed it bothered Lee Roy. My only regret is that the wrestlers were not insulated from the effect the process may have had on their performance.

Lastly, a few words about Steve Combs. I had, and still have, a lot of respect for Steve. He went totally out of character with his censure and his letter to Gable. I didn't understand why there was so much anger vetted against Dan. I think that led to Steve's departure from USA Wrestling.

Rick Tucci

TUCCI was one of the most highly regarded wrestling officials in the world. A resident of Hollywood, Florida, Tucci started refereeing high school matches in 1965. He received his 'E' rating from FILA at the '76 Pan-Am Games in Mexico City, and he refereed every Freestyle World Championship from 1977-1983.

Tucci was the mat official for the second Lewis-Smith bout. He recalls:

I remember parts of the match. The action was back and forth. The deciding move started with Smith on bottom, Lewis on top. There was a bit of a flurry. Lee Roy blocked Randy's arm and sat back into him. Randy was caught off-balance, his hand went back, and his elbow hit the mat. Then he got back on top. I scored it two points for Smith for the exposure and one point for Lewis coming back up. I felt that Lee Roy initiated the pressure and was deserving of the points. However, the points were not confirmed by the mat judge and mat chairman.

It got pretty nasty after that. Gable got intimately involved, fighting for Lewis, his own Iowa wrestler. That left a bad taste in a lot of people's mouth.

One of the things that aggravated me the most occurred at the arbitration hearing. The Lewis team brought in another official, Chad Crow, as an expert witness. He said the call I made was wrong. Crow wasn't regarded as one of our top officials. He did a lot of Iowa's home matches, though. Other senior officials were around — like Evanoff, Garber, Zuaro — who really were the experts. But they didn't get called to testify.

The other bad thing was the California wrestle-off. They started with Randy in the lead, and made it very difficult for Smith to win. He had to give all his Olympic training equipment and everything back after he lost.

It was not a good situation all the way around. It turned many people against Gable for his involvement, which was too bad.

Steve Combs

COMBS was a Big Ten wrestling champion at the University of Iowa and runner-up in the NCAAs at 167 pounds in 1963. He won the National AAUs in 1966 and made the 1968 US Freestyle Olympic team. In 1974, Combs took over the leadership of the USWF and was most instrumental in their successful battle to emerge as the governing body for amateur wrestling in the US.

In 1984, Combs was the Executive Director of the newly formed USA Wrestling organization. He was not present at the Trials but was intimately involved in all the controversy. After the arbitration hearing Combs wrote a personal, 'f**k you, strong letter to follow' type of letter to Gable that was widely reported by the media during the Olympic Games.

Combs talks about his point of view on the whole subject:

The Lewis-Smith controversy was probably the lowest point in what was the greatest experience of my career — heading the USWF and USA Wrestling organizations. I had quite a few encounters in the 12-year period battling the AAU, but nothing like the controversy surrounding the '84 Trials. I am very proud of my accomplishments in finally getting the Federation acknowledged as the US governing body. I felt that what I was doing was in the best interest of wrestling.

The crux of the Lewis-Smith arbitration was the 1978 Amateur Sports Act. What happened with Gable was extremely frustrating and disappointing. The position I had taken with the Board members, 24 to 26 people representing all aspects of wrestling, was at the heart of this disappointment. Let me go back to 1983 in order to frame the whole story about the controversy.

Gable was selected as Olympic team coach well before the Trials. That was a difficult decision for our Federation Board members. The Board at that time was made up of numerous administrators who had fought the AAU for years, plus some new grass-roots members and active athletes. Through the years of battle with the AAU, Dan was both an

active competitor and eventually a coach in Iowa. He was never behind the USWF even though his first international experience was a trip to the Soviet Union under USWF leadership. No one could ever recall him saying that the USWF was doing the right thing for wrestling. Many of our folks saw Dan aligned with the AAU, though no one ever heard him say bad things about us either.

Hence, Dan was not 'one of us' from the beginning and many of the Board members wanted one of 'our people' named as coach. In contrast, Russ Hellickson and J Robinson had been extremely proactive in supporting the USWF and the Federation programs over the years.

I personally considered Russ and J as the two most important people in the wrestling world to go to for advice on issues regarding National level programs. So when it came time for the final selection of our Olympic team coach, I went to Russ and J for their advice. I told them that Gable was a strong candidate but our Board didn't think he was the right man and that they didn't identify with him.

Russ and J both told me that Dan was the best and only guy to coach the team. They were very emphatic about it and said that the athletes identified with him and that he was undoubtedly our best choice. Because of the diverging opinions, I got caught up emotionally in the selection process. Based on the strong support from the active athletes, I went to the Board members and sold Dan's candidacy to them. It was finally resolved; the Board appointed Dan Gable as our Olympic team head coach.

I personally did not go to the Final Trials tournament in Michigan; it was being handled by our Director of National Teams, Greg Strobel. I stayed back in Stillwater at USA Wrestling headquarters. On the first day of competition I received a phone call from my staff in Michigan informing me, 'We have a problem. We are spending a lot of time in the back room reviewing videos of protested matches. And Randy Lewis, with the support of Dan Gable, is protesting Lee Roy Smith's victory.'

It all ended up in my hands. Here I was trying to establish a new organization built on honesty and fair play, something we didn't see exist in the old AAU. And now, we were being accused of the same things by our own head coach.

I was not against the process of going to ar-

bitration. I accepted that as being okay, especially since the Federation used arbitration to win its battle against the AAU years earlier. What I could not understand was Gable's involvement in the process. He was now the Olympic coach, not the coach of Iowa wrestlers. He should not have been involved in the Trials selection process. His job was to train and inspire the wrestlers selected for the team. I can understand J Robinson taking on Lewis's side; after all, he was his coach at Iowa and had not yet been designated a National team coach. But Dan should not have been challenging the organization that appointed him as head coach.

As we know, the arbitration went in Lewis' favor. I was very disappointed and found it difficult to accept on two levels: 1) that Smith lost due to a great extent on Gable's reputation and how vigorously he fought before the Arbitrator on behalf of Lewis, and 2) that the Arbitrator decided to have the two wrestlers re-wrestle from the point of protest. Starting with Lewis ahead and only 84 seconds of wrestling to go made everything more ridiculous to accept. If the Arbitrator didn't want to give Smith the win, then he at least should have given the wrestlers a full match to decide the outcome. It was an absurd, ridiculous verdict.

Even these many years later, as I am reminded of the letter I sent to Gable following the verdict, I am as disappointed and embarrassed by my active support of his selection as Olympic coach as I was then.

Greg Strobel

STROBEL was a three-time All-American at Oregon State University, winning NCAA titles in '73 and '74. He went on to be an assistant coach at Oregon State and also a high school coach prior to joining USA Wrestling. He attended the '84 Trials as Combs' delegate from USA Wrestling and was part of the Protest Committee and the arbitration hearings.

Strobel relates his story about the '84 Trials:

In March of 1983, I took the job as USA Wrestling National Teams Director. I was a full-time staff person, working for Steve Combs.

I had liaison responsibility for the Coach Selection Committees and the Sports Committees, which established the Trials procedures. As the liaison, I did not write or revise any rules, but merely expedited the process. We set up the ladder system and the video system all as part of making things as fair as possible.

I can tell you that the full intent of USA Wrestling's procedures was to make the team selection process fair and equitable for everyone. People were tired of the AAU days when coaches at times interfered in the selection of World and Olympic team members.

As the USA Wrestling liaison at the Trials, I would attend all Protest Committee meetings, but did not have a vote. I was an expert on the process and procedures, but was not a category E official, so I could provide input on the protest process but was really not qualified to vote on bout scoring matters.

Basically, the Protest Committee people felt that the second Lewis-Smith bout was so topsy-turvy that the fairest thing to do was to re-wrestle it. This was not the only bout that the Committee voted to uphold the protest.

USA Wrestling made the mistake of being unprepared for the arbitration. We should have had our attorneys there like the Lewis side did. The other side had all the firepower; we had the short straw. And on top of that, the most famous name in wrestling, Dan Gable, was there representing the other side.

I think Combs and Holzer [USA Wrestling President] didn't believe they needed attorneys there. They thought it was a cut and dried issue — we followed our procedures the way we designed them. They were overconfident. When you go to court anything can happen — and it did. Plus, the Arbitrator can do anything he wants. He was convinced by Lewis and his attorneys and his supporters that he [Lewis] was treated unfairly. The Arbitrator really only heard one side of the story.

Why the judge ruled to start wrestling again with 84 seconds left is beyond me. Lee Roy, being behind by a point, had no chance to win under those conditions. A more fair decision would have been the Arbitrator saying to both wrestlers, 'In one week from today, re-wrestle the match.'

It would have been nice to have both Lewis

and Smith on the team. I knew each of them — Randy from coaching him on a trip to Japan in '83 and Lee Roy from being together in Stillwater. I believe Gable thought he saw an injustice being done and that he had to do something about it. He didn't, and neither do I, see anything wrong with getting involved. That's the way he is.

Dan Gable

GABLE, the 1984 Olympic Freestyle team coach, talks about those Trials and his involvement:

The thing that bothered me the most about the whole controversy in '84 was the way protests were handled. USA Wrestling set up the protest system and it was clearly stated that wrestlers and coaches could not protest judgment calls.

Well, there were lots of protests and most ended up being on judgment calls. The Committee allowed one judgment call to be protested and that opened the gates. Things got way out of hand.

Those protests were a nightmare. In Freestyle and Greco-Roman wrestling, there are always going to be judgment calls. That's just the way Freestyle and Greco-Roman wrestling is. Was it a 90-degree angle or 89 degrees? Who can tell exactly?

In the case of Smith, like the rest, there should not have been a protest allowed, because it was a judgment call. I believe that the Arbitrator based his decision on that breakdown of the process.

I stand by my comment at the time that if the situation had been reversed, I would have said the same on Lee Roy's behalf. What made it even more difficult was the perception of bias — Randy and me being from Iowa, while Lee Roy was working with the USA Wrestling people in Stillwater. I don't know if either side was intentionally biased. Maybe unintentionally, though I hope not.

It ended up with lots of controversy and hard feelings all around. It caused me a lot of personal grief. When I received the letter from

Dan Gable *Photograph courtesy of Amateur Wrestling News*

Steve Combs, I felt very bad that a guy could feel that way; I broke down in tears at the USA Wrestling Directors' meeting after the Olympics when they censured me. I just felt terrible that I was part of this system that caused so much controversy.

The rest of the experience leading up to the '84 Olympics was great. We knew that some of the main competition would be missing due to the Communist boycott. We had to take on the mentality of having all the wrestlers ready to compete. We had to train them to be as good as they could possibly be and not to take the competition lightly.

I felt our guys were very well prepared. I had a great committed group of assistant coaches and had each assistant specifically assigned to at least one wrestler. For instance, I think I had Bill Weick assigned to Baumgartner and Weaver. Everyone had a responsibility and it worked out well.

Excerpts from 1984 Olympic Trials Procedures, approved 01-23-84 by the Executive Committee of USA Wrestling

Statement of Policy

The process of selecting the 1984 Olympic Team must be logical, fair and unbiased.

Members of the Olympic Committee Coaching Staff are prohibited from coaching any US athlete during the Trials competition against another US athlete.

There must be no favoritism towards any athlete at any time.

Final Qualifying Tournaments

5. The top three place-winners in each weight class advance to the Ladder Challenges of the Final Olympic Trials.

8. If the top three place-winners in a weight class are determined by criteria (after each records one victory and one defeat in the round-robin), competition in that weight class at the Final Olympic Trials shall be a four-man round-robin rather than a ladder challenge.

10. Protest procedures for Final Qualifying Tournaments and Final Olympic Trials:

a. The Protest Committee shall comprise:
1) Chief mat official, who shall serve as chairman
2) National Teams Director
3) Chief pairings master
4) An additional referee-judge appointed by the chairman
5) An additional referee-judge appointed by the chairman

b. The Olympic coach of the appropriate style shall be a member ex officio of the Protest Committee. He may participate in the discussions, but shall have no vote in determination of the outcome.

c. Any member of the Protest Committee shall disqualify himself from a protest hearing when he has personal ties to any contestant in the same weight class. All replacements shall be appointed by the chairman.

d. All matches shall be video-taped, and tapes shall be reviewed to determine possible errors in scoring. If tapes other than the official video tape are available, the Protest Committee may consider them also in determination of the facts. (It is recommended that two official video cameras be employed during each match at the Final Olympic Trials.)

e. The protest must be filed in writing by the athlete himself not more than 30 minutes after the conclusion of the match.

f. The protest fee shall be $20.

g. The Protest Committee may reach one of the following conclusions:
1) The protest is without merit and is denied.
2) The protest is correct and the outcome of the match must be reversed. Protest fee refunded.
3) The protest has merit but the effect of the outcome of the match is uncertain. The protested result is discarded and the match is ordered re-wrestled entirely. Protest fee refunded.

Final Olympic Trials

3. Protest procedures same as for the Final Qualifying Tournaments.

THEY ALL CAN'T GO

1988

> *At the start of the Trials my confidence and passion was over the top. I knew I could beat Dave (Schultz) and I would be 'The Man'. I had just one fear – and that was John duPont.*
>
> — Kenny Monday's thoughts about facing 1984 Olympic gold medalist Dave Schultz for the 163-pound spot on the 1988 US Olympic team

IT HAD been 12 years since the United States and the Soviet Bloc countries both participated in the summer Olympic Games. Our Freestyle wrestlers and coaches were confident that this was the Olympiad where the US would finish ahead of the Soviets — something we hadn't accomplished since 1960. The good news was that the US team had exceptional depth at most weight classes. The bad news was that a lot of our world-class wrestlers wouldn't make it through the Trials.

On the international wrestling mats, US wrestlers achieved some brilliant results in the 1985-88 quadrennium. In 1985, Mike Houck won our first Greco-Roman World title; two years later, Dennis Koslowski brought home a World silver medal. In Freestyle, the medals were bountiful. Mark Schultz won gold medals in both '85 and '87. Bill Scherr won a gold medal and a silver medal. Bruce Baumgartner and John Smith won their initial World championships while Dave Schultz, Kevin Darkus, Andre Metzger, Joe McFarland, Jim Scherr and Barry Davis all earned World silver medals in the three-year span.

Several US Freestyle wrestlers distinguished themselves by winning the Tbilisi tournament, often considered the stiffest in the world because one has to defeat so many Russian entries. In 1987 Jim Scherr and Dave Schultz captured the coveted gold medals, while in 1988 Kenny Monday not

Previous spread: The Kenny Monday-Dave Schultz match-ups were one of several marquee bouts at the 1988 Trials *Photograph by Steve Brown, courtesy of Amateur Wrestling News*

only won Tbilisi but was also named the tournament's Outstanding Wrestler.

By the summer of '88, President Ronald Reagan was finishing his second term of office. The 'Reagan Years' — running much in parallel with the 'Thatcher Years' in the UK — saw many baby boomers and middle-class Americans enjoying prosperity, as Reagan introduced a new wave of conservatism that spread like margarine across the country.

The Democrats were keen on stopping this wave and looked to several potential candidates whom they thought could win the White House. Gary Hart and Joe Biden were early front-runners, but both fell on their swords due to strategic mistakes of their own making. The Dems eventually chose Massachusetts Governor Michael Dukakis as their nominee at their National convention in Atlanta. Sidestepping some pressure from the Jesse Jackson camp to add the Reverend Jackson to the ticket, Dukakis picked Texan Lloyd Bentsen as his running mate.

The Republicans had few hard choices. Vice-President George Bush easily won the Republican nomination. He considered Dole as his vice-presidential candidate, but which one? Bob Dole, the popular Senate Republican leader from Kansas, or his wife Elizabeth, the former Transportation Secretary and Federal Trade Commissioner and a favorite among women voters? Bush ended up choosing neither, opting for the youthful Indiana Senator, Dan Quayle.

A case could be made that the highlight of the Bush-Dukakis tussle for the Presidency was the mock debate staged on *Sat-*

urday Night Live late in the summer. Others point to the "Senator, you're no Jack Kennedy" line delivered by Bentsen during his televised vice-presidential debate with Quayle.

In the sports world, the Baltimore Orioles set a mark for futility by losing their first 22 games of the 1988 American League baseball season. Naturally, Baltimore fired their manager, Cal Ripken, Sr. Meanwhile, the Arizona State wrestling team blitzed to the NCAA championship. The Sun Devils became the first school in 21 years located outside of Iowa and Oklahoma to take home the Division I crown.

On Wall Street the stock market had the jitters. The Dow registered an all-time high of 2,700 in August of 1987, but then came the 'Black Monday' crash of October 19, 1987 when the Dow fell by 508 points, or 22.6 percent. The good news was that the 2,100 Dow mark of May, 1988 was practically double the 1,100 high attained five years earlier.

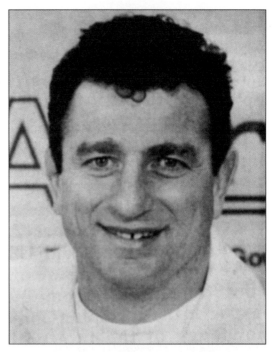

Greco-Roman wrestlers credit Olympic team coach Pavel Katsen for improving the US's stature in international competition
Photograph courtesy of Amateur Wrestling News

The Trials Process

WITH Terry McCann as its President and Gary Kurdelmeier as its Executive Director, USA Wrestling in late '87 announced the 1988 Trials process. The organization's new leadership and creativity was evident in the selection of some non-traditional venues to host the Trials. The powers-that-be chose Reno, Boca Raton, Topeka and Pensacola as the sites for the key Trials tournaments.

The Pensacola spokesperson who headed their city's five-month quest to land the Final Trials remarked to the press that the event hoped to draw at least 8,000 fans — plus wrestlers, their families, officials and media representatives. That number was overly optimistic. Drawing wrestling fans to the humid Florida panhandle in June turned out to be a formidable challenge. Neverthe-

less, the attendance figures reached into the thousands and were a far cry from the couple of hundred in the stands at the Trials in Annapolis in 1964 and at Cleveland in 1976.

Wrestlers aspiring to represent the US in the Seoul Olympics had to initially qualify either through one of eight Regional Trials, the Inter-service tournament, or the National Open tournaments in Freestyle and Greco in April. From there, the top wrestlers would compete in the Final Olympic Qualifier, which was scheduled to be held in Greco on May 12-14 and in Freestyle on May 19-21. The top six in each weight class in each style would then wrestle-off in the Final Trials ladder matches in Pensacola starting June 14.

Approximately 2,000 wrestlers from across the country competed in the preliminary tryouts.

USA Wrestling appointed a pair of colorful head coaches to lead the Olympic teams.

They named University of Indiana coach Jim Humphrey as the head man for the '88 Freestyle team and Dan Gable as his number two. Humphrey and National Freestyle coach Greg Strobel would go on to appoint ten assistant coaches — one for each member of the Olympic Freestyle squad.

Pavel Katsen was selected as the Greco team head coach along with Tom Minkel as his assistant. Katsen was a popular choice.

Greco specialist Mike Houck talks about Katsen, who was the US Greco World team coach in 1985, 1986 and 1987:

As a Greco coach, Pavel took us Americans to another level. He was a huge driving force in having us turn the corner and become world-class caliber Greco wrestlers. He had a concept and a strategy. He taught us that we couldn't go into lock positions with the Europeans.

We had to 'stick and move', use short-arm attacks and defend against turns. He had us work the off-side arm spin and he taught us a lot of edge-of-mat techniques. It was a specific strategy aimed at countering the Russians' strengths and exploiting their weaknesses. It worked.

The Greco Final Olympic Qualifier — Boca Raton, Florida — May 12-14, 1988

THE cozy gymnasium at Florida Atlantic University easily accommodated the enthusiastic crowd that came to watch the Greco-Roman wrestlers. The fans got their money's worth.

Some headline results came out of the 105.5 class. An unheralded 17-year-old wrestler from Missouri, Sammy Henson, defeated former National Greco champion Eric Wetzel along the way to finishing 4th. Two-time Olympian Mark Fuller finished a surprising 2nd behind TJ Jones of the Navy.

At 136.5, Buddy Lee and Dalen Wasmund wrestled a total of 19:58 minutes in overtime before both were disqualified for passivity. An extended match indeed, but still less than half as long as the infamous Wayne Baugh-

man — Willie Williams marathon in the Final Trials 16 years earlier.

Lee, a two-time All-American at Old Dominion, recalls some match details:

In my marathon match with Wasmund, at the 11 minute mark I actually scored with a duck-under, but the referee took the point away. They told me they wanted a more definitive winner. I was the underdog in the match — Wasmund was the guy to beat. At the end, they called it a draw. A half-hour later I had to wrestle again — I beat an opponent from the Army and ended up in 1st place.

Twin brothers Dennis and Duane Koslowski, wrestling at 220 and heavyweight respectively, both qualified for the Final Trials by winning nine matches in a row. In an amazing coincidence, they would go on to join the Scherr brothers (in Freestyle) as two sets of twins from South Dakota to make the '88 US Olympic wrestling team.

Dennis Koslowski tells his story about coming out of a small town in South Dakota, wrestling in Minnesota and advancing along with his twin-brother, Duane, through the 1988 Trials:

I grew up in northeastern South Dakota — the state's wrestling hotbed. My mother died at young age and for awhile my brother and I lived with our aunt and uncle on a farm outside Webster. Right before my high school years we moved to Doland, a village of a couple hundred people. I was a late bloomer physically. As a freshman I wrestled 105, then 119, 138 and 167 in high school. I never won the states; I came in 3rd as a junior and again as a senior in the B [small school] division.

I didn't get looked at one bit by colleges and ended up at a DIII school, Minnesota/Morris. I went on to win the DIII Nationals in 1980 as a junior but in my senior year, I injured my knee and couldn't compete.

I started my studies at chiropractor school in St. Paul in the fall of 1981. I also began rehabbing my knee. It started feeling better so at the end of the first semester I decided to use my last semester of eligibility.

I went back to the Morris campus and wrestled at heavyweight for Minnesota/Morris and

Duane Koslowski throws Craig Pittman en route to winning the 286-pound Greco-Roman Trials
Photograph by Steve Brown, courtesy of Amateur Wrestling News

that's when I won my second DIII crown.

While I was in college, Brad Reinghans would occasionally come over to Morris to work out. That was my introduction to Greco. I couldn't stay with Brad, but I enjoyed the Greco style. I began working with the guys at the Minnesota Wrestling Club where Dan Chandler was running the operation. I went to the '82 Greco Nationals and made it to the finals where Greg Gibson beat me pretty good.

I focused my training on making the '84 Olympic team at 220 pounds. At the '84 Greco National championships in Albany, I beat Jeff Blatnick but during the match he fractured the lower incisor on my tooth. I was in terrible pain. I then had to wrestle Gibson and we were both disqualified for passivity, which was pretty strange. In the Greco Qualifier Gibson beat me

in the finals, 2-0, which meant that I was #2 going into the Final Trials. Blatnick decided to move up to heavyweight since he knew he couldn't beat Greg or me at 220.

At the Grand Valley State Finals, I lost to Gibson in some close matches. Greg was long and strong and was known for his gut-wrench. In the first match I got a lift and throw for three points. Greg got a caution and then he grabbed my leg, which was illegal, and thus he was disqualified. In the next two bouts he beat me — first in overtime and then 2-0 in the final and deciding match.

After the Trials, I went to the Olympic training camp in California and worked out daily with Gibson and Blatnick. Interestingly, I would beat both of them in our scrimmages, which gave me motivation to be ready for the 1988 Olympics.

Meanwhile my twin, Duane, thought he was finished with wrestling after he graduated from Morris. However, while watching the '84 Olympics with me, he brought up the idea of being my training partner to prepare me better for 1988. We agreed on the plan and he moved to the Twin Cities to start training with me.

I was a lot more advanced than Duane was at the international level, so in the beginning he had problems scoring on me. In 1985, we decided that I'd compete at heavyweight while Duane went at 220. We wanted to protect him from getting injured in his first big-time competition. I ended up winning the Nationals; Duane wrestled well, coming in 4th. I went on to get a 6th at the World Championships in Norway. We were both the same size, actually just right for 220 pounds, but it seemed that he had more success with the bigger guys than me. After 1985, Duane usually wrestled at heavyweight while I competed at 220.

In 1986 and 1987 we each won the Nationals. Both years I beat Gibson — who I think was now concentrating more on Freestyle — to win the championship at 220. My big breakthrough came in the 1987 Worlds in France, where I won a silver medal, losing to the Russian in the finals on passivity in overtime. Duane took a 5th at heavyweight.

Our training regime differed from most other wrestlers and it really helped us prepare for the Olympic Trials. First of all, we would spend every other day practicing from the par terre position exclusively, unlike most of the Greco guys, who concentrate their drilling on their feet. We thought it was important to get as much par terre practice as possible. That proved invaluable, especially to Duane, who had to beat out a tough Craig Pittman to make the team. Duane ended up dominating Pittman and didn't even have a close match.

My vigorous stretching program saved me in one of my Trials matches against Chris Tironi, who was my toughest opponent. I considered Chris a good, but not a great, Greco wrestler. In one of our Trials matches, Chris caught me flat-footed with an arm-spin. My knee locked and I felt a terrible burn as it popped. I thought the whole knee was going to bust apart, but nothing really happened. I won the match and was fine afterwards. I am sure that if weren't for the four years of stretching every day, I would have been wiped out and never been able to make it through the Trials.

All in all, it was a very, very special experience to make the Olympic team along with my twin brother. When I won the Olympic bronze medal, I considered that as 'our' medal.

The Freestyle Final Olympic Qualifier — Topeka, Kansas — May 19-21, 1988

CLOSE to 200 of the best US Freestyle wrestlers converged upon Topeka's Expocenter hoping to finish in the top six in their weight class and thus qualify for the Final Trials.

The competition included an impressive array of young guns and fading stars. Alan Fried, just completing his junior year at St. Edward's in the suburbs of Cleveland, entered the tournament as a three-time Junior National champion but he couldn't place among the veterans. Andy Rein, silver medalist in the 1984 Olympics and the coach at the University of Wisconsin in '88, came out of retirement but found the competition too rugged at 149.5 and did not place. Lee Roy Smith could do no better than 4th at 149.5.

The Qualifier finals saw World silver medalist Kevin Darkus lose a close one to Barry Davis; fellow silver medalist Andre Metzger was pinned in just 59 seconds by Nate Carr; 1984 Olympic champion Dave Schultz was upended by Kenny Monday; Mike Sheets pinned World and Olympic champion Mark Schultz.

Fans of high-scoring matches had to look no farther than Ken Chertow's mat in the final round-robin. The young collegian lost a seesaw 15-14 match to Ed Woodburn, came back to defeat Cory Baze 11-6, and ended up losing in the finals to 1984 Olympian Joe Gonzales, 11-9 in sudden-death overtime.

And, in a stunning finals match at 136.5 that had the crowd buzzing, two-time Olym-

> ❝ **We had some tremendous matches, John [Smith] and I. Our match in the National Open in Reno was the first time we ever wrestled each other and was probably the best match to watch. The match was wild and mine to lose.**
>
> **— RANDY LEWIS**

• •

pian Randy Lewis ended World champion John Smith's 131-match winning streak with a 10-8 comeback victory over the Oklahoma State standout.

Lewis talks about his wrestling days following his winning the 1984 Olympic gold medal, his saga of cutting down from 166 pounds to make 136.5, and his showdown matches against old rival Lee Roy Smith's talented younger brother, John:

After winning the Olympics in '84, I retired for a couple of years. I started my comeback in 1986 and wrestled at 149.5 for a few months, but lost to Andre Metzger in the World team tryouts. I was training in Iowa City when I blew out my knee in February of '87. The doctors misdiagnosed the problem and didn't actually operate on me until August. I had major reconstructive surgery and was off the mat a full 11 months, until January of 1988.

I didn't know if I could ever wrestle again, or if I could handle the guys at 149.5 pounds. I was working out with weights and on the machines, but had little mat time. At the end of January I entered a Freestyle tournament and wrestled Jim Jordan at 149.5. I beat him and that gave me a good feeling, since he was ranked #2 in the country at 136.5. Now the question was: could I make it down to 136.5? I was regularly weighing around 166 pounds, but felt that the guys, especially Nate Carr, were too big for me at 149. If I had to do it over, I probably would have gone at 149, but I didn't.

I then wrestled in a dual meet against an all-star Russian team and I beat my guy. I was wrestling very well, not giving up points like I did earlier in my career. I was shutting people out and wrestling more solid than I did in '84.

I had some good workout partners in the Iowa room — guys like Lenny Zalesky, Brad Penrith, and Kevin Dresser — and I would tear after them. I didn't wrestle much with Gable though — he'd beat on me too much.

I decided to try a new weight-making scheme. I was holding around 158 pounds about three weeks before the Regional Trials where I'd have to make scratch weight for the first time. I didn't want to diet the weight off because I didn't have that much body fat and I'd be losing muscle. I decided to sweat the weight off.

I knew my body well and saw where I could sweat off a total of 19 or 20 pounds a day. I'd wrestle for a while, lose some weight, eat and drink, put the plastic suit on and go in the steam room, lose some weight, eat and drink again, and so on. I knew I just had to do this for a short period of time in my life and never again.

I made 136.5 for the one-day Qualifier tournament, coming down from 157 to 136.5 in one day and weighing in the night before the matches. I won the tournament, beating a young Tom Brands, and my weight was back up to 157 by the end of the day. I proved to myself that I could make 136.5. Now the new question was: could I make weight on consecutive days for the three-day Nationals and the Trials tournaments?

At the National Open, I was eight pounds over an hour before weigh-in. I knew from experience that I could lose eight pounds in an hour, which is exactly what I did. Our weigh-ins were always the evening before the matches, so I'd make the weight, go eat and drink, wrestle my matches weighing many pounds over, then sweat off the 10-15 pounds before the evening weigh-in. I remember the evening before my match with John Smith — who was not much of a weight-cutter. When we first checked the scales a couple hours before the final weigh-in, he was three-and-a-half over; I was something like 13 over. I had an easier time losing the weight — he barely made it. I ended up wrestling John the next day weighing 152.

We had some tremendous matches, John and I. Our match in the National Open in Reno was the first time we ever wrestled each other and was probably the best match to watch. The match was wild and mine to lose. I went ahead early but he came back to tie the score, 7-7. I tried a stupid move — a front headlock — which he successfully countered and he ended up winning a 10-8 thriller. I didn't do what I had to do to win that one.

We both got better with each match. Ironically, in all our matches, whoever scored first would lose the match. In the Trials Qualifier in Topeka, I was behind 2-0 but I got a big throw and some turns on him to win, 7-5. We were attacking each other the whole time. No one stalled or backed up; we were each still shooting right up to the end.

The Final Trials — Pensacola, Florida — June 15-18, 1988

THE top 120 Freestyle and Greco wrestlers advanced to the last step towards Seoul in Pensacola's Civic Center for the Final Trials. On the Greco side, the ten winners from the Boca Raton Qualifier were seeded #1, yet only three of them — Shawn Sheldon and the Koslowski brothers — would end up winning the Final Trials. John Morgan would be a fourth, but he did not clinch his Olympic berth until winning a special wrestle-off against Jeff Steubing six weeks later.

Andy Seras earned the Greco 149.5 pound spot the hard way. Unable to compete in the Qualifier due to a tear in his esophagus, Seras was granted an injury hardship invitation to the Final Trials. He first had to wrestle Jim Martinez, the 1984 Olympic bronze medalist, who also received a hardship invitation. Seras defeated Martinez to qualify (at the bottom of the ladder) and then went on to defeat the #6, #5, #4, #3, #2 and #1 seed at 149.5 to make the team.

There were a number of heartbreaker stories coming out of the Final Trials, none more compelling than that of Greco-Roman World champion Mike Houck.

Houck talks about his second straight near-miss of making the US Olympic team:

After losing out on my opportunity to compete in the '84 Olympics, I went back to college at Maranatha. I had a long talk one day with my

coach there, Ben Peterson, and told him that I thought it was time for me to retire from competition. He encouraged me to keep going. He said that he'd personally work with me in the wrestling room — and he did.

1985 was the banner year for me. Even though I had terrible nerve pains in my back, I won the US Greco National Open and went to the Greco World Championships in Norway. I won the gold medal there, becoming the first US wrestler ever to win a World title in Greco.

In the intervening years I had back surgery and took a full year off to recover. I didn't make it back to competition until the 1988 National Open in March, where I dislocated my elbow. I recovered from that and advanced to the Greco Qualifier in Boca Raton in May. I figured my toughest competitor would be Brad Anderson, but I ended up dominating him — and Mike Foy as well. Even though I lost a match to Derrick Waldroup, I won the Qualifier tournament.

Once again I was #1 on the ladder going into the Final Trials at 198. It wasn't Anderson or Waldroup that I would meet in the finals; it was Foy. He was not a pure Greco wrestler like I was. But I will tell you, he was, by far, the best athlete and talented guy I ever wrestled, and that includes all the World champions from Russia and Europe. In the 1988 Final Trials, he wrestled the tournament of his life.

We had a series of high scoring bouts. I won the first one, 8-7. In our second match, Mike ran out to an 8-0 lead and I came back to make it close, losing 9-6. In the last match, he again got a huge early lead, like 9-0. I started coming back and was very close to catching him when the scoreboard clock went dead during the last minute of the match. It took them three minutes or so to fix the clock and that gave Foy the break he needed. The momentum of the match changed and he ended up beating me, 10-9.

Once again I was devastated. It probably wasn't as bad as it was in '84, but I couldn't believe this was happening again — losing by one point in the last match just like four years earlier. I wish I would have had a shot at that Olympic medal, but I have no regrets.

According to Jim Scherr, who was fighting for an Olympic spot in the 198-pound Free-

Jim Scherr and his brother Bill were one of two sets of twins from South Dakota on the US Olympic wrestling team *Photograph courtesy of Amateur Wrestling News*

style division:

There were a number of incredible Freestyle matches to watch — Kenny Monday versus Dave Schultz; Mike Sheets versus Mark Schultz; Kevin Darkus versus Barry Davis. Even though I was focusing on my own matches, plus dealing with a recent personal family tragedy and my dislocated shoulder, I couldn't help but watch these competitors go after each other trying to earn the trip to Seoul.

Scherr and his twin brother Bill were considered favorites to win the Trials. The South Dakota natives were both NCAA champions at the University of Nebraska in 1984 and had won gold [Bill] and silver [Jim] medals at the World Championships. Both were multi-time US Open champions.

The twins, though, had to overcome a horrific family tragedy. In 1988, their sister, 11 months younger than Bill and Jim, was in the final stages of terminal cancer. She died just days before the Final Trials commenced. The boys returned home to South Dakota for the family funeral and then set-off for Pensacola.

Jim Scherr tells his story:

Prior to 1986, Bill and I wrestled at 198 and 180.5. Bill was great at 198, winning the Worlds in '85. I was doing pretty well at 180.5, but I had a tough time beating Mark Schultz consistently. One day Bill and I got together with the Schultz brothers and made this plan. Bill and I would both go up a weight so that the four of us could be on the US team together. We believed we had a good shot at beating the Russians in international competition and that the US team would be strongest with the four of us on it.

I was really in-between weight classes. Normally I weighed 200, so making 198 was easy. I was best wrestling at 186, but that wasn't a weight class and 180.5 was a big pull. Bill normally weighed seven or eight pounds more than me. 198 was the ideal weight class for him. He was small for 220, but we both wanted to be on the team together. Going up to 220 was a huge sacrifice on Bill's part.

The '88 Trials process was very difficult for me. I entered the US Nationals as the defending champion, but I hurt my knee there. I lost to Mike Foy in overtime and ended up 4th, though I didn't wrestle the consolation match since I only had to place in the top six to get into the Trials.

At Topeka I wrestled well. I dominated everyone in the early rounds, including an easy victory in a rematch with Foy. Melvin Douglas was my opponent after Foy. I wrestled Douglas numerous times all during the decade of the '80s. We had many close matches and I always considered him a tough competitor. In the finals, I went on an early leg attack and took him down four times in the first period. Near the end of the period I tried for a fifth takedown. As he kicked out of my single leg attempt, he dislocated my shoulder. It popped out of place and I popped it back in. Although I won the match, I lost the strength in my right arm.

I still had to wrestle Duane Goldman and Dan Chaid. I got one takedown to beat Goldman and then had a tough match against Chaid. I was able to take Dan down with a move that I made up on the spot. He got me in a bad position going for a takedown, but as I was going down to the mat I slipped my good arm around his leg and over the back of his thigh, scooped up

> **I am upset and angry after the match. It was a horrible call on Vinnie's part. The rules clearly state that a wrestler can't initiate a scoring move from outside the 'zone', and Douglas was way outside the 'zone'.**
>
> **– JIM SCHERR**

his ankle and got the takedown to win the match and the tournament.

At Pensacola, it came down to Douglas and me for the 198-pound spot on the team. I was in great shape even though I was still hindered by my dislocated shoulder. My strategy was to wrestle solid and see if I could take advantage of a mistake on the part of Douglas.

– I don't remember much of my first bout with Douglas, other than I won a low-scoring match. In our second bout I felt very strong and confident. I scored a couple of takedowns early and was ahead by three points with just a few seconds to go. We were on our feet and I was trying to push Douglas out-of-bounds and take time off the clock. We went out-of-bounds and I was about to return to the center of the mat, thinking I had the Olympic team made. Douglas then comes at me and throws me to the mat and Vinnie [Zuaro] gives him three points to tie the score. We go into overtime and I am shocked. Douglas gets a legitimate takedown and he wins the bout.

I am upset and angry after the match. It was a horrible call on Vinnie's part. The rules clearly state that a wrestler can't initiate a scoring move from outside the 'zone', and Douglas was way outside the 'zone'. I was worried that the momentum had changed and that Douglas would take confidence from beating me in that second match. I also knew that I didn't have much of an offense with just one good arm.

There was one takedown move that I could do — an inside trip off of a Russian tie. My plan was to look for that opportunity against Douglas. Sure enough, the plan worked as I took him down with the inside trip, catching him with my left leg.

After the match I was physically and men-

tally drained. My brother had already won the Trials at 220, so we met our goal of going to the Olympics together. There was a feeling of euphoria, but considering the constant thoughts about the sister we lost that week, I was more down than up.

Randy Lewis and John Smith met in the 136.5 Freestyle finals. They were 1-1 against each other in their two matches leading up to the Final Trials. Lewis recalls the Pensacola matches and his feelings about competing in the '88 Trials:

In the Trials matches in Florida, Smith had to beat Jim Jordan for the right to wrestle me in the finals. He did beat Jordan rather easily and then he beat me. He won the first match, 8-4. In our second match, I went ahead 2-0; he caught up and was ahead 4-2 when I blew out the ligaments in my bad knee. Referee Rick Tucci correctly stopped the match for my safety and I lost by injury default.

John was way better than I thought he was going to be. I wrestled better than I thought I would. I wrestled my absolute best and better than I wrestled in 1984. John and I wrestled very even. The guy who won was the one who had the most points on the board when the clock stopped.

I am as proud of my accomplishments in 1988 as anything I have ever done. To go pretty even with John Smith after taking so much time off and cutting that much weight was big. I proved a lot to myself going through those 1988 Trials.

Joe Seay coached John Smith during most of his college and Freestyle career. Seay talks about the Smith–Lewis rivalry in 1988:

I started coaching John when I came to Oklahoma State in '84. John took a red-shirt year during the '85-86 season and we began working a lot of Freestyle, because excelling in international competition was definitely his long-term goal.

John was very focused and always well prepared for all his key matches. I knew Randy Lewis from watching him wrestle many, many times over the years. He beat my guy from Cal-State Bakersfield, John Azevedo, back in 1979 in the NCAA finals by a score of 20-14. Randy was

John Smith and Randy Lewis fought and clawed their way through a series of memorable matches in 1988. Smith won the final encounter at Pensacola to clinch a spot on the Olympic team.
Photograph by Ron Good, courtesy of Amateur Wrestling News

always looking to score with the big moves.

In preparation for the Trials, I worked a lot with John on how to best wrestle Randy. We knew we had to try and stay away from his strengths — especially the upper-body moves. We saw certain things in watching videos of Randy's matches where we thought we could capitalize on openings. There was no way we were underestimating Randy Lewis. He was a tenacious Freestyle wrestler.

The first match they wrestled, in Topeka, went back and forth. The guys were going all out. Randy would get ahead by a couple of points but

John would always be back in the match.

In Pensacola, during their first match, it was more of the same. Back and forth it went — huge excitement. John won that one and they wrestled again. Randy hurt his knee. Randy wouldn't quit, as you might expect, and tried to keep on going but the referee had to stop it even though Randy didn't want to. I have always respected Randy for that.

These were two great wrestlers. I was very fortunate to be around the wrestling mats at that time. It was unbelievably exciting to be with such dedicated, talented wrestlers, such intense athletes. They were the two best 136.5 Freestyle wrestlers in the world.

Another Freestyle competitor in the rugged 136.5 pound class was Princeton University graduate John Orr. A native of Altoona, Pennsylvania, Orr played the role of a bridesmaid throughout his wrestling career. He was the runner-up in high school at the Pennsylvania State Tournament, at the Junior Nationals and twice at the NCAAs when he was a student-athlete at Princeton.

Orr recalls giving the '88 Olympics a try:

I entered the Eastern Regionals at East Stroudsburg and beat Jim Jordan for the first time in my career. That victory put me in the running at 136.5, although people asked me why I would want to cut a lot of weight to wrestle in the same weight class as John Smith. I was really too small for 149.5 but had to push very hard to make 136.5. I believed that I had a chance to beat Smith, thinking, 'Who knows, on the right day I could beat anybody.'

I had a terrible tournament at the Topeka Trials. I had a rematch against Jordan and got pinned when I tried a roll-through. I think I also lost to Larry Nugent. I ended up 6th, just enough to qualify for the Pensacola Final Trials.

I wrestled a lot better in Pensacola. I won a couple of matches, including one over my NYAC teammate, Pete Schuyler. However, I wasn't able to defeat Jordan. I gave him a good bout, though. He scored on me when I tripped over some tape sticking up on the mats. Plus, I let him turn me which should never have happened, but it did. I was happy to have wrestled as well as I could. No regrets here. If I had not made it out of the Topeka Trials, it would have stuck in my craw for a long time — leaving wrestling with a poor last effort.

Besides my own experiences, I have this lasting memory of Ken Chertow pulling a lot of weight to make 114.5 pounds. I knew Ken from my days as the graduate assistant coach at Penn State while getting my MBA there. Well, it was the day before the finals and I had already been eliminated. Chertow was having a hell of a time making weight. Before the last weigh-in he's riding this stationary bike and sees my family walk by. In an exhausted voice he tells them to

'get Johnny (me) here quickly'. I get to him and he is about ready to collapse — literally. As he's falling over, I catch him in my arms and get him down off the bike. Somehow he makes the weight and goes on to wrestle in the finals the next day.*

114.5 pounds Freestyle — Ken Chertow vs Joe Gonzales

KEN Chertow was a junior at Penn State in 1988, having finished 3rd in the NCAAs in both '87 and '88. He was known for his aggressive style on the mats, always looking for the pin. In his four bouts in Pensacola, Chertow scored 43 points against Jack Cuvo and Joe Gonzales.

Chertow tells some stories about developing his skills during his wrestling career:

My wrestling career really took off after my sophomore year in high school back in 1982. I was runner-up in the West Virginia states that year and then went to the Junior Nationals in Iowa City. I went 0-4 there, wrestling in both Freestyle and Greco.

I realized then that while I was a good wrestler by West Virginia standards, there was a huge difference on the national scene. If I wanted to get the attention of college coaches, I would need to dramatically improve. That's when I decided to stop participating in all other sports and concentrate on wrestling. I engrossed myself in Freestyle and Greco, training every day for the next two years. I spent my summers training at various camps and that helped me improve significantly each year.

As a junior, I won the State Tournament and it was one of the most important accomplishments of my life. I then went to the Junior Nationals. I won seven matches there but did not place in the top six. However, I was starting to open some eyes of various college coaches. Then in my senior year, 1984, I repeated as a West Virginia state champion and went to the Junior Nationals where I won 21 matches over a five day period. I won both the Freestyle and Greco championship. I won by pin in the Greco finals and technical fall in the Freestyle finals, earn-

Ken Chertow, a junior at Penn State, was always looking for back points. He won several high-scoring matches to make the 1988 Freestyle team.
Photograph courtesy of Amateur Wrestling News

ing the OW in Freestyle. I also won the Junior World championship that summer in my first taste of international competition.

That same summer I vividly remember watching the Olympics on television and seeing guys that I knew from wrestling camps dominating the wrestlers from the rest of the world. Wrestlers like Bobby Weaver, Randy Lewis and the Schultz brothers were winning gold medals, and knowing them personally made it all real for me. That is when wrestling in the Olympics become not just a dream, but a real and concrete goal for me. My goal was to represent our country in the Olympics in 1988, just four years down the road.

A number of colleges recruited me and I chose Penn State. For me, Penn State offered the best combination of academics and wrestling. That was my training ground for the next four years. I worked intensely throughout the year, striving to improve daily. I had some great workout partners in Jim Martin and Tim Flynn, along with our coaching staff headed by John Fritz. The NYAC was also very supportive. I never considered representing Foxcatcher, as I

did not care for duPont. I definitely stayed away from that situation.

In 1986 I won the World Cup for ages 20 and under, defeating the Russian in the finals. I tried out for the US World team and was an alternate to Barry Davis at 125 in both 1986 and 1987. As a sophomore in 1987 I competed at 126 for Penn State and finished 3rd in the NCAAs, then dropped down to 118 for my junior season.

I had a dilemma as the Olympic Trials approached. Should I go at 114 or 125? I felt that I could beat Davis to make the team at 125, but Sergei Beloglazov was competing there for Russia and he would have been very difficult to defeat. The one time we wrestled he beat me by about six or seven points and was unbelievably powerful.

In the spring of 1988 shortly after the NCAAs, I beat one of the best Soviet wrestlers in a US-versus-Russia dual meet at Madison Square Garden. The weight class was 119 pounds. Dan Gable and Al Bevilacqua were the coaches of the team. Afterwards I asked them what they thought about me going down to 114 for the Olympic Trials. They encouraged me to do it. I thought about it long and hard for a week or so and after much soul searching I decided to do it. Though I believed that I could make the Olympic team at 125, my goal was Olympic gold and I felt that 114 gave me the best opportunity to live my dream.

I knew that Jack Cuvo, the NCAA champion, and Joe Gonzales, the '84 Olympian, would be two of the top guys at the Olympic Trials at 114.5. I studied their moves and style extensively. They were both quicker than me. My strategy would be to control the ties to score, and to pressure them into taking bad shots. I would use a variety of under-hook techniques and a variety of combinations from the front headlock. I liked the reverse front headlock and it helped me score a lot of exposure points. I'd go up over the top of the body with it and use it like a gut-wrench. I had other unorthodox counters that I had learned at camps from Randy Lewis and Wade Schalles, amongst others, and wasn't afraid to always be aggressive.

In the Final Qualifier in Kansas, I made it to the finals, where I went up against Gonzales. I had never wrestled or worked out with him before. He was fast and elusive. We went into overtime and he hit me with a leg attack. I threw a belly roll counter and it was scored two-and-two but they ruled that he scored first as he initiated and he won 11-9. I was in 2nd place going into the Pensacola Final Trials.

I went back to the Penn State wrestling room for a month to prepare for the Final Trials. My strategy was to continue controlling the tie-ups, working on numerous counter-attacks, and continuing to relentlessly go for the tilt points both on top and with counters. Sometimes I'd give up points on leg attacks, but my goal was to come out of every flurry with exposure points when practical. In order to offset the guys with more speed than me, I had to set the pace of the match myself. The late, great Dave Schultz often told me to control the tempo and ties and that was my objective. I also knew for me to be successful in Pensacola, I had to be disciplined in my training, nutrition, and weight-control. I would have to weigh-in on multiple days. Having to beat two world-class wrestlers in Cuvo and Gonzales under those conditions was a big challenge.

My dad was in my corner for my matches in Pensacola along with my Penn State coach. My father was there for moral support more than anything else. I beat Cuvo twice in high scoring matches [11-6 and 11-10] and then beat Gonzales twice to make the Olympic team. That was a very satisfying and I had an immense feeling of relief. It was one of the three most memorable moments of my career — up there with winning my first state high school championship and winning the Junior Nationals. It was an awesome feeling.

Joe Gonzales was an NCAA champion at Cal State Bakersfield and a three-time National Open champion. He wrestled for the US in the 1984 Olympics at 114.5.

He tells his story of trying to make the US Olympic team in 1980, in 1984 and again in 1988:

I grew up in East Los Angeles and never saw an amateur wrestling match except on Wide World of Sports until ninth grade. That year I broke my leg playing football. After the season I was walking through the gym and there was

> **[Chertow] beat me fair and square but I don't think he was better than me. My desire just wasn't there. I didn't dig down enough to beat Chertow. His whole mission was to defeat me and he had me in his sights for over a year. I just didn't want it that bad – he wanted it more than I did. I was 31 years old and actually welcomed the loss. It was time for a changing of the guard.**
>
> **– JOE GONZALES**

a wrestling match going on. I liked what I saw, started going to practices and by the end of the season I won a wrestle-off to make the team.

I became dedicated after my sophomore year when I decided to give up everything else to wrestle year-round. I'd go over to the East Los Angeles Junior College wrestling room, where coaches Ben Bolander and Bob Shephard took me under their wing and taught me the finer points of wrestling. That really took me to a whole different level of competing.

I never placed in the California state championships. In my senior year at Montebello High School I was undefeated going into the sectionals. However, I received a head concussion in practice the day before the tournament and I was done for the year. I was devastated. I really wanted to be a state champion.

In those days I was wrestling a lot of Freestyle tournaments during the off-season and doing well. I wanted to have one last shot at doing something spectacular in high school so I made the California team at 114 pounds and went to the Junior Nationals in Iowa City. I had placed 4th at 123 pounds the year before. This year, it was 1975, I won the tournament, beating state champions from all over the country and was named the Outstanding Wrestler. My California buddy and future teammate at Cal State Bakersfield, John Azevedo, also won the Junior National championship that year.

That championship got me the attention of a lot of coaches, like Bobby Douglas and Tom

Chesbro, but it was too late in the recruiting season. They already had their scholarships accounted for. I decided to go to back to the local junior college where the coaches had helped me so much up till then. I wrestled there as a freshman, becoming the California Junior College state champion, and earned myself a scholarship to the University of Oklahoma.

Coach Stan Able was a good talker and the whole aura of wrestling in Oklahoma got to me. I was not happy at Oklahoma. My style, which was based on 'take 'em down, let 'em up' clashed with Abel's philosophy of grinding your opponent into the mat. I also sensed some racism there and wanted to leave and return to California. After my sophomore season, I transferred to Cal State Bakersfield. Coach Able was pissed but I felt much better being back in California.

I had two years of eligibility remaining and made the most of them. I won two Division II national titles. My junior year I made it to the NCAA Division I finals where I lost to Gene Mills, even though I had beaten him a month earlier in the East-West match. In 1980, I won the NCAAs along with my teammate Azevedo.

I went to the first round of Olympic Trials in 1980 in Wisconsin and placed 2nd to Jim Haines. However, I knew that the US was not going to be in the Olympics, so I didn't go to the Final wrestle-offs in New York. I wasn't prepared to lose a lot of weight for a bad cause.

I kept wrestling Freestyle aiming for the '84 Olympics. I made the US World team in '81, '82, and '83, winning a bronze medal in '82. I also won the Tbilisi tournament during that span, which was the highlight of my career. Jim Peckham, the wonderful coach from Massachusetts, helped me and really motivated me to win that tournament. They even wrote a feature article on me in Sports Illustrated.

In '84 I was the favorite to make the US team, but I ruptured my bicep shortly before the Trials. I thought it was all over for me, just like back in my senior year of high school. The local surgeon told me I had to have an operation that would sideline me for months. I went to see the doctors in Colorado Springs and they gave me another option — rehab it and still try to function as best you can. I took their advice.

My plan was to just make it into the final six wrestlers at the Qualifier in Iowa City so that I would be eligible to compete in the Final Trials in Michigan. After winning enough matches to make it to the Final wrestle-offs, I dropped out of the tournament, which Randy Willingham won at 114.5. My arm got better in the interval between tournaments. I came through the wrestle-offs fine, beating several guys before meeting Willingham in the finals. I won the best two-out-of-three to make the Olympic team.

I had the long-time goal of winning an Olympic medal and when I didn't place in '84 in front of the hometown crowd in Los Angeles, it was the low point of my life. Everything seemed to fall apart for me. I felt that I embarrassed myself in front of my friends, fiancée and my family. I wouldn't even stick around for the team picture taken the day after my losses, although Coach Gable consoled me for nearly an hour. I was really down. My life blew up, my fiancée left me and it took several years for me to get over losing my matches in those Olympic Games.

After a while I did get the itch to wrestle again, so I got back into it. I won the National Freestyle at 114.5 in 1986 and decided I'd give the Olympics one more try. I was wrestling well. In February of '88, I won a major international tournament in France, beating the former World Champion from West Germany. From there I wrestled in the World Cup in Toledo and beat my Russian opponent, Anatoli Beloglazov. I went to the National Freestyle Open in Nevada and beat Jack Cuvo in the finals. In the Final Qualifier in Topeka, I went toe-to-toe with Ken Chertow, beating him in overtime. That put me up as the top seed for the Final Trials.

I lost the two matches to Chertow in Pensacola. He beat me fair and square but I don't think he was better than me. My desire just wasn't there. I didn't dig down enough to beat Chertow. His whole mission was to defeat me and he had me in his sights for over a year. I just didn't want it that bad — he wanted it more than I did. I was 31 years old and actually welcomed that loss. It was time for a changing of the guard.

136.5 pounds Greco — Ike Anderson vs Buddy Lee

YOU usually don't find Olympic wrestlers in Hopkins, South Carolina and Richmond, Virginia, but that's where the two Greco finalists at 136.5 originally called home. Anderson wrestled in college at Appalachian State. He qualified at 126 pounds for the NCAAs in 1979, losing in the pigtail round.

[Author's note — 126 was a specially deep weight class that year, with four Olympians — Lewis, Azevedo, Jimmy Carr and Anderson, plus Ricky Dellagatta — competing.]

Anderson talks about his '88 Trials experience:

After college, I picked up Greco and trained under Joe DeMeo for a number of years. I was looking ahead to the '88 Trials but several injuries in '87 prevented me from some competition. I was seeded 3rd at the '88 Greco Nationals and I ended up 2nd to Dalen Wasmund. From there I went to my first Olympic Trials in Boca Raton — this set the ladder for the real Trials.

At Boca, I got hurt again. Wasmund and I were on one side of the bracket; Buddy Lee on the other. I cracked my ribs in the Wasmund match and lost. I kept wrestling, lost again, but won my last bout in the final ten seconds to finish 4th and qualify for the Final Trials in Pensacola. I had a month to recuperate.

I wrestled and beat both the #5 and #6 guys in the mini-tournament. They were relatively easy matches for me. I then wrestled the #3 guy and again won easily. I next had to face the toughest guy — Wasmund. I beat Wasmund two-out-of-three to advance to the finals against Lee. I dislocated my wrist, but not severely. I beat Buddy pretty easily in our first match. In the second match Buddy never came after me. He didn't want to 'open up'. We ended up tied, but I won on criteria. I was elated that I made the team, but I was pretty banged up.

Buddy Lee talks about competing in the '88 Trials and what he learned from the experience:

After Old Dominion, I wrestled for the US

Ike Anderson worked his way through the Trials' mini-tournament to win the 136.5 Greco spot
Photograph courtesy of
Amateur Wrestling News

Marine team, stationed in Quantico, Virginia. I didn't have a personal coach — I was on my own and a lot of my technique was self-taught. I relied on high-intensity training, eight to ten hours a day, rather than utilizing a wide range of Greco techniques. I basically perfected the duck-under, drag-by and head-snap as my go-to moves.

Up to the '88 Trials, I had focused on Freestyle. I was one of the top four in the country in my weight class, but when I didn't do that well in some tournaments early in '88, I said, 'Forget this, I'm putting all my energy into Greco.' I took my Freestyle knowledge and applied it to Greco. I was not a classical Greco wrestler.

At Pensacola, I went in as the #1 guy which was not a good place for me to be. Everyone else was wrestling while I was just sitting around. In my first wrestle-off with Ike Anderson, I received a caution. My coach in my corner went crazy trying to protest the call. They gave Ike an extra point for this and it cost me the match. In the second match, Ike and I went into overtime. Then I got cautioned out. That was a curious call — why didn't they just let us wrestle? Why give a person a ticket to the Olympics on a questionable caution call?

I learned a lot about the politics of the sport from that incident. I had to learn to get to know the officials and let the guys in charge know who I was. Like everyone, coaches and officials have their favorites. Committees of officials meet behind closed doors and decide who would be our best bets to win a medal.

Ike was the biggest guy in the weight class. He was coming down from 160-170 pounds; plus, had a good Greco technique and strategy coach in DeMeo. Joe later coached me at the Pan-Am games and taught me about edge-of-the-mat strategy. Pavel Katsen also helped me along the way. Pavel was a great contributor to the development of Greco wrestling in this country.

After the loss in the '88 Trials wrestle-offs, I did recommit myself to the sport and went on to greater success.

[Author's note: Lee won the Trials in 1992, beating Anderson in the Finals.]

I have no regrets. With the limited Greco knowledge that I had, I was fighting in every match for my dream to become an Olympian. What I remember the most about '88 — it was the beginning of realizing my inner strength, recommitting to a vision, overcoming adversity and learning to fight with all my might to live my dream. At the end of the fight I learned the real meaning of commitment, focus, perseverance, responsibility, balance and the ingredients of becoming a true champion in life.

180.5 pounds Freestyle — Mike Sheets vs Mark Schultz

MIKE Sheets was a native Oklahoman, twice winning an NCAA title at Oklahoma State University. Sheets easily dominated the 167 pound weight class in '83 and '84, with probably the highest match score differential in NCAA history in 1983 — winning by scores of 29-2, 14-0, 6-0, 5-1, and in the finals, 14-0. After graduation, Sheets won the US National Open Freestyle title in 1985.

He tells his story, including his fierce rivalry with the two Schultz brothers:

I started wrestling in fourth grade in Tahlequah, Oklahoma. I kinda liked it and stuck with it. In high school I would wrestle some Freestyle for a couple weeks in the summer. I enjoyed playing football and baseball, too, though I was not very good at either of them. I was good at wrestling, though, and won the State Tournament as a junior and a senior.

I wasn't a blue-chip recruit like Kenny Monday, but Paul Martin and Tom Chesbro recruited me to go to Oklahoma State and that's where I went. When I got to college, Coach Chesbro required freshmen to wrestle in the National Open. The 1981 tournament was at the UNI Dome, and I recall that Lee Roy Smith was in charge of the team going there. I placed but didn't wrestle Freestyle anymore until my senior year at OSU, when I went up against a touring Russian team that came through Stillwater.

Meanwhile I concentrated on wrestling Folkstyle at OSU. As a sophomore I made it to the NCAA finals against Dave Schultz. I made a mental mistake allowing him to get a takedown with just a couple seconds left at the end of a period. We went into overtime and he then beat me on criteria. The next two years I won the title.

In 1984-85, I was a graduate assistant at OSU, trying to get into Veterinary school there and wrestling year-round. I beat Jim Scherr to win the National Open Freestyle, which was held out in Pennsylvania. That was a big deal, being my first Freestyle championship. I wrestled for Sunkist Kids and we easily won the tournament. From 149 through 198 we had Bill Nugent, Kenny Monday, me and Mark Schultz as a murderers' row, all four of us winning National titles.

In the fall of 1985 I entered the Vet school in Stillwater and cut way back on my training. Vet school was a full time job, but I'd take a weekend off here and there and show up at tournaments to wrestle without much practice. I entered the 1986 National Freestyle Open and pinned everyone up to the finals where Mark Schultz beat me by a couple of points. I also lost a match that year to Melvin Douglas who was coming on strong in the 180-pound class.

In 1987, I wrestled in the Sports Festival and

Mike Sheets rallied to upend Rico Chiapparelli but ultimately missed out on an Olympic spot
Photograph by Ron Good, courtesy of Amateur Wrestling News

in the first round I was pinned by Rico Chiapparelli. That was all I could take of losing matches and not training enough. I immediately called my father and told him that I was going to have to take a leave of absence from Vet school so that I could work out full time in preparation for making the '88 Olympic team.

From that point on, I went into serious daily training back in Stillwater. My primary workout partners were Kenny Monday and Rich Cody and they were great for me. I wrestled overseas in Russia, France, and Cuba and also in the World Cup. Art Martori and the Sunkist people were very good to me. I went to a lot of places on their ticket.

I was ready for the Olympic Trials and won the Final Qualifier. I beat Kevin Jackson who was a young up-and-coming guy and then pinned Schultz in the finals. I hit him with a duck-under and then trapped his arm. He tried to roll through but I squeezed hard and got the fall.

After the Qualifier I returned to Stillwater to continue my workouts with Monday. They

were remodeling Gallagher Hall where our training room was, so we moved into an old high school gym in the south end of town. That was a different atmosphere. It was an old auditorium with a stage. We put the mats down, but when Kenny and I wrestled, there was no stopping us. We'd continue wrestling off the mat until one of us got the points. There was no such thing as 'out-of-bounds.'

I went into the Final Trials feeling good about things. I knew that it would either be Mark or Rico facing me in the finals. They were both very good. Heck, Mark was a multiple-time World champion and an Olympic champion. He was a very controlled wrestler, extremely strong with excellent balance. Rico was more of a brawler; he would try to get you out of position but was not nearly as controlled as Schultz.

At the Final Trials they set up a new rule which I didn't like. Since I won the Qualifier, I didn't have to wrestle the first days of the tournament. But they instituted this rule that you had to be there the whole time. I was planning on staying in Stillwater until the day before my matches, then flying in. Instead, I was sitting around there in Florida for three or four days before ever wrestling.

Well, Mark beats Rico twice, so Mark and I face off for a best-of-three series. I was feeling a little stale from sitting around, but I went out as the aggressor and took Mark down to start the match. Mark changed his defensive strategy and wouldn't allow me to get my legs in on him — he has his clamped together. He's the toughest guy in the world to gut-wrench, so I'm not getting any tilt points. Then I made a tactical error while on defense. He turned me for back-points and came back to beat me in a pretty intense bout.

After the match, a lot of people were telling me that I have to do this, change that, and so on. Personally, I don't think I should have changed anything — just gone on out there and wrestled my own match. But I did try to make some adjustments in the second match and it didn't work out. I got behind and started doing desperate things. I got smoked by Mark and end up 2nd, which doesn't do much for you.

If I had to do it over, I would have done two other things differently. First, I would have put

> **After the Qualifier I returned to Stillwater to continue my workouts** with Monday. They were remodeling Gallagher Hall where our training room was, so we moved into an old high school gym in the south end of town. We put the mats down, but when Kenny and I wrestled, there was no stopping us. We'd continue wrestling off the mat until one of us got the points. There was no such thing as 'out-of-bounds.'
>
> **— MIKE SHEETS**

off going to Vet school until after the Olympics and concentrated on wrestling from '85 through '88. And I should not have gone to the Final Trials until the day before weigh-in. Hindsight is 20-20, but it makes me wonder. I'll never know if those strategic mistakes would have made a difference in my making the Olympic team.

Mark Schultz was the defending Olympic champion at 180.5 and a two-time World champion. He recalls his battle to make the '88 US Olympic team and his tumultuous days with John duPont at Foxcatcher:

Up until the 1988 Trials, I was undefeated in the US for five years — winning four National Freestyle titles, two World championships and a Pan American gold medal.

At Wichita, I defeated everyone up until the final match with Mike Sheets. No points were scored early. He got a caution on me. I was put down and he put the legs in. It was a killer, killer Turks ride. He started cranking me and it was like murder it hurt so much. He turned me and while I was on my back, I tried to kick his legs back over him and roll through, but as I rolled the ref called me pinned.

I went to Pensacola as the runner-up and had to first wrestle Rico Chiapparelli, who was tough and very difficult for me to wrestle. He had an unorthodox style and it was hard for me to finish a move on him. He was always throwing stuff really hard and in order to beat him I'd just

have to thrash him.

In my first match with Rico, I was winning 5-0 after one period. I relaxed a bit, got distracted by all the Foxcatcher stuff in the back of my mind, and let Rico come back to beat me, 16-8. I felt horrible, but weighed-in and went back to my hotel. I told myself, 'I quit, let Chiapparelli go against Sheets for the Olympics'. I ordered room service and ate like crazy. A friend of mine, Hal Miles, who coached wrestling in Virginia, stopped by and started talking to me at the hotel. He got me talking about all the bad stuff that John duPont did to me at Foxcatcher. That got me riled up and changed my whole mental attitude. I got out of my funk and went out and pinned Rico twice the next day. I was my old self again.

I then had to wrestle Sheets for the Olympic team spot, but I had a little weight problem. The evening before our match, I go to weigh-in and Sheets is right in front of me. He gets on the scale and makes weight. I get on and I am 12 pounds over — thanks to that big room service meal I ate. It is just 90 minutes to go before the weigh-in final deadline. Sheets is looking at me and I know what's going through his mind: 'I'm going to the Olympics because there is no way Schultz can make weight on time'.

First thing I do is puke. There goes one-and-a-half pounds. Then I put on sweats and run around the hot, humid Florida arena. I don't get to sweat enough, so I find a stationary bike and pull it outside right in front of the arena door, where all the people leaving the tournament can see me. I pedal like a madman and my brother keeps me cooled down with ice chips. I stop with ten minutes to go before the deadline and jump on the scale — I am one-half pound over. I know I'll make it, so I ride the bike for a few more minutes and finally make weight with two minutes to go.

My matches against Sheets were the next day. In the first match he was up by one in the second period when I did a move that I never did before. I was on top of Sheets on the mat when I did a handstand and turned it into a step-through turk. That got me three points and I ended up winning, 6-2. Our next match was in the evening. I took an early lead when he went for a single leg and I

Sooner tops Cowboy: Mark Schultz, right, defeated Mike Sheets en route to repeating his success of '84 by winning the Olympic Trials at 180.5 pounds *Photograph by Steve Brown, courtesy of* Amateur Wrestling News

countered with a whizzer kick-up which put him on his back and it then turned into a massacre, something like 13-1.

Back to my story about Foxcatcher and du-Pont. In 1986 I was working as the assistant coach to Chris Horpel at Stanford along with my brother. It was a terrible job. I only was making $5,500 a year after taxes and no benefits. Dave and I both wanted to get out of there. duPont called Dave from Foxcatcher and asked him if he would come there as the coach. Dave turned him down since he already had an opportunity to coach at Wisconsin. Then duPont called me and asked me to come. He asked what I wanted for a salary and I said $25,000 — much more than I was earning at Stanford. He said he'd get back to me.

While I was at the World Team Trials at Indianapolis in '86, where I beat Sheets twice to make the team, I meet up with duPont. I was wondering what kind of situation I might be getting into if I went to work for him at Fox-catcher.

Well, when I met duPont at Indianapolis, I knew things would be terrible. He was sitting in this room with a glass of alcohol in his hand, food caked to his teeth, hair filled with dandruff

and dyed orange, and he was slobbering his words. It was a scary scene. I asked him the crit-ical question as far as I was concerned — 'What role was he going to take in the Foxcatcher wres-tling program?' He gave me the answer I wanted — he would fund it, I would run it.

I was desperate to get out of Stanford and out of poverty, so I took the Foxcatcher job even though I had a lot of apprehension.

I moved out to Foxcatcher which was in the Philadelphia suburbs. DuPont doesn't show up for the first two months. Then one day duPont does show up, and again the next day, and ev-ery day after that. I can no longer do anything. He then hired Andre Metzger, which I thought was great because Andre was one of my best friends from college at Oklahoma. However, duPont played us against each other and started manipulating us. He ruined our relationship to this day.

DuPont was the devil himself. He was like a vampire, taking drugs all the time. He took ad-vantage of guys who were vulnerable because of the financial situation they were in. He'd make life terrible for us and then when we got fed up and about to leave Foxcatcher, he'd offer us some money and we'd have no choice but to stay.

To compound things, USA Wrestling wouldn't change the status of an 'amateur wrestler' in financial terms, so I and others were put in a desperate situation of financial survival. Our motivation shifted to financial survival rather than winning wrestling matches. I think that because of my situation and my pleading, USA Wrestling later changed their policy and found ways for amateur wrestlers to make some money to survive.

163 pounds Freestyle – Kenny Monday vs Dave Schultz

KENNY Monday talks about his early wrestling days, his duels with Dave Schultz to make the 1988 US Olympic team and his biggest fear – John duPont.

I started wrestling when I was six, back in 1967 at the Tulsa Y after-school program. Charlie Shivers was the coach there and he had 30 to 40 kids on the squad. I loved it from the start.

We'd travel down to Stillwater to watch the Federation matches and the OSU matches. We had some incredible athletes as part of the team; guys like Doug Blubaugh and Wayne Wells would come to workout. I was certainly not one of the best athletes there.

I especially liked the Federation Freestyle environment. They were using those crazy high-flying throws and the older guys would clean the mat up with the younger guys like me. It was a great time to be a wrestler, back in the early '70s in Tulsa. I was hooked and saw when Wells won the Olympics that you could come out of here and actually be among the best in the world. It was exciting for me.

Besides Wells, my childhood heroes in those days were Bobby Douglas and Lloyd Keaser. I had some good people to look up to. Since they were among the best in the world, I made that my goal.

I was successful at wrestling early on. I went undefeated from seventh through twelfth grade and won four Oklahoma state titles at Booker T Washington high school. I did have one tie and that was against Mike Sheets, who turned out to be my best workout partner in college and later

> **"Sheets is looking at me and I know what's going through his mind: 'I'm going to the Olympics because there is no way Schultz can make weight on time'. First thing I do is puke. There goes one-and-a-half pounds. Then I put on sweats and run around the hot, humid Florida arena. I don't get to sweat enough, so I find a stationary bike... I pedal like a madman and my brother keeps me cooled down with ice chips.**
> **– MARK SCHULTZ**

in Freestyle.

I traveled to Freestyle tournaments as a youngster as part of the Oklahoma team. When I was 10 or 11, I met the Smith family from Del City and got to know them well. Lee Roy was a bit older and very talented. His brother, John, was three years younger and we called him the 'little brat'. I loved the Freestyle – especially the throws. It was great to do slams without getting called.

Once I started wrestling in college I mostly focused on Folkstyle. I had a good year wrestling as a true freshman, but lost in the quarter-finals of the NCAAs and did not place. As a sophomore and junior, my intense rivalry with Nate Carr got started. I beat him both years in the Big Eight finals, but he beat me each year in the NCAA finals, both times in overtime. He was very good – in fact he was the fastest guy I ever wrestled and one of the fiercest about winning. But I was a tough competitor, too, so we had some great battles against each other.

As a senior in '84 I finally won the NCAAs. I was pretty tired at the end of the season; that college scene of competing every week is draining. Then, Myron Roderick, as the OSU Athletic Director, fired Coach Tom Chesbro and brought in Joe Seay.

Joe got into a bad car accident and things were in disarray in Stillwater. I was looking for the best wrestling environment to continue my training. I received a call from Bobby Douglas and he offered me a job at Arizona State, where I

> " Before the Trials I went to see Rick Tucci, who I felt was the best of our officials. I told Tucci that I wanted a fair shake in my matches. I also told myself that I had to dominate Schultz, so that no bad call could swing the match.
>
> **— KENNY MONDAY**

Kenny Monday became "The Man" when he beat Dave Schultz to make the Olympic Freestyle team at 163 *Photograph by John Hoke, courtesy of Amateur Wrestling News*

could workout and could compete for the Sunkist Kids club. So, I moved to Arizona and began working under Bobby. Fortunately, Eddie Urbano was there and he was a good, tough workout partner for me.

I entered the '84 Trials but did not do well. I tried to get down to 149.5, but that was too hard for me to make, so the day before the tournament started I decided to go 163. I was really too small for 163. I remember losing to Mike DeAnna and finishing 5th.

In '84 I really wasn't quite ready to compete against the elite guys. The transition from college to international wrestling is huge. It takes a different strategy, different training, a different mind-set. It took me three years to make that transition. For me the '84 Trials were a great learning experience — I watched the top guys be 'The Man'; that was exciting and motivating. I knew then I would be 'The Man' in 1988 to represent the United States in the Olympics.

Things started to fizzle out for me in Arizona. Although I built a very good relationship with the Sunkist Kids leader, Art Martori, I was second fiddle behind Dave Schultz at 163 for the Sunkist team. I wasn't making the progress I thought I should have been making. Joe Seay found an opportunity for me to return to Stillwater as part of the OSU staff in 1986. I took it and we started building up an awesome wrestling environment there with myself, Mike Sheets, John Smith, and others. Schultz left Sunkist to start working with John duPont at Foxcatcher, so Martori said that even though I was living in Oklahoma, he'd still sponsor me on the Sunkist team.

I started training really hard and knew that Carr and Schultz were the guys I had to beat. I lost to Nate at the '86 National Open, but at the World Team Trials in 1987, I beat him, 8-1. I wrestled Dave at those Trials and won a match against him for the first time, although he won two-out-of-three to make the World team. I was closing the gap on him.

After those '87 World Trials, I tried to talk Nate into going down to 149.5 for the Olympics. He said, 'No, you go down', and we went back and forth with a little trash talk. Even though we were fierce competitors we hung out together some. I told him that he could beat Andre Metzger at 149.5 and that way we could both make the Olympic team.

A couple weeks later, Nate calls back and says, 'Okay, I'll go to 149.5.'

I got to go to Russia that year and compete at Tbilisi and some other duals. I went 10-0 against ten different Russians. My breakout tournament was Tbilisi. And who was there watching me — Dave Schultz, who went along as a coach. I believe that after watching me beat the Russians, he knew he'd have a tough-time beating me.

By the way, on the way to Russia, I stopped off in New York primarily to get some advice from Lee Kemp, who was living there at the time. We went to lunch together and I asked him about wrestling Schultz in '84. I wanted to know where Lee's head was back in '84 when he was the established guy, just like Dave was now in '88. Lee was kind and definitely gave me some valuable insights for my upcoming Trials wrestle-offs with Dave.

My training in Stillwater leading up to the Trials was incredible. I think I was in the best training environment in the whole world. We had a great group of guys, shooting for the Olympics and helping each other. We were helping John get geared up to wrestle Randy Lewis and for Mike to face Mark Schultz, as well as my own competition with Dave. The Sunkist people were supporting us and giving us every opportunity to train the right way. It was a good deal all the way around. My biggest disappointment was that Sheets didn't make the team. That broke my heart because Mike had helped me so much.

Let me explain why I was so fearful of John duPont. DuPont was donating big money — $800,000 to $1,000,000 a year — to USA Wrestling at the time and had a huge influence on the sport. He had Schultz training at his Foxcatcher facility in Pennsylvania and he wanted Dave on the 1988 Olympic team. He would exert pressure on USA Wrestling and their Executive Director. There was pressure to appease the guy. I knew it would be tough to overcome that influence. It was a difficult position for everyone.

I felt that the biggest variable was the officials and their calls. In my matches with Schultz in '87 there were some controversial calls that didn't go my way. I wanted to be sure that this time the calls would be fair. Before the Trials I went to see Rick Tucci, who I felt was the best of our officials. I told Tucci that I wanted a fair shake in my matches. I also told myself that I had to dominate Schultz, so that no bad call could swing the match.

Tucci officiated one of my matches against Dave and there was no problem. And I did dominate in the Final Trials in Pensacola, winning 6-1 and 5-1. Those wins were some of the best matches of my life. I was now 'The Man.'

After I made the team, Dave was very helpful to me in the training camp. We'd work out together and we'd let it all hang out. Coach Douglas kept saying, 'He'll try to hurt you, Monday', but I wasn't afraid. I was, at that point, so far ahead of Dave that I could dominate him.

1988 OLYMPIC TEAM MEMBERS

	FREESTYLE	GRECO-ROMAN
105.5	Tim Vanni (4th)	Mark Fuller
114.5	Ken Chertow	Shawn Sheldon
125.5	Barry Davis	Anthony Amado
136.5	John Smith (1st)	Ike Anderson (6th)
149.5	Nate Carr (3rd)	Andy Seras
163	Kenny Monday (1st)	David Butler
180.5	Mark Schultz (6th)	John Morgan
198	Jim Scherr (5th)	Michael Foy
220	Bill Scherr (3rd)	Dennis Koslowski (3rd)
286	Bruce Baumgartner (2nd)	Duane Koslowski

★ THE Soviets proved much too slick and powerful in Seoul. While we applauded our two gold medalists, the USSR claimed eight gold medals combined in Freestyle and Greco, plus four more silvers. Kenny Monday extended our three-decade dominance of the 163-pound weight class.

1988 PRESIDENTIAL ELECTION

★ IN A battle reminiscent of 1960, an incumbent Republican VP was challenged by a liberal young Democrat from Massachusetts. This time the incumbent won - easily. Many attributed Bush's victory to Americans enjoying 'peace and prosperity' during the years that Bush served under Reagan.

THE SCORECARD	
George H. W. Bush Dan Quayle	426 Electoral Votes 53.4% of Popular Vote
Michael Dukakis Lloyd Bentsen	111 Electoral Votes 45.6% of Popular Vote

INDEX

This list contains the names of wrestlers, officials and coaches included in the narrative. Names in bold were interviewed and quoted.

Gagne, Vern 1972
Gallo, Nick 1980
Garber, Steve 1976, 1984A
Gardner, Sprig 1964, 1968, 1972
Giani, Lou 1960, 1968, 1984
Gibbons, Gene 1976
Gibson, Greg 1980, 1984, 1988
Gitcho, Jan 1976
Glass, Brad 1968
Goldman, Duane 1988
Goltl, Walt 1960
Gomes, Joe 1960
Gonzales, Joe 1988
Gonzales, Sergio 1972
Grandstaff, Mike 1960
Gray, Ron 1968
Greenhalgh, Sonny 1976, 1980, 1984A
Griffith, Art 1960
Guira, John 1984
Gust, Brian 1980
Guzzo, Bobby 1964
Haines, Jim 1976, 1980, 1988
Hall, Terry 1972
Hammond, Jay 1980
Hanson, James 1968
Harlow, Bill 1968, 1972
Harman, Maynard 1964
Harman, Mike 1964
Harris, Jonny 1972
Hart, Ed 1984
Hassman, Gordon 1964
Hastert, Denny 1976
Hatta, Masaaki 1968, 1984
Hay, Jack 1972
Hayes, Larry 1964
Hazewinkel, Dave 1964, 1972, 1976
Hazewinkel, Jim 1964, 1968, 1972
Heffernan, Jim 1984
Hellickson, Russ 1972, 1976, 1980, 1984, 1984A
Henson, Geoff 1964
Henson, Josiah 1964, 1968
Henson, Sammy 1988
Hicks, Greg 1972, 1976
Hicks, Wayne 1964, 1972
Hitchcock, Vaughn 1976
Hodge, Dan 1960
Hoke, Jess 1960
Holland, Bob 1976
Holmes, Charles 1968
Holmes, Wayne 1976
Holzer, Werner 1968, 1972, 1984, 1984A

Horpel, Chris 1988
Houck, Mike 1980, 1984, 1988
Houk, Russ 1972, 1976
Houska, Harry 1968
Huff, Tom 1964, 1968
Hughes, John 1980
Hull, Mitch 1980, 1984
Humphrey, Jim 1976, 1980, 1984, 1988
Hunt, Briggs 1960
Hunte, Ken 1968
Hurley, Al 1968
Hutchinson, Tom 1980
Iacovelli, Orlando 1964
Jack, Hubert 1960
Jackson, Jimmy 1980
Jackson, Kevin 1988
James, Joe 1964
Jantzen, Jesse 1984
Jean, Chuck 1968
Johnson, Bob 1964
Johnson, Evan 1984
Johnson, Mark 1980, 1984
Johnson, Morris 1984
Johnson, Okla 1964
Johnson, Wally 1972
Jones, Ron 1980
Jones, T.J. 1980, 1988
Jordan, Jim 1988
Kancsar, Karoly 1976
Katsamura, Yasuo 1972
Katsen, Pavel 1984, 1988
Kauffman, Len 1964
Keaser, Lloyd 1972, 1976, 1988
Keeley, Tom 1976
Keller, Darrell 1972
Keller, Dwayne 1968, 1976
Kelly, Jerry 1976
Kelly, Pat 1968
Kemp, Lee 1976, 1980, 1984, 1988
Kerslake, Bill 1960
Kinseth, Bruce 1976, 1980
Kinyon, Jim 1960
Kinyon, Phil 1960
Kirsch, Dr. Joel 1984
Kleven, Duane 1972, 1980
Knosp, Martin 1984
Kocher, Leo 1972
Koslowski, Dennis 1984, 1988
Koslowski, Duane 1988
Kraft, Ken 1964, 1968, 1972
Kristoff, Larry 1964, 1968, 1972, 1976
Kurdelmeier, Gary 1988
Kuzu, Abdurrahim 1980

Kwiecinski, Czeslaw 1980
Lahr, Dean 1964
Lamphere. Reid 1976
Land, Mike 1984A
Lanzatella, Phil 1980
Lauchle, Larry 1960, 1964
Layton, Bill 1960
Lee, Buddy 1988
Lee, Peter 1988
Leeman, Gerry 1964
Lett, Fred 1968
Lewis, Jess 1968
Lewis, Randy 1980, 1984, 1984A, 1988
Liace, Rocco 1984
Lieberman, Mark 1972, 1980
Lieberman, Mike 1980
Lipien, Kazimierz 1980
Lockwood, Marty 1976
Long, Linn 1960, 1964
Long, Veryl 1960
Lucas, Frank 1960
Lyden, Larry 1980
Malcolm, Ron 1980
Mallory, Ken 1984
Mangianti, Mark 1980
Martell, Bill 1984
Martin, Billy 1960
Martin, Jim 1988
Martin, Mickey 1964
Martin, Paul 1976, 1988
Martinez, Jim 1984, 1988
Martori, Art 1988
Massery, Mike 1976
Mastro, Jim 1976
Matthews, John 1980
McCann, Terry 1960, 1964, 1968, 1972, 1988
McCready, Mike 1976
McCuskey, Dave 1964
McFarland, Joe 1988
McNerney, Andy 1984
Metzger, Andre 1980, 1984, 1988
Miles, Hal 1988
Milkovich, Tom 1972
Miller, Jimmy 1960
Miller, John 1972
Miller, Randy 1972
Milliron, Virgil 1968
Mills, Gene 1980, 1988
Minkel, Tom 1980, 1988
Molino, Carmen 1960, 1964
Monday, Kenny 1984, 1988
Morgan, John 1988
Morgan, Larry 1976

Morley, John 1972
Mousetis, Stan 1976
Murano, Chick 1968, 1980
Murphy, Ray 1976
Murray, Don 1980
Nance, Jim 1964
Nelson, Bill 1976
Nichols, Harold 1964, 1968, 1972, 1980, 1984
Norris, Bernadette 1984A
Northrup, Ben 1960
Northrup, 'Doc' 1960, 1976
Nugent, Bill 1984, 1988
Nugent, Larry 1988
Ogelsbury, Ron 1984A
Olesen, Roger 1960
Orr, John 1988
Osborne, Ray 1960
Owings, Larry 1968, 1972
Pamp, Jerry 1964
Parise, Doug 1980
Parker, Fred 1960
Parker, Ted 1968
Peckham, Jim 1972, 1976, 1984, 1988
Peckham, Tom 1968
Peery, Ed 1964
Peery, Rex 1960, 1964
Peninger, Grady 1960, 1968, 1976
Penrith, Brad 1988
Peterson, Ben 1968, 1972, 1976, 1980, 1984, 1988
Peterson, John 1972, 1976, 1980
Phills, Jim 1984
Pickens, Bob 1964
Pieper, Vern 1972, 1984
Pittman, Craig 1988
Piven, Mark 1968
Powell, Fred 1968, 1976
Pruzansky, Dave 1968, 1972
Raheem-Ali, Abdul 1980
Range, Dave 1976
Raschke, Jim 1964
Redd, Richard 1964
Reding, Mike 1964
Rein, Andy 1980, 1984, 1988
Reinghans, Brad 1976, 1980, 1984, 1988
Reinwand, Jack 1976, 1980
Rice, Alan 1972, 1980
Roberts, Clay 1960
Robertson, Port 1960, 1968
Robinson, J 1972, 1976, 1980, 1984, 1984A
Rockwell, Dean 1964, 1968, 1984

Roderick, Myron 1960, 1964, 1968, 1988
Rodriguez, Mike 1960
Roop, Bob 1968, 1980
Rosado, Bill 1976, 1980
Rosenmeyer, Frank 1960
Rumsfeld, Don 1968, 1984
Rushatz, Al 1960
Ruth, Greg 1960, 1964
Salamone, Richard 1980
Sanchez, Gil 1960
Sanders, Rick 1964, 1968, 1972
Santoro, Dick 1960
Sasahara, Shozo 1960, 1968
Scalzo, Joe 1968, 1980
Schalles, Wade 1976, 1988
Schenk, Henk 1972, 1976
Scherr, Bill 1984, 1988
Scherr, Jim 1984A, 1988
Schultz, Dave 1976, 1980, 1984, 1988
Schultz, Mark 1980, 1984, 1988
Schuyler, Pete 1988
Schyler, Stan 1964
Sciacchetano, Larry 1984
Seay, Joe 1964, 1972, 1980, 1984A, 1988
Seras, Andy 1988
Severn, Dan 1984
Sheets, Mike 1984, 1988
Sheldon, Shawn 1988
Shephard, Bob 1988
Sheppard, Isreal 1984
Sherman, Dan 1972
Shivers, Charlie 1988
Shuler, Don 1980, 1984
Siddens, Bob 1968
Simon, Jeff 1984
Simons, Gray 1960, 1964, 1968
Simons, Wayne 1960
Smith, Bill 1960, 1968
Smith, Bob 1964
Smith, Grant 1980
Smith, John 1988
Smith, Lee Roy 1980, 1984, 1984A, 1988
Snyder, Ken 1976
Sofman, Rich 1968, 1980
Sondgeroth, Don 1984A
Soucie, Laurent 1980
Sparks, Ray 1960
Stagg, Frank 1984
Stensland, Garry 1964
Steubing, Jeff 1988
Stewart, Ricky 1984

Strobel, Greg 1984, 1984A, 1988
Swartz, Ray 1960, 1964
Tanniehill, Jim 1972
Taylor, Chris 1972, 1980
TenPas, Larry 1960
Thomas, Dale 1960, 1964
Thomas, Tony 1984
Thompson, Bruce 1980
Tironi, Chris 1988
Torio, Dick 1976, 1980
Tribble, Charlie 1964, 1968
Trizzino, Scott 1984
Tucci, Rick 1976, 1984A, 1988
Turnbull, Tom 1972
Turner, Thad 1980, 1984 I
Uetake, Yojiro 1968
Urbano, Eddie 1988
Vanni, Tim 1984
Vatch, Ed 1972
Wais, Eric 1980
Waldroup, Derrick 1988
Walsh, Jack 1968
Ware, Lester 1984
Wasmund, Dalen 1988
Weaver, Bobby 1976, 1980, 1984, 1984A, 1988
Weaver, Brad 1976
Weick, Bill 1972, 1976, 1984A
Wells, Joe 1972, 1976, 1984
Wells, Wayne 1968, 1972, 1976, 1988
Wetzel, Eric 1988
Whelan, Keith 1976
Whelan, Khris 1976
Widerman, Paul 1984
Wiley, Harold 1976
Wilkinson, Jim 1964
Williams, Rudy 1960
Williams, Willie 1972, 1988
Willingham, Randy 1988
Wilson, Bruce 1976
Wilson, Dick 1960, 1964, 1980
Wilson, Hallow 1960
Wilson, Shelby 1960, 1964, 1968, 1976
Wittenburg, Henry 1960, 1968
Wojciechowski, Greg 1972, 1980
Woodburn, Ed 1988
Yagla, Chuck 1976, 1980
Young, Mike 1968, 1972
Young, Norm 1960
Yozzo, Pete 1984
Zalesky, Lenny 1984, 1988
Zindel, Jack 1976
Zuaro, Vince 1964, 1984A, 1988

ACKNOWLEDGMENTS

WHEN I began researching this book, in November, 2005, I spoke with **Dave Auble**, who gave me this piece of advice about **Terry McCann**, one of America's wrestling legends and Auble's arch-rival in 1960: "Talk to Terry as soon as you can. He's dying of cancer."

I reached Terry at his home in Dana Point, California that December. Terry was confined to his bed by that stage but could not have been more helpful and encouraging. He put together a file of press clippings and letters for me and answered every question I had, and then some.

That was the first of three conversations we had over the next few months.

Terry passed away in the spring of 2006.

I can't imagine this book without him. I'm honored to have had his input. Thank you, Terry, and thank you, Dave.

I also want to thank the other 88 wrestlers, coaches and officials who took the time to tell me their stories. Without exception — I repeat, without exception — these decorated men were gracious, responsive, courteous and thoughtful in providing the source material for this book.

I'd be remiss if I didn't single out **Wayne Baughman** and **Wayne Hicks**, who especially went out of their way to help. Baughman related first-hand stories of five different Trials and helped me locate some hard-to-find veterans, while Hicks not only recalled stories covering the 1964 Trials, but also guided me on a personal tour of the Naval Academy in Annapolis, including the dorms, mess halls and wrestling rooms where the

'64 Trials took place.

The individuals provided the stories, but I also needed to have some facts about the Trials. For this, I depended upon our sports bible, the *Amateur Wrestling News*, along with digging into the on-line archives of *The Oklahoman* (Oklahoma City's daily paper), and to a lesser extent, *The New York Times* and the *Cleveland Plain Dealer*. For confirming historical wrestling information, I was saved numerous times by the National Wrestling Hall Of Fame's database, the AAU sports database and **Jay Hammond**'s website, www.wrestlingstats.com. **Denny Diehl**'s generosity in loaning me his vast collection of *Amateur Wrestling News* kept me from having to fly to Oklahoma on more than one occasion.

At the initiation of this project, I received needed encouragement from USA Wrestling and the United States Olympic Committee. I thank **Rich Bender** and **Jim Scherr** for their moral support and opening their organizations' doors to me. **Gary Abbott** led me through the voluminous USA Wrestling press files and **Cindy Stinger** shared whatever contact information about the Olympians that the USOC had available.

I needed, and received, special help with the sensitive material and stories brought to bear in the chapter '1984 Addendum'. **Greg Strobel** and the **Dellagatta** family each loaned me their extensive files that contained copies of pointed clippings, letters and formal documents of the times. **Lee Roy Smith** gracefully provided copies of certain key documents. **Randy Lewis** was passionate in his recollection of events.

I am particularly grateful to Gary Abbott, once again, for allowing me to collect and use material from the comprehensive 'Special Report' he wrote in the Fall, 1984 edition of *Wrestling Masters*, entitled 'The 136.5 lb.

Class and the Gable Connection.'

As I neared completion of the narrative, I took the bold step of asking two pros to review and critique a couple of chapters. Both **Mike Chapman** and **John Irving** not only took time from their busy schedule to read what I sent them, they gave me direct and helpful editing advice that I immediately incorporated into the final manuscript. **Jay Hammond** provided much-needed proofreading assistance, always keeping me in line with his mind-boggling collection of amateur wrestling facts. And **Mark Rector**, an accomplished actor, assisted at the finish with some meticulous proofing skills.

Finding photographs for the book was less of a problem than it might have been, thanks to the generous assistance of **John Hoke** (*Amateur Wrestling News*), **Lanny Bryant** (*Scholastic Wrestling News*), **Bobby Douglas** (*Take It to the Mat* and several of his *Technique* books), **Wade Schalles** (*They Call It Wrestling* book), **Mark Palmer**, **Mark Osgood** and items, such as the Dan Gable and Wayne Wells cards, found on **Tom Fortunato**'s website, wrestlingsbest.com. I am also extremely grateful for the assistance of **Frank Bettucci**, who not only encouraged me to write this book but provided me with a file of old news clippings and photographs.

Closer to home, thank you, **Jack Wright**, for taking a chance on me and agreeing to direct the editing, layout and publication of this book. You have a magical touch, my friend.

Artist **Victor Grasso**'s genius gave the cover the right mixture of flair and nostalgia.

And most of all, thank you to my wife – **Betty Moffatt** – for always giving me "another chance" and putting up with seeing the back of my head hovering over the keyboard for the last 21 months. I love you, babe.

Jamie Moffatt, August, 2007

ABOUT THE AUTHOR

★ Jamie Moffatt captained his prep school and college freshman wrestling teams despite being labeled "slow but weak" by his more talented teammates. He is a retired Management Consulting Partner of PricewaterhouseCoopers, LLP, and the former Board Chairman of the College Sports Council, a non-profit advocacy group who oppose the enforcement of the Title IX quota (proportionality) system.

He was the co-author, in 2003, of *A Turning Point*, a story of the 1953 NCAA wrestling championship, won by Penn State.

Jamie and his wife Betty reside in Cape May, NJ.